THE
ALTRUISM
QUESTION

Toward a
Social-Psychological
Answer

THE
ALTRUISM
QUESTION

Toward a
Social-Psychological
Answer

C. Daniel Batson
University of Kansas

LEA LAWRENCE ERLBAUM ASSOCIATES, PUBLISHERS
1991   Hillsdale, New Jersey   Hove and London

Lawrence Erlbaum Associates, Inc., Publishers
365 Broadway
Hillsdale, New Jersey 07642

Library of Congress Cataloging-in-Publication Data

Batson, C. Daniel (Charles Daniel), 1943–
    The altruism question : toward a social psychological answer / C.
Daniel Batson.
        p.   cm.
    Includes bibliographical references and index.
    ISBN 0-8058-0245-2 (c)
    1. Altruism.   I. Title.
    [DNLM: 1. Altruism.   2. Empathy.   3. Psychological Theory.   BJ
1474 B334a]
    BF637.H4B39   1991
    155.2′32—dc20
    DNLM/DLC
for Library of Congress   91-6758
                                                                      CIP

Printed in the United States of America
10 9 8 7 6 5 4 3 2 1

Contents

Part III: Testing the Egoistic Alternatives to the Empathy-Altruism Hypothesis

Part IV: Extensions

Preface

Even casual observation of the human condition prompts the question, "Why do people do what they do to one another?" How do we explain the Holocaust, wars, terrorist attacks, torture, oppression, discrimination, and callous insensitivity to starvation, poverty, and homelessness? But casual observation also prompts a second question: "Why do people do what they do *for* one another?" As real and undeniable as our callousness is, also real and undeniable is our ability to care for and help family, friends, even total strangers. Indeed, most observers find it easier to explain our callousness than our compassion. The former can be attributed to a deeply ingrained impulse to do anything and everything necessary to promote our own welfare. The latter seems to challenge the truism of self-interest, forcing us to ask: Could it be that we are capable of having another person's welfare as an ultimate goal, that not all of our efforts are directed toward looking out for Number One? This is the altruism question. It is the question that this book attempts to answer.

Traditionally, philosophers are the ones who have offered answers to the altruism question. In recent years, however, they have been joined by biologists, especially sociobiologists, and by psychologists, especially developmental and social psychologists. To set the present inquiry in context, I have paid particular attention to classic philosophical discussions, many of which are quite insightful and a delight to read. But my approach is social psychological, because I think social psychology is the scientific subdiscipline best suited to provide an answer to the altruism question. At the same time, I have tried to write not only for social psychologists but also for other psychologists, philosophers, and biologists. I have also tried to write for students, both undergraduate and graduate—indeed, for anyone interested in the question of why we help one another.

To set one's sights on the lofty heights of providing a scientific answer to the question of the existence of altruism may seem to be setting them far too high. It is certainly not a mountain I would have dared try to climb had I known in advance what I was doing. I stumbled onto a path and, before I knew where it was leading, found myself too far along to turn back gracefully. The path has not been easy. It has wound through conceptual briar patches and tangled thickets of data and alternative explanations. I wish there were an easier way to answer the altruism question, but if there is, I missed it.

Of course, I had a lot of help along the way. When I was in graduate school, John Darley introduced me to the idea that one could study scientifically— even experimentally—something as complex and intangible as why we help others. A few years later, Jay Coke, more a colleague than a graduate student, led me to consider empathy as a possible source of altruistic motivation. Jay also served as an important collaborator on an initial conceptual analysis that suggested how we might detect altruistic motivation empirically. Other students since have contributed to the conceptual analysis, as well as to one or more empirical studies: Graduate and postdoctoral students include Bruce Duncan, Janine Dyck Flory, Jim Fultz, Rick Gibbons, Katherine McDavis, Rosalie McMaster, Karen O'Quin, Patricia Schoenrade, Laura Shaw, Miho Toi, Mary Vanderplas, and Joy Weeks. Undergraduates include Paula Ackerman, Kimberly Birch, Michelle Bolen, Randy Brandt, Terese Buckley, Julie Cross, Victoria Fortenbach, Cari Griffitt, Missy McCarthy, Helen Neuringer-Benefiel, Kathy Oleson, Anne Powell, David Schoeni, Jacqueline Slingsby, Peter Sprengelmeyer, and Laurie Varney.

Colleagues have helped by critiquing and suggesting improvements in the conceptual analysis, the research designs, and this manuscript. They include Jack Brehm, Sharon Brehm, Jack Bricke, Bob Cialdini, Malcolm Clark, John Darley, Jack Dovidio, Nancy Eisenberg, Bill Graziano, Fritz Heider, Grace Heider, Alice Isen, Jerzy Karylowski, Dennis Krebs, Malcolm Murfett, Patricia Schoenrade, David Schroeder, Elliott Sober, Abraham Tesser, and Larry Wrightsman. I did not follow all of the suggestions made, so none of these individuals should be held accountable for shortcomings that remain.

Absolutely essential has been the contribution of hundreds of unnamed students who took part in the empirical studies. Quite simply, the information they provided has totally changed my mind about the existence of altruism.

The National Science Foundation provided much appreciated research funds (BNS-8507110 and BNS-8906723), and the University of Kansas a sabbatical leave. Lynn Porter, Jennifer Lamb, and Katia Silva provided great assistance with manuscript preparation.

Finally, my wife, Judy, has been immensely helpful as a research collaborator, manuscript critic, and editor. Even more, she has provided a happy
blend of support and cynicism as I have—day after day—ridden off to joust the
windmill of altruism.

For all of this help, I am deeply grateful—so much so that I shall refrain
from asking why it was given.

C. Daniel Batson

Mr. James Harthouse: *Every man is selfish in everything he does.*

Bitzer: *I am sure you know that the whole social system is a question of self-interest. What you must always appeal to is a person's self-interest. It's your only hold. We are so constituted.*

Mr. Sleary: *There is a love in the world, not all self-interest after all, but something very different.*

—all from *Hard Times* by Charles Dickens

Sherlock Holmes: *When you have eliminated the impossible, whatever remains, however improbable, must be the truth.*

—from "The Sign of Four" by Sir Arthur Conan Doyle

CHAPTER 1

The Question Posed
by Our Concern for Others:
Altruism or Egoism?

W hy do we send money to help famine victims halfway around the world? Or to save whales? Why do we stay up all night to comfort a friend who has just suffered a broken relationship? Why do we stop on a busy highway to help a stranded motorist change a flat?

Why would an intelligent, cool, self-assured young woman, after having a child "just for the experience," find herself saying about her small daughter: "I know that I would do anything for her; I would throw myself under an oncoming car to save her if she was in danger of being run over. I never dreamed that I could feel this way about anybody." Why did Lenny Skutnik risk his life diving into the icy waters of the Potomac to save an airline crash victim, and why did "the sixth man," Arland Williams, surrender his life by giving others his place in the rescue helicopter? Why did Mother Teresa reach out to the dying of Calcutta, the lowest of the low? Why did Miep Gies help hide Anne Frank and her family from the Nazis month after month, risking imprisonment, torture, and even death?

Few of us have not asked ourselves why we help others. Often, the answer is easy. We help because we have no choice, because it is expected, or because it is in our own best interest. We may do a friend a favor because we do not want to lose the friendship or because we expect to see the favor reciprocated. But it is not for such easy answers that we ask ourselves why we help; it is to press the limits of these answers. We want to know if our helping is always and exclusively motivated by the prospect of some benefit for ourselves, however subtle. We want to know if anyone ever, in any degree,

1

transcends the bounds of self-benefit and helps out of genuine concern for the welfare of another.

THE ALTRUISM QUESTION

The question thus raised has been a central one in moral philosophy for many centuries; it is the question of the existence of altruism. Advocates of universal egoism, who are in the clear majority in Western philosophy and psychology, claim that everything we do, no matter how noble and beneficial to others, is really directed toward the ultimate goal of self-benefit. Advocates of altruism do not deny that the motivation for much of what we do, including much that we do for others, is egoistic. But they claim that there is more. They claim that at least some of us, to some degree, under some circumstances, are capable of a qualitatively different form of motivation, motivation with an ultimate goal of benefiting someone else.

Many forms of self-benefit can be derived from helping. Some are obvious, such as getting material rewards or public praise (or escaping public censure). Yet even when we help in the absence of obvious external rewards, we may still benefit. We can receive self-rewards, congratulating ourselves for being kind and caring, or we can avoid self-censure, escaping shame and guilt. In such cases the pat on the back may come from ourselves rather than from someone else, but it is a pat nonetheless. Alternatively, seeing someone else in distress may cause us distress, and we may act to relieve the other's distress as an instrumental means to reach the ultimate goal of relieving our own distress.

Even heroes and martyrs can benefit from their acts of apparent selflessness. Consider the soldier who saves his comrades by diving on a grenade or the man who dies after relinquishing his place in a rescue craft. These persons may have acted to escape anticipated guilt and shame for letting others die. Or they may have acted to gain rewards, such as the admiration and praise of those left behind or benefits expected in a life to come. Or they may simply have misjudged the consequences of their actions. The possibility that such acts are ultimately motivated by some form of self-benefit may seem cynical, but it is real. It lies at the heart of the altruism question.

WHY WE NEED AN ANSWER
TO THE ALTRUISM QUESTION

Clearly, to raise the question of the existence of altruism opens a Pandora's box of complex issues and conceptual traps. Yet, with some trepidation, I believe it is important that we lift the lid and face these issues. The potential for getting caught in one or more of the traps is great, but the need for an answer to this question is also great. It is one of the most fundamental questions we can ask about human nature. And it is important that we understand human nature.

By human nature I do not mean something mystical, nor do I refer to our innate nature as opposed to that acquired by nurture; I simply mean the propensities, motives, and desires that are within the repertoire of normal adult humans living in at least some societies. If altruistic motivation is part of this repertoire, then both who we are as humans and what we are capable of doing are quite different than if it is not. How we answer the altruism question tells us something fundamental about the role of other people in our lives—and of us in theirs. It tells us about our capacity for involvement with and caring about one another.

From the perspective of universal egoism, looking out for "Number One," being your own best friend, is not only prudent, it is inevitable. Other people, however dear, are simply complex objects in our world—sources of stimulation and reward, of facilitation and inhibition—as we each seek our own ends. But from the perspective of altruism, we have the potential to be more interconnected, more closely tied to one another. From this perspective there are, as Adam Smith (1759/1853) claimed long ago, principles in our nature that interest us in the welfare of others, and not just when their welfare affects ours.

Knowing whether or not we are capable of altruism would, then, help us better know ourselves. And that is not all. If we are capable of altruism, then virtually all of our current ideas about individual psychology, social relations, economics, and politics are, in an important respect, wrong. Virtually all of our current ideas explicitly or implicitly deny the possibility of altruism; they are firmly founded on the assumption of universal egoism. From Aristotle and St. Thomas Aquinas, through Thomas Hobbes and Jeremy Bentham, to Friedrich Nietzsche and Sigmund Freud, the dominant view in Western thought has long been that we are, at heart, exclusively self-interested. And today, when we ask why we care for and help others, the answer provided by all major theories of motivation—Freudian, behavioral, and even humanistic theories—is quite clear: Everything we do, including everything we do to benefit others, is ultimately done for our own benefit.

The assumption of universal egoism is so fundamental and widespread in our culture that it is hard to recognize, like water for a fish. It only becomes apparent if we imagine the possible changes if it were not there. Imagine, for example, the possible changes in child-rearing practices and moral education if—instead of assuming that sensitivity to the needs of others must always be made worth a child's while—we assume that the child is capable of genuine interest in the welfare of at least some others. Similarly, imagine the changes in economic theory and models of social change if we drop the assumption that self-benefit alone defines utility and value. Or imagine the consequences for discussions of morality and ethics.

Knowing whether we are or are not capable of altruism will not tell us what is morally right, either in a specific situation or as a general principle. As Scottish philosopher David Hume (1740/1896) pointed out, we cannot reason from an *is* to an *ought,* from an understanding of what our human potential is to what we ought to do.

Our potential does, however, set the boundaries for any consideration of what is morally right. We can be held morally accountable only for those actions that are within our repertoire. We are not, for example, held accountable for harm done by "acts of God," which we have no capacity to control. Similarly, if we are capable of seeking only our own benefit, then we can hardly be blamed for doing so. Morality becomes a matter either of brokering various self-interests (Rawls, 1971) or of trying to convince ourselves and others of one of two possibilities: that there is virtue in selfishness (Nietzsche, 1888/1927; Rand, 1964) or that acts that benefit others are actually better for us than acts that benefit only ourselves (Bentham, 1789/1876; Maslow, 1968; Rogers, 1961). Unless arguments advocating the latter possibility can be made convincing, we cannot be expected to care about the welfare of others. If, on the other hand, it turns out that we are capable of altruism, then our moral horizon—and our potential for moral responsibility—broadens considerably.

Flights of fancy like these suggest how important it could be to know the answer to the question of why we help others. If our belief in universal egoism is wrong and we are actually capable of altruism, then possibilities arise for the development of more caring individuals and a more compassionate, humane society. And in a world so full of fear, insensitivity, suffering, and loneliness, such developments are sorely needed.

Yet we cannot decide that altruism exists simply because our world might be a nicer place if it did. Wishes are not horses. If our concern for others is limited to those situations in which such concern serves our own interests, then it is best we know this, lest the rhetoric and dreams of altruism seduce us into counterproductive sentimentality and doomed efforts at social reform. To build a better society, we need to know the truth about our raw materials. We need to know the correct answer to the question of why we help others, whether we like that answer or not. Moreover, we need a solid basis for the answer, so that it will be persuasive, even if it contradicts our present belief. That is the task before us.

DEFINING ALTRUISM

If we are to make any headway with the altruism question, then we must first clearly specify the difference between altruism and egoism, and do so in a way that does not distort or oversimplify the egoism–altruism debate. We can best do this, I think, by following the lead of Auguste Comte (1798–1857), who is credited with coining the term *altruism*. Before Comte, the question of why we help others was discussed under a variety of headings—benevolence, charity, compassion, and friendship. Comte's differentiation between altruism and egoism brought the question into sharper focus.

Comte's Concept of Altruism

Comte (1851/1875) considered altruism and egoism to be two distinct motives within the individual. He did not deny the existence of self-serving motives, even for helping; the impulse to seek self-benefit and self-gratification he called *egoism*. But Comte believed that some social behavior was an expression of an unselfish desire to "live for others" (p. 556). It was this second type of motivation to benefit others that he called *altruism*.

One popular rejoinder to Comte's proposal of altruism, made by philosophers of his day, went as follows: Even if it were possible for a person to be motivated to increase another's welfare, such a person would be pleased by attaining this desired goal, so even this apparent altruism would actually be a product of egoism. This argument, based on the general principle of *psychological hedonism*, has been shown to be flawed by later philosophers, who have pointed out that it involves a confusion between two different forms of hedonism. The strong form of psychological hedonism asserts that attainment of personal pleasure is always the goal of human action; the weak form asserts only that goal attainment always brings pleasure. The weak form is not inconsistent with the possibility that the ultimate goal of some action is to benefit another rather than to benefit oneself, because the pleasure obtained can be a consequence of reaching the goal without being the goal itself. The strong form of psychological hedonism is inconsistent with the possibility of altruism, but to affirm this form of hedonism is simply to assert universal egoism; as such, it is an empirical affirmation that may or may not be true. (See MacIntyre, 1967; Milo, 1973; Nagel, 1970, for further discussion of these philosophical arguments.)

A Modern Recasting

Comte coined the term *altruism* in juxtaposition to *egoism* over a century ago, and, understandably, his concept is dated. It is an odd alloy of phrenology, conditioning principles, assumptions about emotional contagion, and utopian moralizing. Fortunately, I believe that his concept can be recast and expressed more usefully, without changing its basic meaning, by employing a more modern view of motives as goal-directed forces within the individual.

Employing this view of motivation, I would suggest the following definition: *Altruism is a motivational state with the ultimate goal of increasing
another's welfare.* There are three key phrases in this brief definition, and to
avoid confusion later we need to be explicit about each:

1. "*. . . a motivational state . . .*": Motivation is energy (potential or
kinetic), a force within the individual (Lewin, 1935). The motivation of
interest here is directed toward some goal. Goal-directed motivation has five
key features: the person in question perceives some desired change in his or
her experienced world; a force of some magnitude exists, drawing the
person toward this goal; if a barrier prevents direct access to the goal,
alternative routes are sought; the force disappears on attainment of the goal;
and consistent with the weak form of psychological hedonism, reaching the
goal is likely to be pleasurable for the person.

2. "*. . . with the ultimate goal . . .*": For a goal to be an ultimate goal, it
must be an end in itself and not just an intermediate means for reaching some
other goal. If a goal is an intermediate means for reaching some other goal,
and a barrier arises, then alternative routes to the ultimate goal that bypass
the intermediate goal will be sought. And if the ultimate goal is reached
without the intermediate goal being reached, then the motivational force will
disappear and pleasure will be felt. If, however, a goal is an ultimate goal, it
cannot be bypassed in this way.

3. "*. . . of increasing another's welfare*": This phrase identifies the specific
ultimate goal of altruistic motivation. Three conditions must be satisfied for
increasing another's welfare to be considered an ultimate goal: First, the
motivated person must perceive a negative discrepancy between another
person's current state and potential state on one or more dimensions of
well-being. Dimensions of well-being include the absence of physical pain,
negative affect, anxiety, stress, and so on, as well as the presence of physical
pleasure, positive affect, security, and so on. More simply, we may say that
the person experiencing altruistic motivation must perceive the other to be in
need. *Need* is here defined to include the potential for a person not currently
in distress to benefit (e.g., Maslow's, 1954, growth needs), as well as the
potential for a distressed other to escape suffering (e.g., Maslow's deficiency
needs). Second, the person must desire that the other's need be reduced; that
is, reduction of the need must be a goal for the person. Third, increasing the
other's welfare by reducing the need must be an ultimate goal for the person,
not just an instrumental means of reaching some other goal.

Does Altruism Require Self-Sacrifice?

It is important to understand that, as defined here, altruistic motivation does
not necessarily involve self-sacrifice. To pursue the ultimate goal of in-

creasing the other's welfare may involve cost to the self, but it also may not. Indeed, it can even involve self-benefit and the motivation still be altruistic, as long as obtaining this self-benefit is not the ultimate goal.

Some psychologists have defined *altruism* as requiring self-sacrifice (e.g., Campbell, 1975, 1978; Hatfield, Walster, & Piliavin, 1978; Krebs, 1970, 1982; Midlarsky, 1968; Wispé, 1978). Proponents of such a definition usually cite as examples of altruism the acts of heroes and martyrs, for whom the absolute cost of helping is very high, often including loss of life. It is assumed that in such cases the costs of helping must outweigh the rewards, so the helper's goal could not have been self-benefit. By this definition, diving into shark-infested waters to save an attack victim would be labeled altruistic, whereas giving a lost and frightened child a comforting hug would not.

There are at least two problems with including self-sacrifice in the definition of altruism. First, it almost invariably shifts attention from the crucial question of motivation to a focus on consequences. The more the beneficial act costs the helper, the more altruistic it is assumed to be. But what if the hero or martyr had no intention of risking death, and things got out of hand? Is this altruism? And what about that comforting hug? How do we know it was not at least in part altruistically motivated?

Second, a definition based on self-sacrifice overlooks the possibility that some self-benefits for helping increase as the costs increase. Precisely because the costs are very great, the rewards may be very great as well. It may appear tasteless to scrutinize the motives of a person who risks his or her life to shelter refugees from the Holocaust or a person who dies trying to save a drowning child, but if we are serious about trying to understand why people help, then such scrutiny is necessary. And under scrutiny, we must admit that the hero who helps, even at the cost of his or her life, may be acting to avoid guilt or gain praise and esteem, or may have simply misjudged the seriousness of the situation. These two problems reveal the importance of focusing on benefit to the other, not cost to self, when we define altruism.

DEFINING EGOISM

For Comte, both egoism and altruism were motivational states; the crucial difference between them was the goal of the motivation. Reflecting this difference, and paralleling the definition of altruism, we can define *egoism* as follows: *Egoism is a motivational state with the ultimate goal of increasing one's own welfare.*

What was said earlier about the meaning of "a motivational state" and "the ultimate goal" applies here as well, so we need only consider the specific ultimate goal of egoistic motivation, "increasing one's own welfare." There is a wide variety of egoistic motives, ranging from the desire for physical comfort, to the desire to be loved and to succeed, to the desire to express oneself and be self-actualized. Most important for our discussion are the egoistic motives evoked by perception of another in need. This perception may evoke needs within oneself: It may be personally upsetting to see someone suffer; it may lead one to anticipate feeling ashamed or guilty if help is not given, and so on. More formally, perception of the other in need may lead to awareness of a negative discrepancy between one's own current state and one's own potential state on one or more dimensions of well-being. The relevant dimensions of well-being for the self are the same dimensions considered previously as affecting the well-being of the other. They include the absence of negative affect, of anxiety, stress, anticipated shame and guilt, and so on, as well as the presence of positive affect, of material, social, and self-rewards, and so on. If the person desires to have his or her own need reduced, and, moreover, if doing so is an ultimate goal and not just a means of reaching some other goal, then egoistic motivation is present.

CLARIFYING THE DEFINITIONS
OF EGOISM AND ALTRUISM

As defined here, *egoism* and *altruism* have much in common. Each refers to a goal-directed motivational state; each is concerned with the ultimate goal of this motivational state; and for each the ultimate goal is increasing someone's welfare. These common features provide the context for highlighting the crucial difference between the two terms: Whose welfare is the ultimate goal? For egoistic motivation, the ultimate goal is increasing one's own welfare; for altruistic motivation, the ultimate goal is increasing another's welfare.

These definitions of egoism and altruism may seem straightforward enough, but like most definitions, they have some implications that may not be apparent at first glance. To be sure that these implications are clear, six points should be made:

1. The proposed distinction between egoistic and altruistic motivation is qualitative not quantitative; the ultimate goal, not the strength of the motive, distinguishes egoism from altruism.

2. As long as the motivated individual perceives a distinction between self and the other, a single motive cannot be both egoistic and altruistic. This is because in the present analysis a motivational state is defined by the existence of an ultimate goal. To seek to benefit both self and other (as long as self and other are distinct) implies two ultimate goals, which in turn implies two distinct motives. Of course, an individual may have more than one ultimate

goal at a time and, thus, more than one motive. Both egoistic and altruistic motives can exist simultaneously within a single individual. If the egoistic and altruistic goals are of roughly equal attractiveness and lie in different directions, so that behaviors leading toward one lead away from the other, then the individual will experience motivational conflict.

3. The terms *egoism* and *altruism* are assumed to apply only to the domain of goal-directed activity. If a person acts reflexively or automatically without any goal, then no matter how beneficial the act may be, it is neither egoistically nor altruistically motivated.

4. A person may be egoistically motivated and not know it, may be altruistically motivated and not know it, may believe that his or her motivation is altruistic when it is actually egoistic, and vice versa. This is because a person may have a goal and not be aware of it, or may mistakenly believe that his or her goal is X when it is actually Y. Especially in so value-laden an area as our helping of others, we cannot assume that we know—or if we know that we will report—our true motives.

5. Both egoistic and altruistic motives may evoke a variety of behaviors or no behavior at all. A motive is a force. Whether this force leads to action depends on the behavioral options available in the situation, as well as on the strength of both the motive and of congruent and conflicting motivational forces present at the time.

6. Logically at least, there may be motives that are neither egoistic nor altruistic. There may even be motives for helping that have an ultimate goal other than benefit to self or benefit to another. To illustrate, a person may have an ultimate goal of upholding a principle of justice (Kohlberg, 1976). Pursuit of this goal may lead this person to help others in need, which may bring benefit to the others as well as to the self. Yet, if upholding justice is the ultimate goal rather than an instrumental means to, for example, avoid guilt for failing to live up to one's principles, then the benefits to others and to self are unintended consequences, and the motivation is neither egoistic nor altruistic.

RELATING EGOISM AND ALTRUISM TO HELPING

By these definitions, helping another person might be egoistically motivated, altruistically motivated, both, or neither. To ascertain that some act was beneficial to another and was intended, which is what is meant by helping, does not in itself say anything about the nature of the underlying motivation. We might act in order to increase another person's welfare, even at great personal cost and without obvious reward; yet, this helping is still egoistic if it is motivated by an ultimate desire to increase our own welfare.

For example, if a friend's distress caused you distress, and you stayed up all night providing comfort in order to reduce your own distress, then your motivation was egoistic. True, you sought to make your friend feel better, but that was not your ultimate goal. It was only instrumental in allowing you to reach the ultimate goal of feeling better yourself. Similarly, if you helped in order to avoid feelings of guilt that you anticipated were you to "pass by on the other side," like the Priest and Levite in the Parable of the Good Samaritan, then your motivation was egoistic.

It is also true by these definitions that helping another could increase your own welfare and still be altruistic if the helping was motivated by an ultimate desire to increase the other's welfare. For example, if your friend's distress caused you distress, but you helped in order to relieve the friend's distress as an end in itself, then your motivation was altruistic. True, by relieving the friend's distress you probably relieved your own distress and avoided feeling guilty. Yet, to the extent that these outcomes were not your ultimate goal but only unintended consequences of pursuing the ultimate goal of relieving the friend's distress, your motivation was altruistic. The proposed definitions of egoism and altruism focus on the motivation, not on the behavior or the consequences of the behavior.

I believe that the proposed definitions of egoism and altruism are faithful to the spirit of the egoism–altruism debate. At issue in this debate is whether our motivation for helping is ever, in any degree, directed toward the ultimate goal of increasing the other person's welfare. If it is, then the widespread assumption that the ultimate goal of all human action is some more or less subtle form of self-benefit must be rejected.

But does altruism as defined here exist? We could define a mermaid in detail and assert with confidence that if such a creature exists, then we must make some significant adjustments in our assumptions about biology and the nature of species. Yet to define a mermaid in no way increases the likelihood that mermaids exist—outside of our imaginations. The same is true for altruism. Defining it as we have in no way increases the likelihood that it exists.

Indeed, you may feel that the definition offered only makes it easier to answer the altruism question. You may feel that you can now answer with a confident and resounding, "No! Altruism does not exist." You may even wish to add, "And if it did, we would never be able to know it!"

I do not think we should accept either of these answers, at least not yet. Even though the facts in question concern motives rather than directly observable behavior, the altruism question is still empirical; it asks what the helper's ultimate goal is. To answer this question we can and should appeal to empirical evidence. Thus, to raise the altruism question faces us immediately with another, the question of method: How are we to arrive at a persuasive empirical answer to the altruism question?

THE QUESTION OF METHOD

Philosophical Approaches

Most classic answers to the altruism question come from philosophers. These answers usually employ one, or both, of two strategies. One strategy is to argue for the logical necessity of universal egoism or of altruism, basing the argument on some "obvious" premises about what human nature is or should be. The second strategy is to cite cases of helping—usually dramatic cases—and point out how the helping in each case clearly is or is not self-beneficial.

Neither of these classic philosophical strategies has provided a persuasive answer to the altruism question. A logical argument based on deduction from "obvious" first principles is not likely to persuade someone who does not already agree with those principles. Such logical arguments inevitably seem to hinge on assertions that begin: "It cannot be doubted that. . . ." But what is beyond doubt for someone on one side of the egoism–altruism issue is likely to be far from clear to someone on the other side. Indeed, probably the only point in the egoism–altruism debate that cannot be doubted is that persons of good will and sincerity can and do sharply disagree.

Inductive arguments based on analysis of dramatic examples share the same fate. Take any given instance of helping behavior, including any of those listed at the beginning of this chapter. We can always think of possible self-benefits—thanks, praise, enhanced self-esteem, avoidance of guilt, and so on. Yet, the question is not whether self-benefits are possible, or even present; the question is whether the helper acted solely in order to obtain these self-benefits as an ultimate goal. The likelihood that we will consider the self-benefits to have been the goal will almost certainly be determined by our initial assumptions about whether goals other than self-benefit are possible. Interpretation of the meaning of dramatic examples thus also seems, in the final analysis, to involve deduction from initial assumptions about first principles.

These classic philosophical methods have added much to our understanding of the altruism question, and they have provided us with a rich array of possible answers. They have not, however, provided a persuasive case for which answer is correct. I believe that this is because the altruism question is empirical. It is a question not of what the helper's goal might be, but of what the helper's goal actually is. Because this is an empirical question, I think a scientific approach is likely to be the best source of a persuasive answer. Just as questions about the nature of the physical world have been answered more effectively by the physical sciences than by philosophy (think, e.g., of answers to questions about the movement of the stars and planets), questions about human nature are likely to be answered more effectively by the behavioral and social sciences. To which behavioral or social science should we turn for an answer to the altruism question?

Scientific Approaches

Sociobiology.   The new discipline of sociobiology (Wilson, 1975) has, with adolescent zeal, been quick to nominate itself. Sociobiologists often speak of altruism, and they are fond of claiming to explain it (e.g., Dawkins, 1976; Trivers, 1971; Wilson, 1975, 1978). If, however, we look more closely at what sociobiologists are talking about, we find that they have no intention of even attempting to answer the altruism question.

As Richard Dawkins stated in *The Selfish Gene* (1976): "An entity, such as a baboon, is said to be altruistic if it behaves in such a way as to increase another such entity's welfare at the expense of its own. Selfish behavior has exactly the opposite effect" (p. 4). This definition may seem quite straightforward; yet, as Dawkins explained:

> It is important to realize that the above definitions of altruism and selfishness are *behavioral*, not subjective. I am not concerned here with the psychology of motives. I am not going to argue about whether people who behave altruistically are "really" doing it for secret or subconscious selfish motives. (p. 4)

Sociobiology has been useful in revealing numerous ways in which self-sacrificial behavior can be consistent with the theory of natural selection. That, however, is not the problem before us. We want to know if our ultimate goal when helping others is ever, in any degree, to benefit them. Our question is about precisely those motives that Dawkins and other sociobiologists exclude from their analyses. If we are to answer the altruism question, then we must turn to some other discipline.

Psychology.   As Dawkins implied, psychology is the branch of science that we might expect to address a question about motivation. Yet, perhaps because the altruism question asks for identification of a person's true motives among multiple possible motives, psychologists have been reticent even to consider this question. Far from self-nomination, the stance of psychologists has been closer to a recalcitrant, "If nominated I will not run; if elected I will not serve." They have usually either ruled altruism to be beyond the reach of psychology as a science, or they have finessed the question by redefining altruism as nothing more than a special case of egoism.

In spite of psychology's reticence to address the altruism question, I think psychology is the discipline to which we are best advised to look for an answer. That is where I invite you to look. Specifically, I invite you to consider the approach to science developed over the past 50 years in social psychology, building on the initial insights of Kurt Lewin. Lewin (1951) advocated a two-step approach to answering empirical questions, and his approach seems ideal for addressing the altruism question.

Lewin's approach involves, first, turning one's back on the infinite variety of experience in order to develop one or more general theoretical models of underlying constructs that can account for the infinite variety. This strategy may seem contrary to the popular view that science deals only with facts, but for Lewin, theory lay at the heart of science.

To be of value, of course, a theoretical model must be able to predict observed experience across a range of different situations. This leads us to the second step in Lewin's approach. Alternative theoretical models are tested by generating unique empirical predictions from each model and making relevant empirical observations. Lewin was an innovator in developing ways a researcher could create situations in which relevant empirical observations could be made, even for very complex social behaviors such as helping.

Of course, being a social psychologist myself, my belief that Lewin's method is ideal for addressing the altruism question may be no more than another example of disciplinary chauvinism. In the abstract, the claim that his method enables us to answer this question—or any other fundamental question about human nature—certainly has a hollow ring. It is a statement of faith more than of fact. Unlike the physical scientist who claims to have a method for addressing fundamental questions about the workings of the universe, I cannot quietly point to a long string of successful answers to fundamental questions about human nature. It is my hope, however, that the use of this method in the pages that follow provides a case in point, illustrating by example how the altruism question, and other similar questions, can be addressed scientifically. You can judge.

WHAT LIES AHEAD

Here, in brief, is what lies ahead. We follow as far as we can the trail blazed by those philosophers and psychologists who have contributed to the egoism–altruism debate (chapters 2–4). Even though the word "altruism" is less than 150 years old, the altruism question is not nearly so new. Why we help others has long been a puzzle, one examined with insight, passion, and wit. Few—if any—of our current views are really new. Tracing the history of the egoism–altruism debate will enrich our understanding of the conceptual issues and sensitize us to the range of possible answers to the altruism question. But I do not think you will find any of the answers persuasive.

From this point, we strike out on a new trail, relying on Lewin's approach to science as a guide. As already noted, Lewin's method included, first, turning one's back on the rich variety of experience to develop theoretical models and, second, testing the adequacy of these models by making carefully selected empirical observations, often in quite artificial and contrived experimental settings. Because many people, including many social psychologists, would consider this to be precisely the wrong way to go about doing science, we need to pause and consider the legitimacy of this strategy before going on (chapter 5). Reassured, I hope, we then put this method to work.

Chapter 6 presents a general model of the motivation for helping that differentiates three general classes of egoistic motives from one class of possible altruistic motives. The possible altruistic motives are those evoked by an emotional reaction of empathy, sympathy, or tenderness toward the person in need. The proposal that empathic emotion evokes altruistic motivation has been called the *empathy–altruism hypothesis.* Employing the general model presented in chapter 6, we then derive competing empirical predictions that allow us to determine whether the motivation to help associated with empathy is altruistic, as claimed by the empathy–altruism hypothesis, or egoistic (chapter 7).

Chapters 8–10 review a series of empirical studies designed to test these predictions. Most of these studies have been reported in detail in psychological journals during the last 10 years. Summarizing the evidence all at once here better enables us to evaluate it. Although more tests can and should be made, I believe you will find that the evidence to date provides surprisingly strong support for the hypothesis that empathic emotion evokes altruistic motivation, and fails to support any of the egoistic alternatives to this hypothesis that have been proposed. Of course, the possibility always exists that some as yet unconsidered nonaltruistic explanation may be discovered that can account for all of the evidence appearing to support the empathy–altruism hypothesis. As the quantity and diversity of supporting evidence increases, however, and as one after another plausible egoistic explanation proves inadequate, the likelihood of finding a plausible nonaltruistic explanation becomes smaller and smaller.

In the final two chapters we look up from the trail we have been following to take a broader view. First, we consider whether there might be sources of altruistic motivation other than empathic emotion (chapter 11). Finally, we consider some of the theoretical and practical implications if it is true that empathy can evoke altruistic motivation (chapter 12).

PART
I

THE ALTRUISM QUESTION
IN WESTERN THOUGHT

CHAPTER 2

Egoism and Altruism in Western Philosophy

Two major threads are woven into the fabric from which Western views on egoism and altruism are cut. One comes from Greek philosophy, most notably Plato and Aristotle; the other, from Judeo-Christian religion. It is common to contrast these threads, to juxtapose a Greek emphasis on self-interest and a Judeo-Christian emphasis on loving neighbor as self. It is also common to call the former egoistic, the latter altruistic. But this juxtaposition is misleading. Neither ancient tradition confronts the altruism question directly, perhaps because each assumes that human interactions take place in the context of a larger metaphysical scheme. Human behavior is not judged in terms of the goals of the actor but whether it does or does not conform to some higher standard. Ideas (Plato) or Universals (Aristotle) set the standard for the Greeks; God's law or plan sets the standard in the Judeo-Christian tradition. Still, both traditions show a sensitivity to many of the issues that lie at the heart of the egoism–altruism debate. And both seem at times egoistic, at times altruistic.

CONCERN FOR THE WELFARE OF OTHERS
IN ANTIQUITY

Greek Philosophy

Plato (c. 428–348 B.C.). Plato's most extensive discussion of concern for another's welfare—and the possible self-benefits derived therefrom—

appeared in his early dialogue on friendship, the *Lysis*. Even though Plato may have lacked a notion of loving neighbor as self that extended to all humanity (Kahn, 1981), in this dialogue he considered the possibility of such love in the context of friendship. Specifically, he raised two key questions about friendship: Is concern for a friend's welfare directed toward the friend's benefit as an end in itself, or is it ultimately directed toward one's own benefit?; and does some special tie exist between friends, allowing them to transcend self-interest? Plato raised these key questions and explored both egoistic and altruistic answers; but in the end he left both questions unanswered.

Aristotle (384–322 B. C.).   Aristotle tried to answer Plato's questions about friendship. First, he defined true friendship: "Let being friendly be defined as wishing for a person those things you consider to be good—wishing them for his sake, not your own—and tending so far as you can to effect them" (*Rhetoric*, 1380b35–1381a1—references are by Bekker numbers). The parallel between this statement and the definition of altruistic motivation in chapter 1 is striking. Yet elsewhere Aristotle stated that, "All the friendly feelings extend to others from those that have Self primarily for their object" (*Ethics*, 1168b6).

Resolution of the apparent contradiction in these two statements comes when Aristotle proposed that the good man "feels towards a friend as towards himself (a friend being in fact another Self)" (1166a31). "As his own existence is desirable for each man, so, or almost so, is his friend's existence" (1170b7–8). Aristotle applied a similar analysis to family affections: "Now parents love their children as themselves (since what is derived from themselves becomes a kind of other Self by the fact of separation)" (1161b27).

As even this brief sampling from Plato and Aristotle suggests, the Greeks were well into many of the subtleties of the egoism–altruism debate almost 2,500 years ago. The altruism question certainly was not answered; it was not even clearly asked. Yet the crucial elements of the debate were present: recognition that we act to benefit at least some others, often at considerable cost to ourselves; and recognition that our own welfare seems to be of central concern to us. How can these two elements be reconciled?

Epictetus (60–138 A. D.).   Neither Plato nor Aristotle came down clearly on one side of the issue or the other, although each seemed to lean (with some reluctance) to the egoistic side. A similar teetering stance may be found in the writings of Seneca (c. 4 B.C.–65 A.D.) and Marcus Aurelius (121–180 A.D.), as illustrated by Poplawski (1985). But the Roman Greek Epictetus stood firmly on the egoistic side. Although Epictetus (1877) advocated the brotherhood of man and reasoned self-control, he was convinced that human nature was fundamentally self-serving:

Did you never see little dogs caressing and playing with one another, so that you might say there is nothing more friendly? But that you may know what friendship is, throw a bit of flesh among them, and you will learn. Throw between yourself and your son a little estate, and you will know how soon he will wish to bury you and how soon you wish your son to die. . . . For universally, be not deceived, every animal is attached to nothing so much as to its own interest. Whatever then appears to it an impediment to this interest, whether this be a brother, or a father, or a child, or beloved, or lover, it hates, spurns, curses: For its nature is to love nothing so much as its own interest; this is father, and brother and kinsman, and country, and God. . . . For this reason if a man put in the same place his interest, sanctity, goodness, and country, and parents, and friends, all these are secured: but if he puts in one place his interest, in another his friends, and his country and his kinsmen and justice itself, all these give way being borne down by the weight of interest. For where the I and the Mine are placed, to that place of necessity the animal inclines. (pp. 177–178)

Judeo-Christian Religion

Jewish Law.   Several hundred years before the Golden Century when Plato and Aristotle walked the streets of Athens, Israelite priests created a "Holiness Code," which appears in the second half of the book of Leviticus. This Code outlined moral standards for social behavior. In it, one finds the first statement of the commandment that becomes central to Judeo-Christian morality: "You shall love your neighbor as yourself" (Leviticus 19:18, *Revised Standard Version*). Even at this early date (about 550 B.C.), the concept of "neighbor" is broad: "The stranger who sojourns with you shall be to you as the native among you, and you shall love him as yourself; for you were strangers in the land of Egypt" (Leviticus 19:34; see also Deuteronomy 10:18–19).

Teachings of Jesus.   Jesus repeated, elaborated, and extended the command to love neighbor as self. He asserted that this commandment applies not only to strangers but even to enemies: "Love your enemies, and do good, and lend, expecting nothing in return; and your reward will be great, and you will be sons of the Most High" (Luke 6:35). This commandment was described as second only to the commandment to love God, and "on these two commandments depend all the law and the prophets" (Matthew 22:40; see also Mark 12:31 and Luke 10:27).

Early Christianity.   As Christianity spread, the emphasis on love of neighbor remained central. For example, Paul wrote in his letter to the Romans (c. 56–57 A.D.):

> He who loves his neighbor has fulfilled the law. The commandments, "You shall
> not commit adultery, You shall not kill, You shall not steal, You shall not covet,"
> and any other commandment, are summed up in this sentence, "You shall love
> your neighbor as yourself." Love does no wrong to a neighbor; therefore love is
> the fulfilling of the law. (Romans 13:8–10; see also Galatians 4:14; James 2:8)

It is worth noting that the Greek word translated here as "love"—and throughout the New Testament when referring to love of neighbor—is neither *eros* (romantic love) nor *philia* (friendship), the word used by Plato and Aristotle. It is *agape,* a new word that refers to self-sacrificial or selfless loving kindness, a giving of self to others.

Some early Christians so wished to emphasize the necessity of practicing such love that they at times appear to have reversed Jesus's prioritizing of the two great commandments; love of neighbor seems even to have taken precedence over love of God: "If anyone says, 'I love God,' and hates his brother, he is a liar; for he who does not love his brother whom he has seen, cannot love God whom he has not seen" (I John 4:19–20).

WEAVING THE GREEK AND JUDEO-CHRISTIAN
THREADS: THOMAS AQUINAS

If Greek and Judeo-Christian threads make up the fabric from which Western views on egoism and altruism are cut, then Thomas Aquinas (1225–1274) was the master weaver. He, more than anyone else, attempted to blend these two traditions into a single whole. For him, virtue was to be found by following a two-fold rule for human action: human reason and the will of God. Reason was manifest in the Greek tradition; the will of God, in the Christian tradition. Of course, Aquinas did not give the two traditions equal weight; as he explained in *Summa Theologica* (1270/1917): "God is the first rule, whereby even human reason must be regulated" (II-II, Question 23, Article 6).

Aquinas used the Latin word *caritas* to describe the selfless love (*agape*) of the New Testament; *caritas* is translated into English as *charity.* Aquinas linked this concept to Greek philosophy by asserting that charity is a specific form of the true friendship of which Aristotle spoke: "Charity is the friendship of man for God. . . . The friendship of charity extends even to our enemies, whom we love out of charity in relation to God, to Whom the friendship of charity is chiefly directed" (II-II, 23, 1). Our charitable concern for the welfare of others is thus derivative from our friendship toward God; we love our Friend's friends. Aquinas thought that we ought even to love ourselves out of charity, insofar as we are related to God (II-II, 25, 4).

From these propositions, Aquinas drew one predictable and one rather surprising conclusion: Out of charity, we ought to love God more than ourselves (II-II, 26, 3); and "out of charity, a man ought to love himself more than his neighbor" (II-II, 26, 4). This second conclusion seems entirely consistent with Aristotle's *Ethics*, but how could Aquinas reconcile it with the Judeo-Christian commandment to love neighbor as self? He actually quoted the commandment and argued: "It seems to follow that man's love for himself is the model of his love for another. But the model exceeds the copy. Therefore, out of charity, a man ought to love himself more than his neighbor" (II-II, 26, 4). The apparent contradiction with Judeo-Christian teachings actually posed no special problem for Aquinas; he believed that a divine harmony in nature guaranteed a convergence of the interests of self and others.

Aquinas went on to argue that charity leads us to care for others by causing us to feel mercy (pity). Mercy is an emotional response of "heartfelt sympathy" that is evoked when the disposition to charity confronts another person in misery (II-II, 30, 3). Aquinas gave two possible accounts of how mercy affects behavior, each based on Aristotle's discussion of friendship:

> From the very fact that a person takes pity on anyone, it follows that another's distress grieves him. And since sorrow or grief is about one's own ills, one grieves or sorrows for another's distress, in so far as one looks upon another's distress as one's own.
>
> Now this happens in two ways: first, through union of the affections, which is the effect of love. For, since he who loves another looks upon his friend as another self, he counts his friend's hurt as his own, so that he grieves for his friend's hurt as though he were hurt himself. . . .
>
> Secondly, it happens through real union, for instance when another's evil comes near to us, so as to pass to us from him. Hence the Philosopher [Aristotle] says that men pity such as are akin to them, and the like, because it makes them realize that the same may happen to themselves. (II-II, 30, 2)

The latter account presented here is clearly egoistic; we respond to the threat to ourselves. The former account is less clear. Reflecting the same ambiguity found in Aristotle's treatment of friends as other selves, it could be either altruistic or egoistic. Which it is depends on whether the motivation is to reduce the friend's distress or one's own distress evoked by seeing the friend's distress.

This ambiguity about the nature of the underlying motives was of little concern to Aquinas; he was not trying to draw inferences about human nature from observing human behavior. Instead, he was describing the means whereby the divine purpose was achieved, the way God had chosen to have charity operate. Aquinas's gaze was steadfast on this divine purpose, and he was convinced that all was in order. The order could be clearly discerned by looking back to biblical and Greek texts.

With the Renaissance, however, divine order ceased to be the focus. A new figure moved to center stage: Man (used generically to refer to both men and women). What are we really like? What is our nature? What is our potential? When such issues were raised, the altruism question quickly emerged as central.

EMERGENCE OF THE DOMINANT WESTERN VIEW: UNIVERSAL EGOISM

Machiavelli (1469–1527)

A shift of attention toward what we are really like is apparent in Machiavelli's *The Prince* (1513/1908). Machiavelli might agree with Aquinas that the goal of the good prince should be virtuous concern for his kingdom and his subjects, but he could not agree with Aquinas's assumption of an overarching divine order in which means and end are always in harmony. The world—at least the political world—is out of joint. So Machiavelli sought to provide a cold, hard, unblinking look at social and political behavior as it is, not as it ought to be, believing it "more appropriate to follow up the real truth of a matter than the imagination of it" (1513/1908, p. 121).

Freed from the prescriptive deductions of classical metaphysics and religion, Machiavelli built his political analysis on the proposition of universal egoism:

> This is to be asserted in general of men, that they are ungrateful, fickle, false, cowards, covetous, and as long as you succeed they are yours entirely; they will offer you their blood, property, life, and children, as is said above, when the need is far distant; but when it approaches they turn against you. (1513/1908, p. 134)

Thomas Hobbes endorsed a similar view, and it remains the dominant view in Western thought to this day.

Hobbes (1588–1679)

As Hobbes stated it in his classic, *Leviathan* (1651):

> There is no such *Finis ultimus* (utmost aim) nor *Summum Bonum* (greatest good) as is spoken of in the books of the old moral philosophers. . . . The voluntary actions and inclinations of all men tend not only to the procuring, but also to the

assuring, of a contented life; and differ only in the way; which ariseth partly from the diversity of passions in diverse men and partly from the difference in knowledge or opinion each one has of the causes which produce the effect desired. (Chapter 11)

During the time men live without a common power to keep them all in awe, they are in that condition which is called war; and such a war as is of every man against every man. . . . And the life of man, solitary, poor, nasty, brutish, and short. (Chapter 13)

Hobbes found the only security from this frightful natural state to be a mutual agreement to curb our natural rights. This mutual agreement, or social contract, produced the State, Hobbes's Leviathan.

The State thus created can provide peace and security; but our nature has not changed. Hobbes believed that, "All society . . . is either for gain, or for glory; that is, not so much for love of our fellows, as for the love of ourselves" (1642/1973, Chapter 1, Section 2). Our ultimate goal or desire is forever and always to benefit ourselves; we show concern for another's welfare only when it is in our best interest to do so: "No man giveth but with intention of good to himself, because gift is voluntary; and of all voluntary acts, the object is to every man his own good; of which, if men see they shall be frustrated, there will be no beginning of benevolence or trust, nor consequently of mutual help" (1651, Chapter 15).

Hobbes was by no means unique among his contemporaries in assuming that human nature is fundamentally egoistic. Both Pascal (1670/1952) and Spinoza (1677/1910) said as much. More lighthearted but no less influential in making the same point were the *Moral Maxims and Reflections* (1691) of the Duke de La Rouchefoucauld and *The Fable of the Bees, or Private Vices, Public Benefits* (1714/1732) by Bernard Mandeville.

La Rouchefoucauld (1613–1680)

Voltaire said of La Rouchefoucauld, "His maxims [are] known by heart. . . . Though there is but one truth discussed in the book—viz. that self-love is the motive of all action, yet this is presented under so many aspects that it never fails to interest" (quoted from Powell, 1924, p. x). Here are just two of La Rouchefoucauld's (1691) maxims depicting the egoism of human nature:

2

Self-love is the love of a man's own self, and of every thing else, for his own sake. . . . It never rests, or fixes any where from home, and, if for a little while it dwell upon some other thing, 'tis only as bees do, when they light upon flowers, with a design to draw all the virtue there to their own advantage. . . . When we think it renounces and forsakes its pleasure, it only suspends or changes it. . . . This is the true picture of self-love, which is so predominant, that a man's whole life is but one continued exercise and strong agitation of it. . . .

82

The most disinterested love is, after all, but a kind of bargain, in which the dear love of our own selves always proposes to be the gainer some way or other.

A third maxim reminds us of, but extends, Aquinas's analysis of mercy (pity):

264

Pity and compassion is frequently a sense of our own misfortunes, in those of other men: It is an ingenious foresight of the disasters that may fall upon us hereafter. We relieve others, that they may return the like, when our own occasions call for it; and the good offices we do them, are, in strict speaking, so many kindnesses done to our selves before-hand.

Mandeville (1670–1733)

Bernard Mandeville first published *The Fable of the Bees* in 1714, and from time to time thereafter he added to it. The *Fable* consists of a doggerel poem called "The Grumbling Hive, or Knaves Turn'd Honest," which describes the collapse that would come to our society if individuals practiced virtue rather than vice, followed by two volumes of commentary.

Mandeville argued, much like Hobbes and La Rouchefoucauld before him, that our natural state is one of self-interest, and the underlying motive for any act of public benefit is always self-love, however cleverly disguised or rationalized. Religion and society simply make it worth our while to care for others by appealing to our pride and anticipation of glory:

To define then the reward of glory in the amplest manner, the most that can be said of it is that it consists in superlative felicity which a man, who is conscious of having performed a noble action, enjoys in self-love, whilst he is thinking on the applause he expects of others. (1714/1732, p. 41)

There is no merit in saving an innocent babe ready to drop into the fire: The action is neither good nor bad, and what benefit soever the infant received, we only obliged our selves; for to have seen it fall, and not strove to hinder it, would have caused a pain, which self-preservation compelled us to prevent. . . .

The humblest man alive must confess that the reward of a virtuous action, which is the satisfaction that ensues upon it, consists in a certain pleasure he procures to himself by contemplating on his own worth. (pp. 42–43)

Bentham (1748–1832)

Jeremy Bentham constructed a theory of morality based on "the principle of utility," or "the greatest happiness for the greatest number." To build this theory, he relied heavily upon Hobbes's view of Man as a calculator of self-interest. Bentham's major work, *Introduction to the Principles of Morals and Legislation* (1789/1876), begins:

Nature has placed mankind under the governance of two sovereign masters, pain and pleasure. It is for them alone to point out what we ought to do, as well as to determine what we shall do. On the one hand the standard of right and wrong, on the other the chain of causes and effects, are fastened to her throne. They govern us in all we do. . . . In words a man may pretend to abjure their empire: but in reality he will remain subject to it all the while. (Chapter 1, paragraph 1)

What makes one happiness or pleasure greater than another? Bentham's list of factors that enter into our calculation of the magnitude of a pleasure included the intensity, duration, certainty, and propinquity (closeness) of the pleasure. When the focus shifts from our personal pleasure to the pleasure of the community, Bentham added another factor, the extent of the pleasure, or the number of persons who are affected by it. Why should we choose to focus on the interest of the community at large rather than our own interest alone? Bentham believed that it was the task of lawmakers to ensure that to focus on the community's interests is in our personal best interest. As Plamenatz (1949) observed in *The English Utilitarians:*

It was his [Bentham's] mission in life to teach men how they might contrive a harmony of selfish interests, so that it might at last be possible for them to desire as a means what they ought to promote for its own sake. . . . Bentham's legislator makes the laws that ensure that each man from selfish motives will promote the greatest happiness of the greatest number. (pp. 9, 12)

Mill (1806–1873)

Bentham's famous follower John Stuart Mill went to great pains to try to exorcise the apparent egoism from utilitarianism. In *Utilitarianism* (1861), Mill claimed that: "The utilitarian morality does recognize in human beings the power of sacrificing their own greatest good for the good of others. It only refuses to admit that the sacrifice is itself good" (Chapter 2, paragraph 17).

Where do we get the power to attend to the good of others? Or, in Mill's words, "Why am I bound to promote the general happiness? If my own happiness lies in something else, why may I not give that the preference?" (Chapter 3, paragraph 1). His answer was that we *will* give our own happiness preference "until, by the improvement of education, the feeling of unity with our fellow-creatures shall be . . . deeply rooted in our character" (Chapter 3, paragraph 2). Once this feeling is internalized, Mill claimed, we will feel obliged to act in accord with it, lest we suffer external and internal sanctions.

The external sanctions are "the hope of favor and the fear of displeasure, from our fellow-creatures or from the Ruler of the Universe . . ." (Chapter 3, paragraph 3). The internal sanction is:

> a pain, more or less intense, attendant on violation of duty. . . . This feeling . . . is the essence of Conscience . . . , all encrusted over with collateral association, derived from sympathy, from love, and still more from fear; from all the forms of religious feeling; from the recollections of childhood and of all our past life; from self-esteem, desire of the esteem of others, and occasionally even self-abasement. (Chapter 3, paragraph 4)

Mill's argument, then, is that we ought to care for the happiness of others, and we will, once we have been socialized to (a) anticipate social (including Divine) approval if we do and (b) fear social and self-censure if we do not. The underlying motivation remains egoistic.

Nietzsche (1844–1900)

Utilitarians like Bentham and Mill may have been convinced that our own self-interest or happiness is the force controlling our actions. Yet they were also convinced that, ideally, we ought to show an equal concern for the happiness of others. They considered the principle of utility to be entirely consistent with the admonition to love neighbor as self, the core of Judeo-Christian morality.

Friedrich Nietzsche took a far more radical stance. He questioned this very "morality of unselfing," arguing that it was actually immoral. In his autobiography, *Ecce Homo* (1888/1927), written only weeks before his complete mental collapse, Nietzsche asserted:

> My experiences give me a right to feel suspicious in regard to all so-called "selfless" tendencies, in regard to the whole "love of one's neighbor" which is ever ready and waiting with deeds and advice. It seems to me that they are signs

of weakness. . . . The overcoming of pity I reckon among the noble virtues. (pp. 824–825)

Morality, the Circe of mankind, has falsified everything psychological, from beginning to end; it has demoralized everything, even to the terrible nonsense of making love "altruistic." (p. 862)

First I deny the type of man who formerly passed as the highest—the *good*, the *benevolent*, the *charitable;* and on the other hand, I deny that kind of morality which has become recognized and dominant as morality-in-itself—the morality of decadence, or, to use a cruder term, *Christian* morality. (pp. 925–926)

Clearly, Nietzsche had taken a bold step beyond the formulations of Aquinas, Hobbes, Mandeville, and the Utilitarians. For him, our callousness to those who are downtrodden and suffering was not a problem to be overcome through the higher call of morality; self-interest is a moral virtue. The "higher" call to selfless concern for others is actually the vice. Authentic morality demands that we be truthful, recognize this, and pledge allegiance only to ourselves.

The complete triumph of egoism expressed in Nietzsche's work may have been shocking in its day, but not for long. It became widely accepted in the 20th century, especially among psychologists.

AN ALTERNATIVE VIEW:
EGOISM AND ALTRUISM

The argument of Hobbes and his followers that human nature is exclusively self-interested did not convince everyone. No one disputed that self-interest was a powerful motive, but there were those who felt that it was not all there was to human motivation and human nature. They felt that to some degree, under some circumstances, concern for the welfare of at least some others was an end in itself and not simply a means to the ultimate end of self-benefit. They argued for the existence of altruism as well as egoism.

Bishop Butler (1692–1752)

The first major response to Hobbes was made by Anglican Bishop Joseph Butler. In a series of tightly reasoned sermons, Butler argued that self-love, in the sense of a general desire for one's own happiness, must be distinguished from the particular affections, passions, and appetites that are directed toward some object (e.g., food, when we are hungry), which are the primary source of our motives. Moreover, Butler argued, the *particular desires* are logically prior to self-love, because if we had no particular desires, there would be nothing to constitute our happiness, and self-love would have no object. Having thus placed self-love, or the general desire for our own happiness, in a derivative position, Butler concluded that it cannot be our sole motive.

Butler (1729/1896) then introduced benevolent motives as one class of particular desires, those directed toward the object of another's welfare. Further, he argued that these benevolent motives are entirely consistent with self-love, as he defined it. If we desire another's welfare, then to seek it is to seek what will make us happy, even though it is not sought *because* it will make us happy: "Every particular affection, even the love of our neighbor, is as really our own affection, as self-love; and the pleasure arising from its gratification is as much my own pleasure, as the pleasure self-love would have, from knowing I myself should be happy some time hence, would be my own pleasure" (Sermon 11, paragraph 7).

Through this argument, which distinguishes between the strong and weak forms of psychological hedonism, Butler succeeded in showing that there is no logical contradiction between altruistic motivation and desiring to reach our goals. This success has been considered by some to undercut Hobbes's argument (see Milo, 1973) because Butler made it clear that for Hobbes to affirm the universality of such a desire did not exclude the possibility of altruistic motivation as well.

But Hobbes was affirming more; he was affirming that altruistic motives do not, in fact, exist. For Butler to show that altruism is not logically impossible in no way assures us that it actually exists. Unfortunately, Butler did not even attempt to address the empirical question of the actual existence of altruism.

Rousseau (1712–1778)

Jean Jacques Rousseau advocated a more empirical approach. Based on careful reflection, he thought he could discern two fundamental characteristics of human nature, one egoistic and one altruistic:

> Contemplating the first and most simple operations of the human soul, I think I can perceive in it two principles prior to reason, one of them deeply interesting us in our own welfare and preservation, and the other exciting a natural repugnance at seeing any other sensible being, and particularly any of our own species, suffer pain or death. (1755/1950, Preface, paragraph 11)

Rousseau quickly moved on to build his political philosophy on these two natural rights; he did not tarry to dwell upon the nature of our repugnance at seeing another suffer. David Hume did.

Hume (1711–1776)

David Hume shared Rousseau's conviction that moral philosophy must be based on a clear understanding of human nature. He also shared the conviction that such understanding was possible only through careful observation of human behavior. And when Hume looked to experience he believed, like Rousseau, that he saw more than self-interest motivating our concern for others. He also saw universal and extensive benevolent principles based on sympathy. In *A Treatise of Human Nature* (1740/1896), Hume explained:

> No quality of human nature is more remarkable, both in itself and in its consequences, than that propensity we have to sympathize with others, and to receive by communication their inclinations and sentiments, however different from, or even contrary to our own. . . . Hatred, resentment, esteem, love, courage, mirth and melancholy; all these passions I feel more from communication than from my own natural temper and disposition. . . .
>
> When any affection is infus'd by sympathy, it is at first known only by its effects, and by those external signs in the countenance and conversation, which convey an idea of it. This idea is presently converted into an impression, and acquires such a degree of force and vivacity, as to become the very passion itself, and produce an equal emotion, as any original affection. (II, i, 11)

Hume thought this sympathetic reaction—closely akin to what is today called emotional contagion—was especially strong in response to the plight of relations and those close or similar to ourselves. Still, the scope of sympathy could be broad:

> 'Twill be easy to explain the passion of *pity*, from the precedent reasoning concerning *sympathy*. We have a lively idea of every thing related to us. All human creatures are related to us by resemblance. Their persons, therefore, their interests, their passions, their pains and pleasures must strike upon us in a lively manner. (*Treatise*, II, ii, 7)

Hume explicitly argued against the possibility that self-love underlies all benevolence in Appendix 2 to *An Enquiry Concerning the Principles of Morals* (1751/1902), entitled "Of Self-Love." He began this appendix by noting the principle, "supposed to prevail among many, . . . that all *benevolence* is mere hypocrisy" and that "all of us, at bottom, pursue only our private interest; we wear these fair disguises, in order to put others off their guard, and expose them the more to our wiles and machinations." Hume was severe in his repudiation of this principle, which he believed to be the product of "the most careless and precipitate examination" of the facts. Deserving more serious consideration, however, is:

Another principle, somewhat resembling the former; which has been much insisted on by philosophers, and has been the foundation of many a system; that, whatever affection one may feel, or imagine he feels for others, no passion is, or can be disinterested; that the most generous friendship, however sincere, is a modification of self-love; and that, even unknown to ourselves, we seek only our own gratification, while we appear the most deeply engaged in schemes for the liberty and happiness of mankind. By a turn of imagination, by a refinement of reflection, by an enthusiasm of passion, we seem to take part in the interests of others, and imagine ourselves divested of all selfish considerations: but, at bottom, the most generous patriot and most niggardly miser, the bravest hero and most abject coward, have, in every action, an equal regard to their own happiness and welfare. (*Enquiry*, Appendix 2)

In response to this "selfish hypothesis" Hume raised two objections. The first involved a retreat from his earlier insistence that all arguments appeal to experience; he appealed instead to Butler's logical differentiation between appetites and self-love. The second objection was based on common sense and obviousness: the selfish hypothesis is "contrary to common feeling and our most unprejudiced notion. . . . To the most careless observer there appear to be such dispositions as benevolence and generosity; such affections as love, friendship, compassion, gratitude" (Hume, *Enquiry*, Appendix p. 2).

The weakness of this appeal to common sense and obviousness is revealed in a passage that subsequent technological developments have made ironic indeed:

A man that grieves for a valuable friend, who needed his patronage and protection; how can we suppose that his passionate tenderness arises from some metaphysical regards to a self-interest, which has no foundation or reality? We may as well imagine that minute wheels and springs, like those of a watch, give motion to a loaded wagon, as account for the origin of passion from such abstruse reflections. (*Enquiry*, Appendix 2)

Since the invention of the internal combustion engine, we have no difficulty imagining minute parts giving motion to a loaded wagon. Similarly, with our increased understanding of the complexity and richness of human motivation, we have no difficulty imagining that self-interest should underlie friendship for a dependent other. If anything, common sense and obviousness are today on the side of the selfish hypothesis, not a hypothesis proposing that concern for others is independent of self-interest.

Smith (1723–1790)

Twelve years before publishing his classic *On the Wealth of Nations* (1771/1872), Adam Smith published a work in moral philosophy, *The Theory of Moral Sentiments* (1759/1853). This earlier work showed a large debt both to the Stoics, including Epictetus, and to David Hume, who was Smith's long-time friend.

From the Stoics, Smith borrowed the ideas of (a) a natural harmony or order and (b) the primacy and virtue of self-preservation:

> Every man is, no doubt, by nature, first and principally recommended to his own care. . . . And to hear, perhaps, of the death of another person, with whom we have no particular connection, will give us less concern, will spoil our stomach, or break our rest much less than a very insignificant disaster which has befallen ourselves. (II. ii. 2. 1)

In this passage Smith's view seems purely egoistic; but Hume's influence introduced an altruistic component, leading Smith to assert that "the great division of our affections is into the selfish and the benevolent" (VII. ii. intro. 3). Indeed, the first paragraph of *The Theory of Moral Sentiments* affirms the independence of altruistic from egoistic impulses:

> How selfish soever man may be supposed, there are evidently some principles in his nature, which interest him in the fortune of others, and render their happiness necessary to him, though he derives nothing from it except the pleasure of seeing it. Of this kind is pity or compassion, the emotion which we feel for the misery of others, when we either see it, or are made to conceive it in a very lively manner. (I. i. 1. 1)

Smith believed that pity or compassion are based on sympathy, which, following Hume, he defined as "our fellow-feeling with any passion whatever" (I. i. 1. 5).

But Smith did not believe that all—or even most—helping was prompted be benevolence. In a section entitled "Of the Sense of Duty," he revealed a clear awareness of the important role played by self-punishment and self-reward in promoting our attention to the needs of others:

> When we are always so much more deeply affected by whatever concerns ourselves, than by whatever concerns other men; what is it which prompts the generous, upon all occasions, and the mean upon many, to sacrifice their own interests to the greater interests of others? It is not the soft power of humanity, it is not that feeble spark of benevolence which Nature has lighted up in the human heart, that is thus capable of counteracting the strongest impulses of self-love. It is a stronger power, a more forcible motive, which exerts itself upon such occasions. (III. 3. 4–5)

The "stronger power" to which Smith referred is conscience and concern for our image; it leads us to act not out of interest in the other's welfare but to conform to our own sense of duty and, thereby, avoid social and self-censure. Recognizing the egoism in this motive, Smith argued that it is morally better to show compassion in spite of, rather than because of, duty: "With regard to all such benevolent and social affections, it is agreeable to see the sense of duty employed rather to restrain than to enliven them, rather to hinder us from doing too much, than to prompt us to do what we ought" (III. 6. 4). Immanuel Kant took just the opposite view.

Kant (1724–1804)

In the *Fundamental Principles of the Metaphysic of Morals* (1785/1889), Kant argued that a person should act "not from inclination but from duty, and by this would his conduct first acquire true moral worth" (Section 1, paragraph 12): "It is in this manner, undoubtedly, that we are to understand those passages of Scripture also in which we are commanded to love our neighbor, even our enemy. For love, as an affection, cannot be commanded" (Section 1, paragraph 13). The motive to serve duty described by Kant is neither egoistic nor altruistic. The ultimate goal is neither one's own nor the other's welfare; the goal is simply to do one's duty.

Kant was, however, ready to recognize that even when the concern we show for others appears to be prompted by duty, it may actually be prompted by self-love:

> Sometimes it happens that with the sharpest self-examination we can find nothing beside the moral principle of duty which could have been powerful enough to move us to this or that action and to so great a sacrifice; yet we cannot from this infer with certainty that it was not really some secret impulse of self-love, under the false appearance of duty, that was the actual determining cause of the will. We like to flatter ourselves by falsely taking credit for a more noble motive; whereas in fact we can never, even by the strictest examination, get completely behind the secret springs of action. . . . A cool observer, one that does not mistake the wish for good, however lively, for its reality, may some-times doubt whether true virtue is actually found anywhere in the world, and this especially as years increase and the judgment is partly made wiser by experience and partly, also, more acute in observation. (1785/1889, Section 2, paragraphs 2–3)

Whether made wiser by experience—including two world wars—or more acute in observation, 20th-century thought has certainly moved in the skep-tical direction Kant described. This is clearly reflected in psychology's assess-ment of our motives for showing concern for others.

CHAPTER 3

Egoism and Altruism in Early Psychology

Psychological answers to the altruism question are cut from the fabric of Western thought, so, predictably, they reflect the pattern and style of the philosophical tradition. Especially influential for psychology have been the ideas of Hobbes, the Utilitarians Bentham and Mill, and Nietzsche. But psychological answers are colored by a bold new influence as well: the theory of natural selection.

OUR CONCERN FOR OTHERS
IN LIGHT OF NATURAL SELECTION

Darwin (1809–1882)

With the publication in 1859 of Charles Darwin's *On the Origin of Species,* a whole new approach to the study of human nature seemed possible. If one could trace the evolution of physical structures and behavior patterns in other species—whether beetles in England or tortoises in the Galapagos—then could not the same be done for man? Instead of looking around us and within for consensus as had Hobbes and Hume, instead of trying to discern the true form of human nature beneath the shroud of social pressure as had Rousseau, could not human nature be found in the bundle of instincts that we inherited from our primate ancestors?

Darwin thought so, as have many of his followers. Indeed, eminent pale-ontologist George G. Simpson (1966), after posing the question "What is Man?," went so far as to assert: "The point I want to make now is that all attempts to answer that question before 1859 are worthless and that we will be better off if we ignore them completely" (p. 472). Darwin himself was far too modest and too knowledgeable of earlier thought to make so bold a claim; he knew his debt to his predecessors. Yet he was also firmly convinced that the theory of natural selection gave him a powerful new tool. Employing this tool, Darwin presented a multifaceted view of the motivation behind our concern for the welfare of others in Part I, chapter 4, of *The Descent of Man* (1871/1952).

Is the view Darwin presents in *The Descent of Man* egoistic or altruistic? An answer is difficult. To the extent that the concern we show for others is based on instincts that operate to ensure survival through the pull and push of personal pleasure and pain, as Darwin said instincts often do, the motivation seems egoistic. Yet, Darwin also argued that instinctive love based on pa-rental and filial affections and "the all important emotion of sympathy" evoke other-oriented benevolent actions within the community and outward to-ward an ever expanding community that may eventually include other species (1871/1952, p. 308). This motivation seems altruistic. Finally, Darwin suggested a third possibility: We often care for others from blind instinct or habit, not directed by pleasure, pain, love, or sympathy, and without any conception of a goal. If our concern for others is a product of these reflexive impulses, then terms like *selfish* and *selfless, egoistic* and *altruistic,* do not really apply. As noted in chapter 1, these terms assume an actor who is pursuing a goal, not simply acting reflexively.

The multifaceted complexity of Darwin's analysis was largely lost on early psychologists purporting to follow him. Typically, one facet was seen, and the other two were overlooked. As a result, Darwin's theory of natural selection was used to provide the foundation for three very different—even con-flicting—answers to the altruism question: (a) all our actions, including those benefiting others, are directed toward survival and personal pleasure and, hence, are ultimately egoistic; (b) our concern for others is at times altruistic; we have social instincts based on parental and filial affections and on sym-pathy that lead us to care for the welfare of at least some others; and (c) our actions that benefit others are neither egoistic nor altruistic because they are not goal-directed at all—we act impulsively, from blind instinct or habit. Psychologists advocating each of these answers could—and did—claim sup-port from Darwin's theory of natural selection.

EARLY EGOISTIC APPROACHES IN PSYCHOLOGY

James (1842–1910)

In his *Principles of Psychology* (1890), William James focused on the first facet of Darwin's argument noted previously; our instinctive impulse for survival makes us egoistic:

> Each mind, to begin with, must have a certain minimum of selfishness in the shape of instincts of bodily self-seeking in order to exist. This minimum must be there as a basis for all further conscious acts, whether of self-negation or of a selfishness more subtle still. All minds must have come, by the way of the survival of the fittest, if by no directer path, to take an intense interest in the bodies to which they are yoked. . . .

> And similarly with the images of their person in the minds of others. I should not be extant now had I not become sensitive to looks of approval or disapproval on the faces among which my life is cast. Looks of contempt cast on other persons need affect me in no such peculiar way. Were my mental life dependent exclusively on some other person's welfare, either directly or in an indirect way, then natural selection would unquestionably have brought it about that I should be as sensitive to the social vicissitudes of that other person as I now am to my own. Instead of being egoistic I should be spontaneously altruistic (pp. 323–324).

Freud (1856–1939)

Sigmund Freud, influenced by Nietzsche, also focused on the first facet of Darwin's argument, viewing all our actions as ultimately self-serving. Although "altruistic" motives can develop, they are really only strategic expressions of more fundamental egoistic ones. In *A General Introduction to Psychoanalysis* (1917/1920), Freud outlined his early position:

> The child loves itself first, and later learns to love others, to sacrifice something of its ego for another. Even those persons whom the child seems to love from the very beginning, it loves at the outset because it has need of them, cannot do without them, in other words, out of egoistical motives. Not until later does the love impulse become independent of egoism. *In brief, egoism has taught the child to love.* (p. 171)

Unlike Darwin, Freud did not give independent, biological status to parental affection and other social instincts; he saw them as products of socialization:

"The egoistic instincts are transmuted into social ones. We learn to value being loved as an advantage for which we are willing to sacrifice other advantages" (1915/1959, p. 297).

In his later years, Freud dwelled increasingly on the importance of aggression in human life, depicting a cosmic struggle between the creative life force, *eros,* and the destructive death force, *thanatos.* This new emphasis on aggression injected additional tension into the socialization process and created the need for a powerful moralizing agent, the *super-ego.* The socializing effect of the super-ego is not through the child learning to extend love outward from the self to others but through turning aggression that the individual would like to direct toward others back on the self, producing guilt. In *Civilization and Its Discontents* (1930), Freud argued:

> Aggressiveness is introjected, internalized; in fact, it is sent back where it came from, i.e., directed against the ego. It is there taken over by a part of the ego that distinguishes itself from the rest as a super-ego, and now, in the form of "conscience," exercises the same harsh aggressiveness against the ego that the ego would have liked to enjoy against others. The tension between the strict super-ego and the subordinate ego we call the sense of guilt; it manifests itself as the need for punishment. (p. 105)

Freud argued that civilized man endures this punishment as part of a Hobbesian social contract; it is acceptable only because society in the same way inhibits the aggression of others.

It is in this context, claimed Freud (1930), that we must understand the call to love our neighbor as ourself. This call is so important in our culture precisely because "nothing is so completely at variance with original human nature as this" (p. 87). Concern for the welfare of others is something that civilization can extract from the individual only with the sharp whip of guilt:

> Individual development seems to us a product of the interplay of two trends, the striving for happiness, generally called "egoistic," and the impulse towards merging with others in the community, which we call "altruistic." . . . In individual development, as we have said, the main accent falls on the egoistic trend, the striving for happiness; while the other tendency, which may be called the "cultural" one, usually contents itself with instituting restrictions. (p. 134)

There have been many extensions, criticisms, and revisions of Freud's ideas, both by Freud himself, and by others. Later psychotherapists have moved beyond Freud's focus on survival instincts to an emphasis on "higher" needs such as self-realization, self-expression, and self-actualization (Fromm, 1947; Horney, 1950; Maslow, 1954, 1968; Rogers, 1951, 1961). Yet, as Wallach and Wallach (1983) pointed out, even within these neo-Freudian and humanistic views, egoism still reigns. The individual may be viewed as self-determining instead of merely brokering the expression of instinctual impulses, but the realization, expression, or actualization to which the individual is called is still ultimately directed toward meeting the needs of the self.

Behaviorism

Speculation about the interplay of complex biological and cultural forces deep within the psyche of the individual—the sort of theorizing of which Freud was so fond—was precisely what John B. Watson (1878–1958) and other behaviorists argued should be eliminated from psychology. In their view, if psychology is to be a science, then it should restrict its attention to observables. The thoughts, feelings, and impulses of the individual cannot be observed, so they must go. What *can* be observed is the individual's behavior—including motor responses, facial expressions, body posture, verbal expressions, and the like—as well as the environmental conditions under which the behavior occurs. Psychology should direct its attention to these.

In its extreme expression in the work of radical behaviorists like Skinner (1953), behaviorism claims that we cannot meaningfully ask whether a given helpful act was egoistically or altruistically motivated. All talk of motives is out of bounds; the act just is. The only appropriate questions to ask are those about the probability that the helpful act will occur again, either in this or in some other situation.

Behavioral Analysis of Motives.   But most psychologists who responded positively to the behaviorist call that psychology rely on observables did not go as far as Skinner. Most did not believe that questions of motivation could simply be ruled out of bounds. Our actions seemed to be driven or directed in a way not reflected in the statement of stimulus–response relations. To illustrate this point, Woodworth (1918) used the example of a hunting dog following a scent. If the dog loses the scent (the stimulus), it does not stop responding; it actively searches and seems delighted when it picks up the trail once again: "This seeking, not being evoked by any external stimulus (but rather by the absence of an external stimulus), must be driven by some internal force" (p. 41). What kind of internal force? If it is to be part of the science of behavior, can it not—indeed must it not—be tied to observables?

The most influential response to such questions came from Clark Hull (1884–1952). Hull (1943) argued that the tendency of an organism to respond—or as Hull called it, the "reaction-evocation potentiality"—is a multiplicative function of habit strength and a relevant drive; both must be present for a response to occur. *Habits* are the product of the reinforcement history. *Drives* are the internal motivating force that Woodworth sought; they are internal stimuli derived from physiological needs. Satisfying the behaviorist principle of observability, Hull claimed that these needs could be defined empirically, at least in theory, in terms of their physiological effects.

When a behavior evoked by habit and drive succeeds in reducing the physiological need, the drive stimulus is reduced, leading to the cessation of activity. In addition, the habit strength of this behavioral response increases because it is reinforced, making the response more likely to occur in the future when the same drive state and environmental conditions are present.

Motivation to Help.   How are we to explain the motivation to help, according to Hull's analysis? In most cases, it seems unlikely that a physiological need evokes the helping response. Still, Hull and his followers had little difficulty accounting for such behavior; they argued that one can develop secondary or acquired drives (Brown, 1953; Dollard & Miller, 1950). Presumably, helping is the result of one or more such drives.

Paraphrasing Judson Brown's (1953) explanation of the acquired drive for money, we can imagine how a secondary drive to help might function: An individual first learns to become anxious in the presence of cues indicating that another person is suffering or in need. This anxiety serves as a secondary drive. Helping automatically terminates or drastically alters the cues of suffering and, in so doing, causes a decrease in the anxiety. The helping response is reinforced by this decline in anxiety. As a result of the reinforcement, helping is more likely to occur the next time the individual witnesses another person suffering.

In this analysis, it is the reduction of one's own aversive arousal (anxiety) that is reinforcing. Because the arousal reduction benefits the self, it is often assumed that Hull and his followers believed that the motivation to help is always and exclusively egoistic (see, e.g., Wallach & Wallach, 1983). But, strictly speaking, this is not true. In Hull's (1943) system, drives provide a blind push to behavior; they are not goal directed. Drives impel *some* action, and through the particular configuration of drive stimuli, they may provide "a considerable measure of distinctiveness and specificity in the determination of action" (Hull, p. 241). But *what* action they impel is primarily determined by habit (reinforcement history). Trying to stick as close as possible to observables, Hull and his followers wished to avoid assuming that we have goals. As Brown (1953) stated it, drives "activate or energize," but "any capacity to elicit *directed* behavior is specifically denied to drives" (p. 18); "neither learned nor unlearned drives *per se* can be said to be directed toward, or for that matter, away from, any object" (p. 17).

Thus, if egoism and altruism refer to goal-directed motives, as suggested in chapter 1, then the position developed by Hull and his followers is neither egoistic nor altruistic because it does not allow for goal-directed motives. Their position, instead, represents that third possibility suggested by Darwin: In many instances our responses are controlled by blind impulse and habit.

Purposive Behaviorism and Social Learning Theory: An Emergent Egoism. It would be misleading, however, to suggest that all behaviorists fail to give attention to the goals of behavior. Edward Tolman (1932) explicitly included goal-directed activity in his "purposive behaviorism." And within social learning theory (Bandura, 1977; Dollard & Miller, 1950; Mischel, 1973), which is currently the most robust descendant of the behaviorist tradition, talk of goals is commonplace.

When social learning theorists talk about the goals of helping, their explanations are consistently egoistic (see Wallach & Wallach, 1983, for a review). Concern for the welfare of others is explained as motivated by a desire to: (a) acquire material, social, or self-rewards for helping; (b) avoid material, social, or self-punishments for not helping; or (c) relieve the aversive arousal caused by witnessing another's suffering (see, e.g., Bandura, 1977; Cialdini & Kenrick, 1976; Rushton, 1980). In the words of Hatfield, Walster, and Piliavin (1978):

> The majority of scientists—[us] included—are fairly cynical. They interpret apparent altruism in cost–benefit terms, assuming that individuals, altruists included, learn to perform those acts that are rewarded . . . and to avoid those acts that are not. Either self-congratulation or external reward, then, must support apparently altruistic behavior. . . . Most often scientists attribute apparent altruism to more selfish motives. (pp. 128–129)

This seems a fair and accurate description of the majority view throughout the history of psychology. Early on, however, there was also a minority opinion. Some psychologists pursued the second possibility suggested by Darwin, that through parental and filial afections and through sympathy natural selection offers a scientific basis for altruism.

EARLY ALTRUISTIC APPROACHES IN PSYCHOLOGY

Spencer (1820–1903)

Herbert Spencer was the first to build a psychology based on Darwin's theory of natural selection. In his two-volume classic, *The Principles of Psychology* (1870, 1872), Spencer found no difficulty in making room for altruism, although he firmly believed that it must be kept in its proper place: within the family. Spencer believed that affiliative urges originate in the sex instinct, and they lead to the institution of the family, the essential unit of survival for humans. Within the family, the emotion of sympathy operates to arouse concern for the welfare of others. Children do not survive because they are strong and fit, but because their defenselessness and need arouse the sympathy of parents and siblings.

Spencer recognized that there were tendencies to feel sympathy for people in need outside the family, but he felt that these tendencies should be resisted. Failure to do so only increased the likelihood that the weak in society would survive at the expense of the strong. Outside the family, one's actions should be "red in tooth and claw."

Kropotkin (1842–1921)

In *Mutual Aid* (1902), Petr Kropotkin provided a quite different analysis of our concern for others, but an analysis still founded on principles of natural selection. Kropotkin claimed to have evidence for a much broader altruistic impulse than that recognized by Spencer. Born into the Russian aristocracy, Kropotkin based his argument on his observation of the gentility and compassion of the serfs in his childhood, as well as on anecdotes. He concluded that our concern for one another is not based on love and sympathy for specific individuals, but on a species-wide instinct of human solidarity:

> To reduce animal sociability to *love* and *sympathy* means to reduce its generality and its importance, just as human ethics based upon love and personal sympathy only have contributed to narrow the comprehension of the moral feeling as a whole. It is not love to my neighbor—whom I often do not know at all—which induces me to seize a pail of water and to rush towards his house when I see it on fire; it is a far wider, even though more vague feeling or instinct of human solidarity and sociability which moves me. (p. xii)

This instinct of human solidarity is, argued Kropotkin, the primary fact in human evolution.

McDougall (1871–1938)

Far more influential in early psychology than either Spencer or Kropotkin was William McDougall. He too set out to build a psychology founded on the theory of natural selection, a psychology that would account for human goodness. To do so, McDougall (1908) focused on the parental instinct, which he considered to be the most powerful of all instincts, and the associated tender emotion.

Although admitting that instincts and primary emotions cannot really be described, McDougall (1908) painted a clear picture of what he meant by the parental instinct and tender emotion. The impulse of the parental instinct:

. . . is primarily to afford physical protection to the child, especially by throwing the arms about it; and that fundamental impulse persists in spite of the immense extension of the range of application of the impulse. . . . Tender emotion and the protective impulse are, no doubt, evoked more readily and intensely by one's own offspring, because about them a strongly organized and complex sentiment grows up. But the distress of any child will evoke this response in a very intense degree in those in whom the instinct is strong. There are women— and men also, though fewer—who cannot sit still, or pursue any occupation, within the sound of the distressed cry of a child. . . . The emotion is liable to be evoked, not only by the distress of a child, but by the mere sight or thought of a perfectly happy child; for its feebleness, its delicacy, its obvious incapacity to supply its own needs, its liability to a thousand different ills, suggest to the mind its need of protection. By a further extension of the same kind the emotion may be evoked by the sight of any very young animal, especially if in distress. (p. 61)

In a similar direct fashion the distress of any adult (towards whom we harbor no hostile sentiment) evokes the emotion; but in this case it is more apt to be complicated by sympathetic pain, when it becomes the painful, tender emotion we call pity; whereas the child, or any other helpless and delicate thing, may call it out in the pure form without alloy of sympathetic pain. It is amusing to observe how, in those women in whom the instinct is strong, it is apt to be excited, owing to the subtle working of similarity, by any and every object that is small and delicate of its kind—a very small cup or chair, or book, or what not. (p. 63)

As implied here, McDougall made a sharp distinction between the tender emotion and sympathetic pain. He used the latter term to refer to the pain immediately evoked in us by the spectacle of another's pain (p. 66), closely paralleling Hume's and Smith's conception of sympathy in chapter 2. McDougall illustrated the distinction between sympathetic pain and the tender emotion with an intriguing, fanciful interpretation of the Parable of the Good Samaritan:

No doubt the spectacle of the poor man who fell among thieves was just as distressing to the priest and the Levite, who passed by on the other side, as to the good Samaritan who tenderly cared for him. They may well have been exquis- itely sensitive souls, who would have fainted away if they had been compelled to gaze upon his wounds. The great difference between them and the Samaritan was that in him the tender emotion and its impulse were evoked, and that this impulse overcame, or prevented, the aversion naturally induced by the painful and, perhaps, disgusting spectacle. (pp. 66–67)

McDougall believed that the motivation to help associated with sympa- thetic pain is egoistic; the goal is to reduce the helper's own sympathetic pain. The motivation to help associated with the tender emotion is altruistic: "From this emotion and its impulse to cherish and protect spring generosity, gratitude, love, pity, true benevolence, and altruistic conduct of every kind; in it they have their main and absolutely essential root without which they would not be" (p. 61).

McDougall's instinct-based psychology enjoyed great popularity during the first two decades of this century. By 1920, however, it had been severely undercut by behaviorist criticisms. Just as they criticized Freud, behaviorists argued that McDougall's theories consisted of speculation about unobservable internal processes—thoughts, feelings, desires, goals, and instincts—that had no place in a scientific psychology. Unfortunately, unlike Freud's theories, McDougall's did not have the redeeming virtue of clear clinical application. Soon, opposition to McDougall's ideas was sufficiently strong and widespread that his name and his theories were rarely mentioned without derision.

With McDougall's views discredited, the explanations offered by Freud, his followers, and by the behaviorists, dominated psychology. As we have seen, their accounts of our motivation to help were all explicitly or implicitly egoistic. By 1930, the question of the existence of altruism was shelved by mainstream psychologists; it was assumed either to be clearly answered in the negative, or to be clearly unanswerable.

CONCLUSION

From 1930 to 1970, the term *altruism* rarely appeared in the psychological literature. There was, said Gordon Allport (1968), a "flight from tenderness." Even in the 1960s, when a dramatic upsurge of interest in and research on helping behavior occurred (see Krebs, 1970; Latané & Darley, 1970; Macaulay & Berkowitz, 1970, for reviews), there was no parallel upsurge of interest in the classic question of whether at least some helping might be altruistically motivated. Donald Campbell summarized the situation in his widely acclaimed and controversial 1975 Presidential Address to the American Psychological Association: "Psychology and psychiatry . . . not only describe man as selfishly motivated, but implicitly or explicitly teach that he ought to be so" (p. 1104).

CHAPTER 4

The Altruism Question in Contemporary Psychology

In spite of the dominance in psychology of exclusively egoistic views, the term *altruism* began to reappear about 1970. Yet most contemporary psychologists who use the term have no intention of questioning universal egoism. They accept the view that all human behavior, including all the help we offer others, is the product of self-serving, egoistic motives. They simply redefine altruism so that it fits within this egoistic view. Accordingly, the approaches of these psychologists might most appropriately be called *pseudoaltruistic;* they are really egoistic, not altruistic.

PSEUDOALTRUISTIC APPROACHES

Pseudoaltruistic approaches to the question of why we help others can be classified into the following three types.

Altruism as Helping Behavior, Not Motivation. First, there are researchers who ignore the issue of motivation altogether, equating altruism with the act of benefiting another organism relative to oneself (i.e., helping). This first pseudoaltruistic approach has been popular with developmental psychologists, especially those studying children from a social learning perspective (see Rushton, 1980, for a review). It has also been popular with sociobiologists, who wish to apply the term altruism across a very broad phylogenetic spectrum—from the social insects to man (Dawkins, 1976; Hamilton, 1964, 1971; Trivers, 1971; Wilson, 1975).

To illustrate this approach, consider the definition of altruism employed by sociobiologists Ridley and Dawkins (1981):

> In evolutionary theory, altruism means self-sacrifice performed for the benefit of others. In everyday speech the word altruism carries connotations of subjective intent. . . . We do not deny that animals have feelings and intentions, but we make more progress in understanding animal behavior if we concentrate on its observable aspects. If we use words like altruism at all, we define them by their effects and do not speculate about the animal's intentions. An altruistic act is one that has the *effect* of increasing the chance of survival (some would prefer to say "reproductive success") of another organism at the expense of the altruist's. . . . It follows that an indubitably unconscious entity such as a plant, or a gene, is in principle capable of displaying altruism. (pp. 19–20)

I admire the clarity with which Ridley and Dawkins stated their definition. Yet one wonders why someone would want to use the term *altruism* in this unusual way—unless it is to trade on the motivational connotation of the term while at the same time denying this denotation? If altruism is equated with helping behavior, then it obviously exists. But the question remains whether this behavior is ever, in any degree, directed toward benefiting the other as an ultimate goal. No matter how one chooses to redefine altruism, this motivational question will not go away.

Altruism as Helping in Order to Gain Internal Rather Than External Rewards. Pseudoaltruistic approaches of a second and third type do address the question of motivation for helping, but rather than treating altruistic motivation as an alternative to egoistic motivation, these approaches treat it as a special form of egoistic motivation. The second approach—by far the most common among contemporary psychologists—redefines altruism to include seeking self-benefits that are internally rather than externally administered.

For example, Robert Cialdini and his associates (Cialdini, Baumann, & Kenrick, 1981; Cialdini, Darby, & Vincent, 1973; Cialdini & Kenrick, 1976) have spoken of an internalization process through which by adulthood "altruism . . . comes to act as self-reward" (Cialdini et al., 1981, p. 215). Daniel Bar-Tal and his associates (Bar-Tal, 1976; Bar-Tal, Sharabany, & Raviv, 1982) also focused on self-rewards for altruism—"feelings of self-satisfaction and . . . a rise in . . . self-esteem" (Bar-Tal et al., 1982, p. 387). For them, altruism is helping that is (a) self-chosen rather than chosen in compliance to external authority and (b) self-reinforced rather than externally reinforced. Shalom Schwartz and his associates (Schwartz, 1977; Schwartz & Howard, 1982) viewed altruism as "motivated by *personal* (as opposed to social) norms, situation-specific behavioral expectations generated from one's own internal-ized values, backed by self-administered sanctions and rewards" (Schwartz & Howard, 1982, p. 329). Joan Grusec (1981) defined altruism as "the develop-ment of consideration for others which no longer depends on external surveillance" (p. 65); instead, it depends on internalized values. Ervin Staub (1978, 1979) presented a similar but more elaborate definition:

> A prosocial act may be judged altruistic if it appears to have been intended to benefit others rather than to gain either material or social rewards. Altruistic prosocial acts are likely to be associated, however, with internal rewards (and the expectation of such rewards) and with empathic reinforcing experiences. (1978, p. 10).

It seems clear that none of these views describes what has traditionally been meant by altruism, for in each case the ultimate goal is some form of self-reward. Benefiting the other is simply instrumental to reaching this egoistic ultimate goal. In chapter 2 we saw that views of this kind were presented as arguments against altruism in the writings of the Duke de la Rouchefoucauld, Bernard Mandeville, David Hume, Adam Smith, John Stuart Mill, and Immanuel Kant. As a result, the considerable empirical evidence for "altruism" presented by contemporary psychologists who use the term in this way does not permit an affirmative answer to the altruism question. Rather than clearly demonstrating altruism, the evidence only serves to document one of the more subtle forms of egoism.

Altruism as Helping in Order to Reduce Aversive Arousal Caused by Witnessing Another's Suffering. A third pseudoaltruistic approach assumes that altruism is helping that is motivated by a desire to reduce some internal state of aversive arousal or tension caused by witnessing someone suffer. The idea that helping is motivated by the desire to reduce one's own distress has a long history in Western thought; we saw it expressed by Thomas Aquinas, Thomas Hobbes, Bernard Mandeville, and William McDougall. But none of these writers considered it altruistic.

The best-known contemporary expression of this idea is the arousal-reduction model originally developed by Jane and Irving Piliavin (1973) and later revised by Jane Piliavin, John Dovidio, Samuel Gaertner, and Russell Clark (1981, 1982). Although its authors are careful to call this a model of bystander or emergency intervention rather than of altruism, it has often been accepted as an account of altruistic motivation by others (e.g., Kary-lowski, 1982). The heart of the Piliavin model is summarized in two proposi-tions:

> *Proposition II:* In general, the arousal occasioned by observation of an emer-gency and attributed to the emergency becomes more unpleasant as it in-

creases, and the bystander is therefore motivated to reduce it. *Proposition III:* The bystander will choose that response to an emergency that will most rapidly and most completely reduce the arousal, incurring in the process as few net costs (costs minus rewards) as possible. (Piliavin et al., 1982, p. 281)

One way for a bystander to reduce his or her unpleasant arousal is to help, because helping removes the stimulus causing the arousal. The motivational process described clearly reflects Hull's view of motivation as arousal or tension reduction. But contrary to Hull's view, here the reduction of aversive arousal is presented as a sought goal, not simply as a reinforcing consequence.

Variations on the theme of altruism as arousal reduction are provided by Harvey Hornstein (1976, 1978, 1982), Janusz Reykowski (1982), and Melvin Lerner (1970). Hornstein (1978) claimed:

In some circumstances human beings experience others as "we," not as "they." When this happens, bonds exist that permit one person's plight to become a source of tension for his or her fellows. Seeking relief, they reduce this tension by aiding a fellow we-grouper. . . . Self-interest is served and tension is reduced when one acts on the other's behalf. (p. 189)

Hornstein called this aversive arousal "promotive tension." We saw early precursors of such a view in the writings of Aristotle on friendship and Aquinas on mercy, where it was suggested that we are distressed by the suffering of the friend, who is "another self."

Janusz Reykowski (1982) proposed a quite different source of prosocial motivation, but still one that involves reduction of an aversive tension state: "The sheer discrepancy between information about the real or possible state of an object and standards of its normal or desirable state will evoke motivation" (p. 361). Specifically, if one perceives a discrepancy between the current state and the expected or ideal state of another's welfare, this will produce cognitive inconsistency and motivation to reduce the upsetting inconsistency. Reykowski called the result "intrinsic prosocial motivation."

Melvin Lerner's (1970) just-world hypothesis led him to a similar but more specific view. Lerner claimed that most of us believe in a just world—a world in which people get what they deserve and deserve what they get—and that the existence of a victim of innocent suffering is inconsistent with this belief. In order to reduce the arousal produced by this inconsistency, we may help the victim.

According to each of these arousal-reduction approaches, the potential helper's ultimate goal is to reduce his or her own unpleasant arousal or tension. Increasing the other's welfare is simply an instrumental means of reaching this egoistic goal.

ALTRUISTIC APPROACHES

Each of the foregoing pseudoaltruistic approaches involves redefinition of the term altruism in a way that begs the altruism question. There are, however, several contemporary psychologists who use the term altruism in a manner more consistent with its use in earlier Western thought. Most of these psychologists argue for the existence of altruism, so I shall call their approaches altruistic. Lest false hopes arise, however, it must be admitted at once that these contemporary altruistic approaches tend to share two problems. First, they tend to be unstable, changing into one or another of the pseudoaltruistic approaches just described. Second, the empirical evidence presented in support is unconvincing; it can easily be accounted for by one or more egoistic explanations. These problems may be illustrated by taking a close look at the best known contemporary discussions of the existence of altruistic motivation—those by Martin Hoffman, Dennis Krebs, David Rosenhan, Jerzy Karylowski, Melvin Lerner, and Jane Piliavin.

Hoffman

Probably the best known contemporary psychological argument for the existence of altruism has been provided by Martin Hoffman (1975, 1976, 1981a, 1981b). Hoffman proposed that empathy, which he defined as "an affective response appropriate to someone else's situation rather than one's own" (1981b, p. 44), is the basis for an altruistic motive that is independent of egoistic, self-serving motives.

Hoffman considered empathy to evolve through a developmental sequence. Beginning with the reactive cries of infants to the cries of other infants (Sagi & Hoffman, 1976; Simner, 1971), the development proceeds with emergence of a clear sense of other as distinct from self, whereby the individual "imagines how he or she would feel in the other's place" (Hoffman, 1981b, p. 47). If the other is in distress, this leads the individual to experience *empathic distress*, which may eventually be generalized beyond the immediate situation to the other's general plight (e.g., feeling sad at seeing a happy little girl who is unaware of her own terminal illness); it may even be generalized to the plight of an entire group or class of people (e.g., the poor or oppressed).

Out of empathic distress emerges a second vicarious emotion: *sympathetic distress*. It is sympathetic distress that Hoffman claimed evokes altruistic motivation:

Once people are aware of the other as distinct from the self, their own empathic distress, which is a parallel response—a more or less exact replication of the victim's presumed feeling of distress—may be transformed at least in part into a more reciprocal feeling of concern for the victim. That is, they continue to respond in a purely empathic, quasi-egoistic manner—to feel uncomfortable and highly distressed themselves—but they also experience a feeling of compassion, or what I call sympathetic distress for the victim, along with a conscious desire to help because they feel sorry for him or her and not just to relieve their own empathic distress. (1982, p. 290; see also 1981b, p. 51)

Hoffman maintained that the motivation to help associated with empathic distress is egoistic; the helper's goal is to relieve his or her own distress:

Empathic distress is unpleasant and helping the victim is usually the best way to get rid of the source. One can also accomplish this by directing one's attention elsewhere and avoiding the expressive and situational cues from the victim. Such a strategy may work with children but provides limited relief for mature observers who do not need these cues to be empathically aroused. (1981b, p. 52)

The motivation associated with sympathetic distress is truly altruistic; it is directed toward increasing the other's welfare as an ultimate goal.

Hoffman's analysis is elaborate and rich in heuristic potential. It contains themes that can be traced as far back as Aquinas's discussion of mercy, themes that are even more clearly reflected in David Hume's and Adam Smith's discussions of sympathy (Hoffman's empathic distress) and pity (Hoffman's sympathetic distress) and William McDougall's differentiation between the motivational consequences of sympathetic pain (Hoffman's empathic distress) and the tender emotion (Hoffman's sympathetic distress). Yet Hoffman's view also clearly illustrates both problems typical of contemporary altruistic arguments.

First, Hoffman's argument has proved unstable, tending to change from altruistic to pseudoaltruistic. In his early writings on altruism, Hoffman (1975, 1976) made a sharp distinction between the vicarious emotions of empathic distress and sympathetic distress, as well as between their associated egoistic and altruistic motivation. Over the years, however, these distinctions have tended to recede into the background, and another theme has become dominant. The term *empathic distress* is used "generically to refer to both empathic and sympathetic distress" (Hoffman, 1981b, p. 52; also 1982, p. 281), and the clear distinction between egoistic and altruistic motivation is blurred: "Empathy is uniquely well suited for bridging the gap between egoism and altruism, as it has the property of transforming another person's misfortune into one's own distress and thus has elements of both egoism and altruism" (1981b, p. 55).

On what grounds has Hoffman inferred that this generic empathic distress evokes an altruistic motive?

> First, it is aroused by another's misfortune, not just one's own; second, a major goal of the ensuing action is to help the other, not just the self; and third, the potential for gratification in the actor is contingent on his doing something to reduce the other's distress. It is thus more appropriate to designate empathic distress as an altruistic motive—perhaps with a quasi-egoistic component—than to group it with such obviously self-serving motives as material gain, social approval, and competitive success. (1981b, p. 56)

As we know from reviewing the egoism–altruism debate in Western thought and from examining contemporary pseudoaltruistic approaches, these three characteristics apply to a variety of subtle egoistic motives for helping. Hoffman's argument, which began as an argument for an altruistic motive independent of egoistic motives, has over time become indistinguishable from an argument for a combination of two pseudoaltruistic motives: subtle self-rewards and reduction of one's own aversive arousal.

The second problem with Hoffman's argument is the empirical evidence that he has cited as support for an independent altruistic motive. The evidence, which he claimed must necessarily be circumstantial, is the following (Hoffman, 1981b, p. 42):

1. Most people across a wide range of ages and cultures try to help others in distress (see also Hoffman, 1982, pp. 291–293);
2. people are less likely to help when approval needs are aroused; and
3. helping can occur relatively quickly (e.g., in some bystander intervention studies the average response time is 5–10 seconds).

Elsewhere, Hoffman has referred to two more pieces of evidence:

4. Latency of helping decreases as the intensity of the victim's distress cues increases, and
5. following helping there is a decrease in the helper's arousal (1981a, p. 131; also 1982, p. 293).

The first, third, fourth, and fifth of these statements are empirically correct, but they say nothing about the nature of the motivation to help; the motivation could as easily be egoistic as altruistic. The second statement is only correct under some circumstances (see Cialdini et al., 1981; Reis & Gruzen, 1976), and it is easily handled by an egoistic explanation that includes internalized self-reward, for which there is considerable evidence (see Bandura, 1977; Thomas & Batson, 1981; Thomas, Batson, & Coke, 1981).

Hoffman (1981a) has also presented some biological evidence for the existence of altruistic motivation, but this evidence is equally unpersuasive. It is either purely hypothetical or easily amenable to egoistic interpretations. The same is true for the circumstantial evidence that Hoffman has offered for the transformation of empathic distress into sympathetic distress (1982, p. 290).

How could Hoffman conclude that altruism exists based on this equivocal empirical evidence? He reasoned as follows: Empirical evidence for the view that "altruism can ultimately be explained in terms of egoistic, self-serving motives . . . has not been advanced," and as a result, "the burden of proof rests as much on an egoistic interpretation as on an interpretation that humans are by nature altruistic" (1981b, p. 41). Given these premises, Hoffman chose to interpret the evidence as supporting altruism.

Unfortunately, both Hoffman's premises here seem false. First, there is ample evidence that increased potential for self-benefit can increase prosocial behavior (see Dovidio, 1984; Krebs & Miller, 1985; Piliavin et al., 1981; Rushton, 1980; Staub, 1978, for reviews). That egoistic motives can underlie prosocial behavior—as well as many other behaviors—cannot be denied. The issue in doubt is whether egoistic motives are the whole story, or only part. Second, given that egoistic motives exist and altruistic motives may or may not exist, parsimony clearly favors an exclusively egoistic view. If all we can do is muster evidence that is equally consistent with egoistic and altruistic explanations, then we have no good reason for claiming that altruistic motives exist.

Krebs

Like Hoffman, Dennis Krebs (1975) argued that empathic emotion leads to altruistic motivation. Also like Hoffman, his argument proved unstable. In the beginning of his article, Krebs clearly asserted that empathy leads to altruistic as opposed to egoistic motivation, but by the end, he changed to an arousal-reduction pseudoaltruistic view. Initially, Krebs made the motivational distinction clear:

> Psychologists have manipulated various antecedents of helping behaviors and studied their effects, and they have measured a number of correlated prosocial events; however, they have done little to examine the extent to which the acts that they investigated were oriented to the welfare of either the person who was helped or the helper. It is the extent of self-sacrifice, the expectation of gain, and the orientation to the needs of another that define acts as altruistic. People help people for a variety of reasons. Some of them may be altruistic; some of them may not. (1975, p. 1134)

Later on, however, Krebs (1975) blurred this clear motivational distinction into a pseudoaltruistic view: "When the pains and pleasures of others become intrinsically tied to the affective state of observers, it can be in their best interest to maximize the favorableness of the hedonic balance of others in order to maximize the favorableness of their own hedonic state" (pp. 1144–1145). Krebs apparently felt that the latter view is all that can be meant by altruism, because one can never show that an act is not motivated by expectation of reward:

> The main reason why classical debates about human capacity for altruism have flourished is because scholars have defined altruism as helping behavior that is not motivated by expectations of reward. As Krebs (1970) pointed out, the existence of altruistic behavior can never be proved when defined in this manner because it requires proving the null hypothesis (i.e., establishing the absence of expectation of reward). (1975, pp. 1134–1135)

I think Krebs made a logical slip here. As pointed out in chapter 1, an actor can expect reward yet still not be motivated by this expectation, as long as obtaining the reward is not the actor's goal. Krebs failed to make the crucial distinction between the goals and the consequences of an action. Failing to make this distinction, his initially altruistic view changed into an arousal-reduction pseudoaltruistic view.

Krebs's (1975) empirical evidence is more suggestive than that cited by Hoffman, although it too is amenable to egoistic explanations. Krebs conducted an experiment and found that participants observing someone similar to themselves undergo positive and negative experiences were more likely than participants observing someone dissimilar (or someone undergoing affectively neutral experiences) to experience empathy: They (a) showed more physiological arousal, (b) reported identifying with the other more, and (c) reported feeling worse while waiting for the other to experience pain. They were also more willing to help the other at some cost to self. Krebs claimed that because helping in this situation was personally costly, it provided an index of altruistic motivation. But there seems no reason to make this assumption, any more than there is reason to assume that helping was an index of egoistic motivation to—as Krebs himself suggested—maximize the favorableness of the helper's own hedonic state. Krebs demonstrated that empathy was associated with increased motivation to help, but he provided no clear evidence about the nature of that motivation. It could have been egoistic or altruistic.

Rosenhan

Unlike Hoffman and Krebs, David Rosenhan and his associates (Rosenhan, 1970, 1978; Rosenhan, Salovey, Karylowski, & Hargis, 1981) have not focused specifically on empathy or sympathy; they have spoken more generally of affect and emotion as sources of altruistic motivation:

> The ordinary laws of reinforcement seek to maximize rewards to the self. Technically speaking, they forbid altruism, which by definition is behavior directed towards the welfare of others at the expense of one's own welfare, even of one's life. . . . As we shall see, certain affects are the fulcra upon which the ordinary laws of reinforcement are violated. While experiencing those affects, people are led away from stances that maximize their own rewards and find instead that their attention, cognitions, and behaviors are directed toward the needs of others, often without regard for the quid pro quo. (Rosenhan et al., 1981, p. 234)

Like the arguments of Hoffman and Krebs, the argument of Rosenhan et al. (1981) has proved unstable, and the empirical evidence equivocal. Rosenhan et al. quickly shifted away from the stringent definition of altruism just quoted and instead used the term to apply to any prosocial behavior (1981, pp. 235ff.).

For empirical evidence, Rosenhan et al. relied primarily on two studies. In the first, Thompson, Cowan, and Rosenhan (1980) found that research participants who imagined the worry, anxiety, and pain of a friend dying of cancer subsequently spent more time trying to answer difficult multiple-choice questions for a graduate student in Education than either control participants who did not imagine a friend dying or participants who imagined their own pain and sorrow caused by the friend's death. In the second study, Rosenhan, Salovey, and Hargis (1981) found that participants who imagined their own joy at being given a trip to Hawaii subsequently spent more time answering multiple-choice questions for the graduate student in Education than control participants, who in turn spent more time than participants who imagined a close friend's joy at being given a trip to Hawaii.

At least in the Thompson et al. study, one might assume that high empathy or sympathy resulted when participants were instructed to imagine the friend dying of cancer (although no measures of emotions other than sadness were reported) and that this vicarious emotion either (a) sensitized participants to feel empathy (sympathy) for the graduate student, (b) predisposed participants to take the perspective of the graduate student and to feel empathy as a result, or (c) led participants to misattribute some of their empathy for the friend to the graduate student. Although each of these interpretations goes well beyond the data, each would be quite compatible with the relationship between empathy (sympathy) and altruism proposed by Hoffman and Krebs.

Instead, Rosenhan et al. (1981) suggested a pseudoaltruistic interpretation of the Thompson et al. and Rosenhan et al. findings: "It seems reasonable that altruism should occur only when there is a perceived imbalance of resources between self and other, and when that imbalance is weighted in favor of the self" (p. 244). Although Rosenhan et al. (1981) did not clearly specify why this imbalance should motivate helping, the underlying mechanism could easily be a personal need to conform to some internalized standard of equity (Hatfield, Piliavin, & Walster, 1978) or justice (Lerner, 1970). Once again, an altruistic view of motivation to help has changed into a pseudoaltruistic view, and the empirical evidence proves as compatible with an egoistic as an altruistic interpretation.

Karylowski

Jerzy Karylowski (1982, 1984) proposed a distinction between doing good to feel good about oneself (e.g., by maintaining or heightening a positive self-image) and doing good to make someone else feel good. He called the former *endocentric* altruism and the latter *exocentric* altruism. Endocentric altruism is clearly pseudoaltruistic, but exocentric altruism appears to be truly altruistic; the goal seems to be to increase the other's welfare: "Exocentric approaches assume that improvement of the partner's condition may possess inherent gratification value for the observer, regardless of whether it has been caused by him or not" (1982, p. 399). "The source of gratification lies only in the improvement of the conditions of another person in need" (1984, p. 141). Exocentric altruism is said to develop when attention is focused on the person in need rather than on the self.

On closer inspection, however, even Karylowski's exocentric altruism is indistinguishable from a pseudoaltruistic approach. This becomes apparent when he enumerates contemporary views of prosocial motivation that he thinks describe exocentric altruism. Included are the views of Hornstein, of Piliavin and Piliavin (including Piliavin, Dovidio, Gaertner, & Clark), of Lerner, of Reykowski, and of Hoffman (see Karylowski, 1982, pp. 399–403). It soon becomes clear that although exocentric altruism does not involve a desire to gain rewards or to avoid punishments, however subtle, no attempt is made to differentiate between acting in order to reduce one's own aversive arousal caused by witnessing another's distress and acting in order to reduce the other's distress. Yet this distinction seems crucial if we are to answer the question of the existence of altruism. The former is self-serving; the latter is not.

Karylowski's empirical evidence for the existence of exocentric altruism is also weak. Relying on self-reports of what research participants consider the most likely thoughts and feelings of a potential helper, Karylowski found that more exocentric (as opposed to endocentric) choices were made by partici- pants who experienced those socialization practices thought to increase sensitivity to the needs of others. Egoistic interpretations of this finding come readily to mind. To mention only the most obvious, the finding may reflect no more than differential socialization for what are the "right" responses to another's need, the responses for which one can self-reward. In general, it seems unlikely that self-reports of thoughts, feelings, and reasons for doing good are going to move us any closer to an answer to the question of whether altruistic motivation exists. Such reports can tell us that people differ in systematic ways in their prosocial values, but they cannot tell us the nature of these people's prosocial motivation. Those who espouse exocentric values could easily be endocentrically motivated to act in accord with them.

Lerner

In the 1980s, Melvin Lerner (1982; Lerner & Meindl, 1981) sought to go beyond his initial analysis of motivation to help, which was based on a pseudoaltruistic desire to maintain belief in a just world. He suggested that the form of justice operative in a given situation depends on the perceived relationship among the participants in the encounter. Accordingly, he iden-tified a variety of forms of justice, one of which—the justice of need—transcends self-concern for justice and is oriented instead to the welfare of the other.

The justice of need is evoked when we perceive an identity relationship, in which "we are psychologically indistinguishable from the other and we experience that which we perceive they are experiencing" (Lerner & Meindl, 1981, p. 224). Paralleling Hoffman's developmental view, Lerner claimed that there is a prototype for such identity relationships in early childhood in "the persistent and powerful empathic experience of sharing the emotional state of others," which is especially likely to occur when those with whom one is closely associated (e.g., family) transmit affective cues (Lerner & Meindl, 1981, p. 224). With maturation, this prototype becomes elaborated to include goal-directed activity. Specifically, when those with whom we perceive an identity relation desire some resource, we may engage in "identity-based activities":

> The "identity" activities are those activities designed to allow another person to acquire a desired resource. Our only "acquisition" of the resource in question under these circumstances occurs vicariously, as we experience some form of that which the other, who having gained the resource, is experiencing. (Lerner & Meindl, 1981, p. 225)

Lerner's analysis here may seem to imply a model of altruistic motivation based on identity relations. He certainly leads one to expect such a model, both by his sweeping indictment of the egoistic "economic" assumptions underlying every "well recognized theory of prosocial or altruistic behavior" (Lerner, 1982, p. 251) and by his listing of the emergent activities in identity relations as "nurturant concern for the other's welfare" and "meeting other's needs" (Lerner & Meindl, 1981, p. 228).

A closer look, however, suggests that the implied model is at least as amenable to a pseudoaltruistic interpretation as an altruistic one. For, when we help in an identity relation, it seems that the goal sought is our own vicarious experience of rescue: "If the empathic tie is dominant it would be natural for us to engage in acts which we or others might label as self-sacrificial or martyrdom. However, with that emotional bond we of course vicariously share in their fate. We experience their pain or rescue" (p. 227). This statement suggests a view much like Hornstein's (1978, 1982) pseudoaltruistic view, in which a cognitive link of "we-ness" leads us to feel tension over another's need, which we are then motivated to reduce. This is the same tension discussed by Aquinas as underlying our mercy for our true friend, who is another self.

Perhaps the most appropriate interpretation of Lerner's argument here is that it is neither egoistic nor altruistic. As noted in chapter 1, these terms assume a distinction between self and other: At issue in defining motives as egoistic or altruistic is whether the ultimate goal is the self's welfare or the other's welfare. In contrast, Lerner's identity relation appears to assume a dissolution of the self–other distinction; "we are psychologically indistinguishable from the other." Although it seems unlikely that such a dissolution ever fully occurs, except perhaps in some mystical states, if it does, then motivation to benefit the resulting self–other identity cannot properly be spoken of as either egoistic or altruistic. The question of whether the ultimate goal is to increase one's own or the other's welfare cannot meaningfully be asked; the two welfares have become one.

Piliavin, Dovidio, Gaertner, and Clark

In their revision, expansion, and update of the earlier Piliavin and Piliavin (1973) aversive arousal-reduction model, Piliavin et al. (1981, 1982) differentiated two subcategories of costs arising from a bystander's knowledge that a person in need has received no help: (a) *personal costs* associated with the bystander's failure to intervene include "self-blame for one's inaction, public censure, recriminations from the victim, and in some countries even prosecution as a criminal" (1981, p. 85); and (b) *empathy costs* are "unrelated to bystanders' actions on behalf of the victim, but [depend] solely on their knowledge that the victim is continuing to suffer" (p. 85). Piliavin et al. (1982) implied that the motivation to help evoked by empathy costs is more altruistic than the clearly egoistic motivation evoked by aversive arousal reduction or by anticipated personal costs: "To the extent that arousal is interpreted as alarm and concern for another person, rather than personal distress and upset, and the salience of empathic considerations associated with the victim's plight (e.g., the victim is suffering) exceed personal cost considerations, the motive for helping has a sympathetic rather than a selfish tone" (p. 286).

A closer look at the Piliavin et al. (1982) discussion of empathy costs suggests that the associated motivation is, once again, pseudoaltruistic rather than altruistic. In describing the sympathetic motives induced by empathy costs, Piliavin et al. stated that ". . . the needs of another can become undifferentiated from one's own, . . . can become coordinated with those of the bystander or become incorporated into the bystander's self-interest . . ." (p. 286). Piliavin et al. noted the similarity of their position here to Hornstein's promotive tension analysis. They then added: " 'Empathy costs' involve internalizing the need or suffering of the victim and include continued unpleasant arousal related to the perceived distress of the victim" (p. 288). "The more clear and more severe the emergency is, the more unpleasant and costly the continued suffering of the victim will be for the bystander" (1981, p. 99). "We-ness," similarity, and attraction are all assumed to increase empathy costs, which are related to a "disposition to take instrumental action for relief of one's own distress" (1981, p. 203). These statements suggest that the motivation to help associated with "empathy costs" is directed toward the egoistic goal of reducing these empathy costs, not the altruistic goal of reducing the victim's distress.

There is an additional ambiguity in the Piliavin et al. (1981, 1982) discussion of empathy costs. Sometimes, the emphasis is on reduction of unpleasantness that the potential helper is currently feeling as a result of knowing that the victim is suffering. At other times, the emphasis is on unpleasantness that the potential helper anticipates feeling in the future if he or she does not help. These different emphases imply two different egoistic motives: (a) escape from present aversive arousal, and (b) avoidance of anticipated future aversive arousal. The former is akin to the motivation of a rat on a charged grid trying to escape shock; the latter, to the motivation of a rat bar-pressing to escape before the shock is turned on. Learning is necessary for the latter motivation to occur; it is not for the former. These two motivational processes are distinct, but not mutually exclusive. They may even occur simultaneously.

Finally, in their 1981 discussion, Piliavin et al. introduced yet another view of the motivation to help evoked by empathy costs. They suggested that " 'empathy costs' involve internalizing the need or suffering of the victim and include a continued and perhaps increasing level of unpleasant arousal related to the perceived distress of the victim and associated feelings of inequity or unfairness" (p. 85). This statement seems less reminiscent of Hornstein's view than of Reykowski's (1982) suggestion that another's suffering can violate one's standards and expectations and so evoke motivation to avoid unpleasant cognitive inconsistency. Like Reykowski's view, this unfairness view of empathy costs is easily amenable to a pseudoaltruistic interpretation: The knowledge that the other is continuing to suffer is unpleasant because it violates my sense of justice, and I am therefore motivated to help in order to reduce this unpleasantness.

In summary, the differentiation in motives for helping made by Piliavin et al. (1981, 1982) does not seem to be between egoistic and altruistic motives but between three different egoistic motives: (a) egoistic motivation to reduce one's feelings of disgust, anxiety, and upset caused by seeing someone suffer (aversive arousal reduction); (b) egoistic motivation to avoid shame, guilt, and recrimination for a failure to help (personal costs); and (c) egoistic motivation to reduce one's own present or future empathic distress produced by witnessing the suffering victim (empathy costs). The self-benefit may be more subtle in the last case than in the first two, but the motivation still seems egoistic. Whichever version of the Piliavin et al. empathy cost analysis one considers—the version that emphasizes present and future empathic distress or the version that emphasizes unfairness—the result seems the same. Although these authors imply that empathy costs introduce sympathetic motives that transcend selfishness, the specific motivational processes described seem easily amenable to pseudoaltruistic, egoistic interpretations.

CONCLUSION

Overall, contemporary psychological discussions of altruism seem to involve either intentionally or unintentionally redefining the term so that the altruism question is not clearly addressed. As a result, the evidence cited in these discussions provides us with no good basis for claiming that the motivation to help another is ever truly altruistic.

Does this then mean that the recent work is of no value? Not at all. The recent work makes two very important contributions. First, it supplements the earlier philosophical and psychological discussions, making explicit a number of subtle pseudoaltruistic forms of egoism and revealing how easy it is to slip from discussing altruism to discussing one or another of these pseudoaltruistic alternatives. In so doing, the recent work makes it clear that if we are to pursue the question of altruism scientifically, then we must first develop an explicit and detailed map of how any altruistic argument both relates to and differs from various egoistic alternatives, especially from those subtle forms of egoism reflected in the pseudoaltruistic arguments. Such a map seems essential if we are to have any hope of generating empirical predictions from the altruistic argument that differ from predictions made by one or more of the egoistic arguments. And until clear differential predictions can be made, the empirical evidence for altruistic motivation will necessarily remain unconvincing.

Second, in conjunction with the earlier philosophical and psychological writings, the recent work offers a clear hint as to where we might be likely to find altruism, if it exists. Altruistic motivation is most frequently claimed to be the product of an other-oriented emotional reaction to seeing someone suffer, a reaction variously called empathy, sympathy, tenderness, pity, or compassion. This emotional reaction, which I simply call *empathy*, is named as a source—if not *the* source—of altruism by Martin Hoffman, Dennis Krebs, Jerzy Karylowski, Melvin Lerner, and Jane Piliavin et al. It is also the source of altruism most frequently named by earlier philosophers and psychologists, including Thomas Aquinas, David Hume, Adam Smith, Charles Darwin, Herbert Spencer, and William McDougall.

Taking seriously this hint from those who have gone before, the present attempt to answer the altruism question focuses on the possibility that empathic emotion evokes altruistic motivation. The goals of Part II of this book are, first, to provide an explicit and detailed conceptual map that locates this empathy–altruism hypothesis in relation to various egoistic explanations of why we help—highlighting similarities and differences—and, second, to use this conceptual map to derive empirical predictions from the empathy–altruism hypothesis that differ from predictions made by egoistic explanations of the motivation to help evoked by empathy. Then, in Part III, we review research designed to test these empirical predictions.

PART
II

TOWARD AN ANSWER:
THE EMPATHY–ALTRUISM
HYPOTHESIS

CHAPTER 5

A Scientific Method for Addressing the Altruism Question

Our review in Part I traced the high points in the long history of the egoism–altruism debate. The issue of whether we ever care for others for their sake rather than our own was raised as early as the fourth century B.C. in Greece, and even earlier in the Judeo-Christian tradition. In both traditions, there was awareness of the human capacity to sacrifice self-interest for the interest of a friend or neighbor; there was also awareness of an array of self-benefits that might thereby accrue.

The egoism–altruism debate came sharply into focus with the Renaissance, when attention was turned toward the nature of man—flesh and blood men and women stripped of the cloak of metaphysical and theological preconception. Many Renaissance scholars, like Thomas Hobbes, concluded that human nature was fundamentally and universally egoistic. Hobbes did not deny the existence of self-sacrificial behavior or concern for the welfare of others, but he was convinced that self-sacrifice and concern were always in the service of some more or less subtle form of self-benefit. From Hobbes and his contemporaries, the assumption of universal egoism flowed through the Utilitarianism of Bentham and Mill and the writings of Nietzsche into the mainstream of early psychology. There, the current of universal egoism was strong, both in Freud's psychoanalytic theories and in behaviorism—when behaviorism considered issues of motivation at all. In contemporary psychology, the current of egoism is still strong.

The Renaissance also spawned an alternative view, represented by Butler, Rousseau, Hume, and Smith. These writers argued that, in addition to an undoubted concern for one's own welfare, there was within human nature the capacity for genuine concern for the welfare of others. The Scottish philosophers Hume and Smith and, following them, Charles Darwin linked this altruistic motivation to an other-oriented emotional reaction to seeing someone else in distress—to feeling compassion, pity, or sympathy. In early psychology, McDougall labeled this source of altruism the *tender emotion,* and distinguished it from a more self-oriented emotional reaction that he called *sympathetic pain.* By 1930, however, with the demise of McDougall's influence, there were no major advocates of altruism left in psychology; universal egoism reigned supreme.

The renewed talk of altruism in psychology since 1970 has, for the most part, not implied a challenge to the reign of universal egoism. The territory that has been allotted to altruism is no more than a quaint province in an egoistic empire; altruism is spoken of not to reopen the egoism–altruism debate, but to make it go away. Yet, the question of our capacity for genuine concern for others has not gone away. A small group of contemporary psychologists has begun once again to take seriously the possibility that altruism may be part of human nature.

Unfortunately, the arguments for the existence of altruism offered by these psychologists share two problems. First, they seem inevitably to drift from discussion of altruism to discussion of one or another pseudoaltruistic form of egoism. Second, the empirical evidence cited as demonstrating the existence of altruism remains unconvincing. It can easily be explained by one or more of the subtle versions of egoism recognized since antiquity.

WHERE DO WE GO FROM HERE?

Having reached this point, it may seem that we are at an impasse. We have found no satisfactory answer to the altruism question. And, given the number of attempts that have been made, we may despair of ever finding one. The complexity of the issues involved, issues about the nature of human motivation and human potential, seems to place an answer beyond reach. Should we not be honest and declare the question unanswerable, or else admit that any answer is nothing more than an affirmation of belief, derived from untested and untestable assumptions about human nature? The question of the existence of altruism seems no more answerable than the question of the existence of God. If this is so, then our search for an answer is at an end.

But are we really stuck? Are we really limited to recognizing that (a) we care for one another and (b) this care is associated with subtle and varied forms of self-benefit—without being able to ascertain the nature of the underlying motivation? Must we really choose between universal egoism and altruism as assumptions about human nature, basing our choice on nothing more than personal predilection and preference? Given that the altruism question is a question about what *is*, and moreover, about something that is in this world and not in some other, then it should be amenable to a scientific answer. The remainder of this book is based on the premise that it is. I ask you to accept this premise, at least as a working hypothesis.

As Einstein pointed out, belief in our ability to answer seemingly unanswerable questions about the nature of things is a necessary premise of scientific discovery. Without this belief, progress is limited to either filling in the details of what we already know or awaiting the serendipitous happy accident that shows us something new. Filling in details and serendipity are both important in science, but neither is the essence. The essence is the audacious enterprise of seeking answers to questions that at the time seem unanswerable. Many efforts fail, but only when we assume that we can answer a question, even if we do not yet know how, do we have much chance. Science begins with this leap of faith.

Yet faith is not enough. Before attempting a scientific answer to the altruism question, we also need to think with some care about how such an analysis might best proceed. That is our task in the present chapter.

A FALSE TRAIL: SEEKING OUT PARAGONS OF HELPFULNESS

It might seem that the most natural path to follow in search of scientific evidence for altruism would be to seek out those paragons of helpfulness celebrated by our society—the Mother Teresas, Albert Schweitzers, Mahatma Gandhis, the rescuers of Jews from the Nazis, the heroes who risk their lives helping in emergencies. After all, if anyone is altruistic, is it not people like these?

A little reflection reveals that this path is a false trail, for two reasons. First, it focuses on behavior, not motivation. Paragons of goodness are clearly outstanding for their helpfulness. But the altruism question is not about helpfulness; it is about the nature of the motivation for helping. We cannot assume any necessary relationship between the amount of helping an individual displays and the nature of his or her motivation. The amount may reveal something of the quantity of underlying motivation, but it does not reveal the quality.

Second, seeking out paragons of helpfulness blurs the important distinction between scientific and moral perspectives on altruism. From a moral perspective, one may legitimately affirm that a Mother Teresa or an Albert Schweitzer is a better person than the rest of us, a saint perhaps. The altruism question is not, however, a moral question; it is a question about human motives and potential. It asks whether, when we help, our goal is ever to benefit the other as an end in itself, or whether our goal is always, ultimately, some form of self-benefit. From a moral perspective, it is possible to assert that altruism, if it exists, is morally good. This assertion cannot, however, be reversed: Moral goodness need not be altruistic. Feeding the hungry, housing the homeless, and comforting the sick are likely to be seen as morally good, regardless of the underlying motive. Such goodness certainly sharpens the altruism question because the motivation *might* be altruistic, but it provides no answer.

THE HARD CLIMB: INFERRING THE NATURE OF THE MOTIVATION TO HELP

How, then, are we to pursue the altruism question scientifically? As we have said, the issue is one of motivation—specifically, the *nature* of the motivation to help, whether it is exclusively egoistic or at least in part altruistic. In chapter 1, it was suggested that the nature of a motive is defined by its ultimate goal. Benefiting the other is, by definition, a goal of helping. But it may be an instrumental goal on the way to the ultimate goal of benefiting oneself. If it is, then the motive in question is egoistic. On the other hand, just because self-benefits follow from a helpful act does not prove that these self-benefits are the helper's goal. The self-benefits could be unintended consequences of the helper reaching his or her ultimate goal of benefiting the person in need. If they are, then the motive is altruistic. Or perhaps both the self-benefits and benefiting the person in need are ultimate goals. If they are, then we have multiple motives, both egoistic and altruistic. The key to the altruism question lies, it seems, in our ability to distinguish between ultimate and instrumental goals of helping.

Table 5.1 outlines the formal structure of the problem: Helping typically

TABLE 5.1
Formal Structure of the Altruism Question

Nature of the Motive to Help	Outcomes of Helping	
	Relieving the Other's Suffering . . .	And Receiving Self-Benefits
Egoistic	Instrumental goal	Ultimate goal
Altruistic	Ultimate goal	Unintended consequence

Note: Adapted from Batson (1990).

benefits both the person in need and the self. If benefiting the other is an instrumental goal on the way to the ultimate goal of self-benefit, then the motive to help is egoistic. If benefiting the other is the ultimate goal and the self-benefits are unintended consequences, then the motive is altruistic. To answer the altruism question, we must determine whether benefiting the other person is an instrumental goal or an ultimate goal.

Making this determination is especially complicated because certain self-benefits seem to follow automatically from benefiting someone in need. These include: (a) a reduction of one's own disquieting feelings of pity or compassion (Aquinas), (b) anticipated reciprocity (Hobbes, La Rouchefoucauld), (c) feeling good about oneself (Aristotle, La Rouchefoucauld, Mandeville), or (d) avoiding guilt (Mill, Nietzsche, Freud). So how are we to determine whether the helper's ultimate goal was to benefit the other or to benefit the self? The task before us seems difficult indeed. An answer seems to require mind reading, and mind reading of a particularly tricky form. As noted in chapter 1, we cannot even assume that the helper knows his or her own ultimate goal.

Such mind reading may seem impossible, but, in fact, we do it all the time. Consider a simple example far removed from altruism. Suzie and Frank work together. One morning, music-loving Suzie is unusually attentive to homely but well-heeled Frank. "Why?" Frank wonders, "Is it because my prayers have been answered, and Suzie is smitten by my charms? Or is she broke and wanting me to take her to the concert this weekend?" Frank's dilemma is to determine the nature of Suzie's motivation; he wants to know her ultimate goal. As matters stand, however, Frank lacks the information to make a clear inference—though wishful thinking may provide one. Now imagine that Suzie comes back from lunch, opens her mail, and finds that her father has sent her two tickets to the concert. If she coolly passes Frank on her way to invite John, then Frank can infer with considerable confidence—and chagrin—the ultimate goal of her earlier attentions. He knows her motive.

This simple example suggests a general strategy for disentangling instrumental and ultimate goals. Three principles are involved. First and most obvious, we do not observe another person's goals or intentions directly; we infer them from the person's behavior. Second, given a single behavior that moves the person toward more than one possible ultimate goal, the true ultimate goal cannot be discerned. It is like having one equation with two unknowns; a single, clear answer is impossible. Third, we can draw reasonable inferences about a person's true ultimate goal if we can observe the person's behavior in two or more different situations that involve a change in the relationship between the different possible ultimate goals. The behavior should always be directed toward the true ultimate goal.

Everyday use of this disentanglement strategy when inferring the motives underlying other people's behavior has been discussed in some detail by attribution theorists like Heider (1958) and Jones and Davis (1965). We use it to infer when a student is really interested or only seeking a better grade (What happens to the interest after grades are turned in?), why a friend chooses one job over another, and whether a politician is sincere or merely pursuing votes. Psychologists studying motivation also use this strategy, as has been nicely demonstrated in cognitive dissonance (Festinger, 1957) and reactance (Brehm, 1966) experiments.

Employing the Suzie-and-Frank example as a model, there seem to be two steps in the process of inferring the nature of a person's motivation from his or her behavior. First, we must conduct a conceptual analysis of the potential alternative goals of the person's action. Unless we have some idea that a given goal may have been the person's aim, there is little likelihood of concluding that it actually was. Frank realized that Suzie might be after the concert rather than after him. Second, we must observe the person's behavior in varying circumstances. Specifically, the circumstances must vary in a way that disentangles the relationship between the potential ultimate goals, making it possible for the person to obtain one goal without having to obtain the other, just as after lunch Suzie could get to the concert without Frank. The person's behavioral choices in these different situations should prove diagnostic, telling us which goal is ultimate. This two-step process provides, I believe, an objective basis for inferring the nature of a person's motives.

Applying this inference process to the altruism question, we must first consider the possible self-benefits of a given helping act. Then we must vary the helping situation in a way that disentangles the confounding of the benefit to other and the benefits to self. We might do this by, for example, providing a behavioral means of obtaining the self-benefit that does not involve helping and, moreover, is less costly than helping. If we do this and the individual no longer helps, then we have reason to believe that his or her ultimate goal was the self-benefit, and the motivation egoistic. If the individual still helps, then we have reason to believe that this self-benefit was not an ultimate goal. The ultimate goal may have been some other self-benefit, or it may have been benefiting the person in need. If the latter, the motivation was altruistic.

Note the asymmetry in the inferences that can be drawn. When we help, the self-benefits that accrue follow from our efforts to benefit the person in need, not the other way around. There is an ordering of the two possible ultimate goals—benefit to other is a condition for benefit to self. Because of this ordering, any conclusion that the motivation for helping is altruistic necessarily involves a weaker inference than a conclusion that the motivation is egoistic. We can find positive evidence that some proposed self-benefit was or was not the person's ultimate goal; we cannot do the same for benefiting the other. Even if we find positive evidence that benefiting the other was not an instrumental goal on the way to some proposed egoistic ultimate goal, it might have been instrumental in obtaining some other self-benefit.

Although it is important to recognize the difference in strength of the two inferences, this asymmetry should not trouble us too much. Similar asymmetries are common in science. For example, empirical evidence that the speed of light is a constant involves the same kind of weak inference. After a number of tests under circumstances where variability should have appeared but did not, it was accepted that the speed of light is constant. Still, it remains possible that the speed will prove variable in some not yet tested medium or under some not yet conceived condition. Until such a medium or condition is found, however, the conclusion that the speed is constant is justified. Analogously, if in some situation or circumstance we find that all plausible self-benefits of helping were not the ultimate goal, then it is appropriate to conclude that the ultimate goal was to benefit the person in need. Of course, as with the speed of light, this conclusion will have to be re-evaluated if and when a new plausible egoistic explanation for the observed helping is proposed.

ARISTOTELIAN VERSUS GALILEAN SCIENCE

The general strategy that I have outlined for addressing the altruism question assumes a particular approach to science, one that Kurt Lewin (1935) called Galilean as opposed to Aristotelian. Lewin borrowed this distinction from Ernst Cassirer (1910/1921). Because much psychological research takes a more Aristotelian approach, the difference between these two approaches deserves some comment.

The most obvious difference between Aristotelian and Galilean science is in the role of empirical observation. Aristotelian science relies on classical induction; it begins with observation of particulars, moves to conceptual ordering and classification of these into types, and finally, explains the behavior of the particulars as a result of the attributes of the types. Galilean science relies instead upon a hypothetico-deductive method (Popper, 1959); it begins with an explanatory model, derives empirical predictions from the model, and finally, tests these predictions through empirical observation. William McGuire (1973) nicely summarized the logic of this hypothetico-deductive method:

> We not only generate delusional systems, but we go further and test our delusional systems against objective data as well as for their subjective plausibility.... Even when our theory seems plausible and so ingenious that it

deserves to be true, we are conditioned to follow the Cromwellian dictum (better than did the Lord Protector himself) to consider in the bowels of Christ that we may be wrong. (pp. 452–453)

Although this difference in the role of empirical observation between Aristotelian and Galilean approaches to science is profound, Lewin (1935) argued that the distinction between these two approaches goes even deeper. They differ in underlying logic and, even more fundamentally, in their concept of reality.

Aristotelian Science

For Aristotle, the focus of attention is observed phenomena, which are grouped into classes on the basis of common attributes. Lawfulness or regularity is conceived historically, in terms of frequency of occurrence. Observing on a number of different occasions that heavy objects fall quickly but light objects fall more slowly or even rise, as do the flames in a fire, Aristotle concluded that light objects have as part of their essential nature a tendency upward, whereas heavy objects have a tendency downward. Historical invariance in the behavior of observed phenomena is taken as evidence that these phenomena are obeying natural laws. Moreover, concepts in Aristotelian science often have a valuative character. There is, for example, the highest form of motion—circular—that occurs only in the heavens.

Galilean Science

Galilean science departs from Aristotelian science in each of these respects; it rejects the emphasis on classification of observed phenomena into types, on historical frequency of phenomena, and on valuative concepts. The concepts that one uses in Galilean science are more dynamic and relational. For example, motion of objects is no longer explained in terms of attributes of types of objects—light objects rise, heavy objects fall—but in terms of intangible yet still empirical concepts that focus on motion itself—velocity and acceleration.

Lewin (1935) called these intangible concepts "conditional-genetic" or "genotypic," because they specify the underlying conditions for generating observable, or phenotypic, phenomena:

For Aristotle the immediate perceptible appearance, that which present-day biology terms the *phenotype,* was hardly distinguished from the properties that determine the object's dynamic relations. The fact, for example, that light objects relatively frequently go upward sufficed for him to ascribe to them an upward tendency. With the differentiation of phenotype from *genotype,* or more generally, of descriptive from conditional-genetic concepts and the shifting of emphasis to the latter, many old class distinctions lost their significance. The orbits of the planets, the free falling of a stone, the movement of a body on an inclined plane, the oscillation of a pendulum, which if classified according to their phenotypes would fall into quite different, indeed into antithetical classes, prove to be simply various expressions of the same law. (p. 11)

Other examples of conditional-genetic concepts include geometric figures and chemical elements. A circle and an ellipse are defined geometrically not by the phenotypic attributes of size and color but by the movement in a plane of a point equidistant from either one (circle) or two (ellipse) points in the plane. Chemical elements are defined and ordered not by the phenotypic properties of color, taste, or smell, but by atomic number, the number of protons and electrons that make up the element's atom.

In Galilean science, lawfulness is not determined on the basis of frequency of occurrence, as in Aristotelian science. Lawfulness is assumed to be, at once, more universal and more specific. It is more universal in that the laws or relationships postulated are assumed to be trans-situationally invariant. The same laws of motion apply to heavy bodies as apply to light bodies; there is "a comprehensive, all-embracing unity of the physical world. The same law governs the courses of the stars, the falling of stones, and the flight of birds" (Lewin, 1935, p. 10). Lawfulness is more specific in that the laws apply to each individual case, regardless how unusual. The same laws of motion apply to a flame sucked toward the ground by a strong downdraft as apply to one that rises toward the sky.

Finally, the concepts of Galilean science are not valuative. They attempt to account for the natural order as it is, without drawing inferences about that natural order from preconceived beliefs about the way it ought to be.

From an Aristotelian perspective, conditional-genetic concepts may seem shockingly unscientific. To what empirical reality do concepts like velocity, acceleration, force, goal, and power refer? One cannot point to any one phenomenon to define them. Yet they can still be operationalized. Miriam Lewin, Kurt Lewin's daughter, explained with reference specifically to psychological concepts:

A genotype is a capacity whose form depends on the rest of the situation. However, these are not mystical powers. The genotype is measurable in two steps: (1) Measurement of the form or structure (the phenotype) in systematically varied settings and (2) conceptualization of the requisite characteristics which would lead to the different forms in the differing settings. The psychologist asks, "What characteristics could lead to this behavioral outcome in setting A, and that behavioral outcome in setting B?" (1977, p. 166)

This is the same inference process I outlined earlier with the Suzie-and-Frank example for operationalizing the distinction between instrumental and ultimate goals.

RESEARCH METHODS IN GALILEAN SCIENCE:
ARTIFICIAL LABORATORY STUDIES

Once the Galilean scientist proposes relations among conditional-genetic concepts to account for some observed (phenotypic) phenomenon, how is he or she to know whether the hypothesized relations are correct? Galileo's method for testing his ideas about acceleration of falling bodies provides the model. After Galileo had developed concepts that allowed him to postulate general and universal principles for the behavior of falling bodies, he tested the validity of these principles in the laboratory, not in the field. Moreover, to test his principles, he did not even allow the bodies free fall. He constructed totally artificial situations, virtually nonexistent in the world outside the laboratory: He rolled balls of different weight down inclined planes; he attached these balls to threads of equal length and swung them through equal pendulum arcs. Galileo explained his strategy:

> The experiment made to ascertain whether two bodies differing greatly in weight will fall from a given height with the same speed offers some difficulty; because, if the height is considerable, the retarding effect of the medium, which must be penetrated and thrust aside by the falling body, will be greater in the case of the small momentum of the very light body than in the case of the great force of the heavy body; so that, in a long distance, the light body will be left behind; if the height be small, one may well doubt whether there is any difference; and if there be a difference it will be inappreciable.
>
> It occurred to me, therefore, to repeat many times the fall through a small height in such a way that I might accumulate all those small intervals of time that elapse between the arrival of the heavy and light bodies respectively at their common terminus, so that this sum makes an interval of time which is not only observable, but easily observable. In order to employ the slowest speeds possible and thus reduce the change which the resisting medium produces upon the simple effect of gravity, it occurred to me to allow the bodies to fall along a plane slightly inclined to the horizontal. For in such a plane, just as well as in a vertical plane, one may discover how bodies of different weight behave. (1638/1952, pp. 166–167)

From the perspective of Aristotelian science, Galileo's strategy was totally wrong. Not only did he create an artificial event, one all but unknown in the world outside the laboratory, but also this event did not even involve the phenomenon in question—the free fall of objects—in its pure form. Galileo's experiments totally lacked what is today called ecological validity. As Lewin notes, in Galilean science "one declares that one is striving for general validity and concreteness, yet uses a method which, from the point of view of the preceding [Aristotelian] epoch, disregards the historically given facts and depends entirely upon individual accidents, indeed upon the most pronounced exceptions" (1935, p. 25).

Aristotelian criticisms are often made of laboratory experiments in psychology today, including experiments conducted to test whether the motivation to help is altruistic or egoistic. If, for example, we set up a laboratory experiment in which we confront introductory psychology students with an opportunity to help another student in need under conditions that systematically vary the relationship between benefiting the other and benefiting themselves, we may be bombarded with Aristotelian questions like: "Would non-students respond in the same way to the student in need?" "Would people from another culture?" "What if the person in need were not a student?" "What if helping were more costly?" And, most often, "Would this need situation ever occur in real life?"

From an Aristotelian perspective, questions like these are central; they concern the historical frequency, universality, and representativeness of the phenomenon. From a Galilean perspective, such questions are quite beside the point. The Galilean approach involves no assumption that everyone would or should respond similarly in this situation, or that anyone would or should respond similarly to a different situation. Nor is there a concern to study naturally occurring events. As Lewin (1935) observed, to insist that one's science be conducted only on naturally occurring events introduces "a requirement which, if transferred to physics, would mean that it would be incorrect to study hydrodynamics in the laboratory; one must rather investigate the largest rivers in the world" (p. 21).

The Galilean scientist is concerned with a very different matter from ecological validity; he or she is testing hypothesized invariant relations among underlying constructs. If an $A-B$ relation is hypothesized, then to the degree that Variable A is present in some situation, whether naturally occurring or artificially created, we should see the hypothesized manifestation of Variable B—so long as the $A-B$ relation is not overwhelmed or counteracted by other events. If, however, Variable A is not present for some individuals or in some situations, or if other confounding variables are introduced, then we would not expect to observe the $A-B$ relation. Failure to observe the $A-B$ relation under these conditions does not count against the hypothesis any more than does finding that a feather and a lead ball dropped from a balcony do not hit the ground at the same time count against the hypothesis that the acceleration of falling bodies due to gravity is independent of weight.

From a Galilean perspective, laboratory experiments can be criticized as lacking validity only to the degree that they either (a) fail to include the variables involved in the hypothesized relation or (b) fail to exclude potential confounding variables. Whether they involve frequently observed or unusual events, naturally occurring or artificially created situations, is totally irrelevant.

On the other hand, from a Galilean perspective it is no longer possible to take exceptions lightly. As Lewin said, exceptions "do not in any way 'prove the rule,' but on the contrary are completely valid disproofs, even though they are rare, indeed, so long as one single exception is demonstrable" (1935, p. 24). Failures to find the hypothesized relation are so important in Galilean science because empirical observations are not made as a basis for a probabilistic inductive generalization; they are made to test deductions from hypotheses concerning invariant relations.

A GALILEAN APPROACH
TO THE ALTRUISM QUESTION

The strategy of attempting to answer the altruism question by seeking out paragons of helpfulness, the strategy rejected at the beginning of this chapter, is Aristotelian. It rests on the assumption that the extreme helpfulness of these individuals is due to their being exemplars of a class of which altruism is an attribute. The analysis remains at the level of phenotypic, surface empiricism. If we are to understand the motivation underlying this or any other helpfulness, then it seems necessary to employ conditional-genetic motivational concepts such as force, goal, and conflict—concepts that refer to the dynamics that lie beneath and behind the phenotypic manifestations of helpfulness. We must adopt a Galilean approach.

The two-step strategy for determining a person's ultimate goal outlined earlier in this chapter using the Susie-and-Frank example provides the basis for a Galilean approach to the altruism question. Recasting this strategy in light of our subsequent discussion, we can say that the conceptual analysis, which is the first step, should involve specification of relations among underlying psychological constructs to account for the phenotypic manifestations of helpfulness. Moreover, this analysis should specify these relations with sufficient precision that we can discern the nature of the motivation from different patterns of helping across systematically varying situations. Providing such a conceptual analysis is our goal in the next two chapters. Chapter 6 offers a three-path model of egoistic and altruistic motivation for helping. The model incorporates the empathy-altruism hypothesis introduced at the end of chapter 4, which proposes that altruistic motivation is produced by feeling empathy for a person in need. This hypothesis specifies an invariant relation of these two concepts: As empathic feeling for a person in need increases, altruistic motivation to have that person's need relieved increases.

Chapter 7 outlines strategies for testing the empathy-altruism hypothesis against different egoistic alternatives.

The second step involves actually testing the empathy-altruism hypothesis by making empirical observations in systematically varied situations that allow us to infer the nature of the motivation to help associated with empathic emotion: Is it egoistic or altruistic? Following the Galilean model, we have not conducted these tests by interviewing the rescuers of Jews during the Holocaust or by rushing to the scene of disasters and observing those Good Samaritans who help. Instead, we have entered the laboratory and created artificial situations in which one person is unexpectedly confronted with an opportunity to help another perceived to be in need.

Our reason for turning to the laboratory was much the same as Galileo's. There we could slow things down so we could see what is going on. That is, we could introduce changes in the situation—manipulations—that enabled us systematically to disentangle the relationship between different potential ultimate goals of helping, permitting us to make inferences about the true ultimate goal, much as Galileo used the inclined plane and pendulum to make inferences about the true rate of fall. Chapters 8, 9, and 10 report a number of laboratory experiments that have used this general strategy to test the empathy-altruism hypothesis against one or more of its egoistic alternatives.

CHAPTER 6

A Three-Path Model of Egoistic and Altruistic Motivation to Help: The Empathy-Altruism Hypothesis

With Lewin's (1935, 1951) Galilean approach to science in mind, we can begin our attempt to answer the altruism question. The first step is to provide a conceptual analysis that specifies the psychological constructs and processes involved in egoistic and altruistic motivation to help. The three-path model presented in this chapter (see also Batson, 1987) does this. In doing so, it provides a framework for understanding the empathy-altruism hypothesis, the hypothesis that feeling empathy for a person in need evokes altruistic motivation to help that person. The model highlights similarities and differences between the hypothesized empathy-induced altruistic motivation and major egoistic explanations of the motivation to help. Recognizing these similarities and differences is crucial if we are to know how to vary helping situations in order to determine whether the ultimate goal of empathically aroused helpers is to benefit the other, as the empathy-altruism hypothesis claims, or to benefit the self, as egoistic explanations claim.

TWO EGOISTIC ACCOUNTS OF WHY WE HELP: PATHS 1 AND 2

Our review of various philosophical and psychological contributions to the egoism–altruism debate suggests that one or both of two egoistic motives are usually invoked to explain why we help others. Using modern terminology, one of these motives is based on social learning and reinforcement; the other, on arousal reduction. These two egoistic motives are summarized in Paths 1 and 2 of the flow chart in Fig. 6.1. The reinforcement path (Path 1) is further subdivided to differentiate (a) reward-seeking and (b) punishment-avoiding motives. Let us trace each of these paths from beginning to end—from the instigating situation through the resulting motive to a behavioral response. Along the way, we can identify key underlying constructs and psychological processes involved in the different motives. To highlight these underlying processes, the analysis does not focus on specific examples but on general, formal properties of the helping process. These formal properties, if rightly identified, should be applicable to any specific example you choose.

Instigating Situation

Perception of Another in Need. Each path begins with perception of another person in need. Formally, perception of another in need involves recognition of a negative discrepancy between the other's current and potential states on one or more dimensions of well-being. Dimensions of well-being include being free from unpleasant states—physical pain, negative affect, anxiety, and stress—as well as experiencing pleasant states—physical pleasure, positive affect, satisfaction, and security.

Perception of need seems to be a threshold function of three factors: (a) a perceptible discrepancy (real or apparent) between the other's current and potential states on some dimension(s) of well-being; (b) sufficient salience of these states, so that each can be noticed and a comparison made (Clark & Word, 1972, 1974; Latané & Darley, 1970); and (c) the perceiver's attention being focused on the person in need, not on the self or some other aspect of the environment (Duval & Wicklund, 1972; Gibbons & Wicklund, 1982; Mathews & Canon, 1975; Weiner, 1976; Wicklund, 1975). All three of these conditions must be satisfied simultaneously before another's need can be perceived. Yet satisfying these conditions does not guarantee a perception of need; they are necessary, not sufficient, conditions. A variety of cognitive and situational factors—such as misinterpreting the need (Is the scream a plea for help or only playful?)—may lead the perceiver to minimize or even deny the apparent need.

Given that some need is perceived, it can vary in magnitude. Magnitude of the perceived need appears to be a function of three factors: (a) the number of dimensions of well-being on which discrepancies are perceived, (b) the size of each discrepancy, and (c) the potential helper's perception of the importance of each of these dimensions for the person in need (Schaps, 1972).

Expectation of Rewards and Punishments. Perception of another as in need is all that is required to instigate Path 2 egoistic motivation, but this percep-

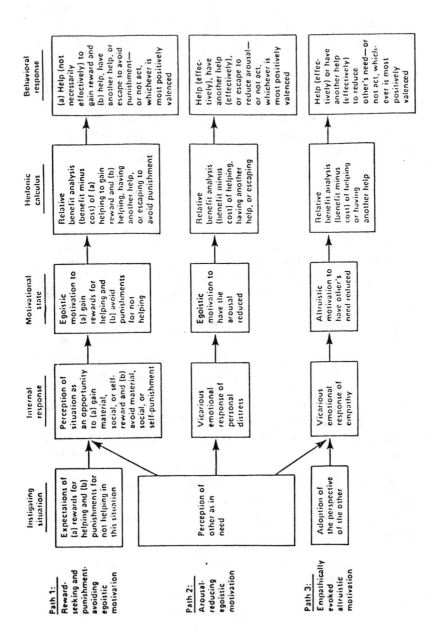

FIG. 6.1 Flowchart of egoistic and altruistic paths to helping (from Batson, 1987).

tion alone is not sufficient to instigate Path 1 motivation. Before motivation to help can be elicited along Path 1, the potential helper must also have the expectation of either receiving rewards for helping or punishments for not helping—or both—in the particular situation. These expectations are the product of the potential helper's learning history, including rewards and punishments received in similar situations, as well as rewards and punishments he or she has observed others receiving in similar situations. (Bandura, 1977; Cialdini et al., 1981; and Eisenberg, 1982, have all presented useful reviews of research on the socialization processes by which such expectations are learned.)

Internal Response

Path 1.   Perceiving the other's need, combined with expectations based on one's learning history, can lead to anticipating rewards for helping or punishments for not. The anticipated rewards and punishments may be obvious and explicit, such as being paid (Fischer, 1963), gaining social approval (Baumann, Cialdini, & Kenrick, 1981; Gelfand, Hartmann, Cromer, Smith, & Page, 1975; Kenrick, Baumann, & Cialdini, 1979; Moss & Page, 1972), or avoiding censure (Reis & Gruzen, 1976). They may also be more subtle, such as receiving esteem in exchange for helping (Hatfield, Walster, & Piliavin, 1978), complying with social norms (Berkowitz, 1972; Gouldner, 1960; Leeds, 1963; Staub, 1971), complying with internalized personal norms (Lerner, 1970; Schwartz, 1975, 1977; Zuckerman, 1975), seeing oneself as a good person (Bandura, 1977; Cialdini et al., 1973; Cialdini & Kenrick, 1976; Weyant, 1978; Wilson, 1976), or avoiding guilt (Hoffman, 1976, 1982; Steele, 1975). This internal response of anticipating rewards and punishments is represented on Path 1 of Fig. 6.1.

Path 2.   Independent of the anticipated rewards and punishments on Path 1, seeing another in need may cause an individual to experience personal distress—to feel upset, anxious, disturbed, and the like (cf. McDougall's sympathetic pain and Hoffman's empathic distress). The magnitude of this aversive vicarious emotion appears to be a function of three factors: the magnitude of the perceived need, its salience, and its personal relevance to oneself (Piliavin & Piliavin, 1973; Staub & Baer, 1974). As Piliavin et al. (1981) have noted, the salience and personal relevance of another's need seem to increase as a result of perceived "we-ness," similarity, and attraction. This second internal response is represented on Path 2 of Fig. 6.1.

Reward and punishment anticipation (Path 1) and feelings of personal distress (Path 2) are distinct internal responses to perceiving another in need, but they are not mutually exclusive. In many helping situations—such as emergencies—each of these internal responses will be instigated, and in proportional magnitudes. In other helping situations—such as making a routine annual contribution to a charity—a person may be very aware of the rewards for helping and punishments for not, yet feel little personal distress. In still other situations—such as witnessing a gory accident—much distress may be aroused, and little or no attention paid to the possible reward and punishment opportunities of the situation.

Motivational State

Reward anticipation, punishment avoidance, and feelings of distress each evoke their own form of egoistic motivation.

Path 1. On Path 1, perception of the opportunity to get rewards or avoid punishments evokes motivation to gain the rewards (Path 1a) or avoid the punishments (Path 1b). Magnitude of the reward-seeking or punishment-avoiding motivation appears to be a function of two factors: (a) magnitude of the anticipated rewards and punishments and (b) the potential helper's current need for the anticipated rewards and punishments. The potential helper's current needs might include, for example, a particular need for enhanced self-esteem (Steele, 1975), for relief from feeling bad (Cialdini et al., 1973; Weyant, 1978), or for continuance of feeling good (Isen & Levin, 1972).

Path 2. On Path 2, experiencing personal distress leads to motivation to have this distress reduced. Magnitude of this arousal-reduction motivation appears to be a direct function simply of the magnitude of the distress experienced (Gaertner & Dovidio, 1977; Hoffman, 1981a; Piliavin et al., 1981).

The egoistic motives on Path 1 and Path 2 are distinct but not mutually exclusive; they may be experienced simultaneously. When they are, obtaining their goals may be compatible or incompatible. Sometimes, actions that move a person toward gaining reward or avoiding punishment also reduce that person's distress—as when the person saves someone trapped in a burning building by putting out the fire. At other times, acting to gain reward or avoid punishment increases distress—as when a person helps by comforting a mangled accident victim. If perception of another in need simultaneously evokes Path 1 and Path 2 egoistic motivation, then to the extent that the goals of the motives are compatible, their magnitudes will sum.

Hedonic Calculus

If the magnitude of one or more egoistic motives is above some minimal threshold, then the individual will consider various behavioral means of reaching the goals of these motivational states. Helping may be one means of reaching the goal(s), but often there are other means as well. Before acting, a *hedonic calculus* is performed; the motivated individual conducts a relative-benefit analysis, weighing benefit against cost for each potential response.

Benefits and Costs. The magnitude of the benefit in the hedonic calculus is a function of the magnitude of the motivational state, because the benefit is to reach the goal. The magnitude of the cost is the sum of the various costs perceived to be associated with the behavior. Perhaps the simplest way to think about these costs is in terms of conflict with other egoistic motives. It is likely that a potential helper, in addition to experiencing one or more motives evoked by perception of the other in need, simultaneously experiences motives to avoid pain or risk of pain, to save time, to keep his or her money, and so on (Piliavin, Piliavin, & Rodin, 1975). As a general principle, if more than one motive exists, and if a given behavior can reach the goal of one of these motives but not others, then failure to obtain the incompatible goals is the cost associated with this behavior. The magnitude of this cost will be a function of the magnitude of the motivational force to reach the unobtained goals.

Benefits and Costs on Path 1. On Path 1a, the desired rewards are associated with being helpful, so the motivation to obtain these rewards specifies a single behavioral means: The motivated individual must try to help. Yet, many of the rewards may be obtained even if one's helping is not effective. We do not usually insist on knowing that our charity dollars are well spent before collecting our social and self-rewards for contributing; as people say, it's the thought that counts. On the other hand, if someone else helps, even effectively, we will receive no reward—unless we can somehow take credit for the other person's helping (e.g., "I talked her into contributing"), and so claim to have helped indirectly.

The behavioral options are quite different on Path 1b. We may avoid possible punishments by trying to help, but there are other possibilities as well. If another person helps effectively before we have a chance, then we are free from any threat of social censure, guilt, or shame, because our help is no longer needed. Alternatively, if we can psychologically escape from the need situation by, for example, becoming involved in a distracting task, then we may successfully escape self-inflicted punishments such as guilt and shame. Thus, whereas the hedonic calculus on Path 1a focuses on helping as the only behavioral means of obtaining the desired rewards, there are three means of avoiding punishment on Path 1b: helping, another person helping, and escaping.

Escaping deserves some additional comment. In general, escape may be accomplished by eliminating any of the three conditions necessary for perceiving need. That is, we can (a) redefine the situation so that no perceptible discrepancy exists between the other's current and potential states of well-being ("He chooses to live homeless"), (b) reduce the salience of the other's need through increasing the physical or psychological distance from it ("Thank goodness that sort of thing doesn't happen around here"), or (c) shift the focus of attention away from the person in need toward some other aspect of the environment ("It's so tragic; I'm going to switch channels"). In order to escape self-inflicted punishments of shame and guilt on Path 1b, it may not be enough for us to physically escape the need situation; we may take the situation with us in memory. To reach the goal of avoiding punishment, we need to escape psychologically. Of course, the old adage, "Out of sight, out of mind," reminds us that physical escape often permits psychological escape as well.

Because many of the rewards can be obtained and the punishments avoided simply by trying to help, Path 1 egoistic motivation should produce a bandwagon effect. The person who arrives at the scene of an accident after the ambulance and busily begins helping can obtain many of the same rewards and avoid many of the same punishments as the person first on the scene, who used her new jacket to wrap the victim's bleeding arm, keeping him alive. If the preferred behavior is the one that maximizes benefit relative to cost, then the safe, clean, low-cost helping of the late arriver looks more attractive. Recognizing this, societies try to increase the attractiveness of dangerous, dirty, high-cost helping by labeling initial helpers "heroes," lavishing on them extra social and even material rewards, such as the Carnegie Hero Fund Commission awards.

Benefits and Costs on Path 2. The same three behavioral options that can be used to avoid punishment on Path 1b can reduce aversive arousal on Path 2. The cause of one's distress can be removed either by helping or by another person helping. Alternatively, contact with the cause of one's distress can be removed by escaping, although the potential helper is escaping something different on Path 2 than on Path 1b. On Path 1b the escape is from anticipated punishment, especially self-punishment in the form of shame and guilt; on Path 2 the escape is from the stimulus causing one's distress. Given this difference, physical escape may be even more effective on Path 2 than Path 1b.

Unlike on Path 1, helping on Path 2 must be effective if the goal of arousal-reduction is to be reached. The help must reduce the other's need, because that is what is causing one's distress. Moreover, having someone else help can be just as effective in removing the cause of one's distress, and it is probably less costly than being the helper oneself. Therefore, the motivation to help aroused on Path 2 should produce quite the opposite of a bandwagon effect.

If no one else can help, Path 2 motivation should lead the potential helper either to help or to escape, whichever is the less costly means of reducing one's distress. Typically, escaping is less costly than helping. So, when escape is possible, Path 2 motivation is likely to lead to little helping.

Considering Paths 1 and 2 Simultaneously.   The hedonic calculus is often even more complicated than suggested thus far, because the distressed individual has almost certainly also been socialized to expect rewards for helping and punishments for not. As a result, he or she will likely experience Path 1a and 1b motivation at the same time as Path 2 motivation. Piliavin et al. (1981) highlight this point through attention to the simultaneous evocation of aversive arousal (Path 2), personal costs (Path 1a & b), and empathy costs, including both present empathy costs (Path 2) and anticipated ones (Path 1b). The goals of motivation on Paths 1a, 1b, and 2 can all be reached by helping, but escaping brings no rewards. Thus, the anticipated loss of praise and esteem is part of the cost of escaping in a more comprehensive hedonic calculus that deals with Path 1 and Path 2 motives simultaneously.

Time Required for the Hedonic Calculus.   How much time is required to compute this hedonic calculus? Carefully weighing the pros and cons of behavioral alternatives may take some time, but it seems likely that various problem-solving heuristics are available, permitting a rough hedonic calculus to be performed, when necessary, in less than a second. If so, then contrary to the suggestions of Hoffman (1975, 1981a) and Piliavin and Piliavin (1973) that rapid, impulsive helping is too quick to involve a hedonic calculus, it seems more likely that a relative-benefit analysis is performed even when helping occurs very rapidly. This high-speed analysis may be crude, being limited both in the number of response options entertained and in the consideration given to the benefits and costs of these options, but that should not lead us to conclude that no analysis was made.

To illustrate: Imagine that you witness a serious auto accident and, as a result, experience a quick and sizable increase in aversive arousal and a quick and sizable increase in motivation to reduce that arousal. The benefit of reducing the arousal, and of doing so before it gets any more intense, is likely to be the most prominent, perhaps the only, factor considered in the hedonic calculus. As a result, you may almost instantly run forward to help, and may afterward report—as do many who rush into burning buildings or dive into dangerous waters—that you "didn't think" before you acted. In spite of this report, it seems likely that you, and they, did think. Otherwise, these impulsive responses would not be as adaptive as they are, allowing the helper to circumvent barriers to reach the goal.

Another individual confronted with the same situation might employ a very different heuristic, one that focuses on the cost of helping to the exclusion of benefit, and leads him impulsively to respond, "No way!" Once again, his impulsive response likely involves thought, even if it is not well thought-out.

Behavioral Response

Moving to the last step on Paths 1 and 2, the motivated individual will help, let someone else help, or escape, whichever available response has the greatest perceived relative benefit to self. If no available response is perceived to have relative benefit; that is, if the anticipated cost of each exceeds the benefit, then the individual will not respond. He or she will pursue some unrelated goal or will do nothing. If no need-related response occurs, then the force of the need-related egoistic motivation should slowly dissipate.

Summary

Paths 1 and 2 are primarily a summary and integration of the work of other researchers (most notably, Bar-Tal, 1976; Cialdini & Kenrick, 1976; Hoffman, 1981a, 1981b; Latané & Darley, 1970; Piliavin et al., 1981; Schwartz, 1977). No doubt, one or more of these researchers would disagree about some of the details of my portrayal. Yet, we need not focus on these disagreements because none is relevant to what follows, and I believe there would be general agreement on the major themes and logic presented.

Much can be said in favor of using these two egoistic paths to account for the motivation to help. Each path makes considerable intuitive sense; each is internally consistent; each is complex, yet permits relatively precise behavioral predictions; each is based on a classic approach to motivation—reinforcement (Path 1) or arousal-reduction (Path 2); and finally, each is supported by much empirical research. Some key studies were cited along the way; Eisenberg (1982), Dovidio (1984), Krebs and Miller (1985), Piliavin et al. (1981), Rushton and Sorrentino (1981), and Staub (1978, 1979) provide more extensive reviews.

In spite of these virtues, philosophers like Hume and Smith, early psychologists like Spencer and McDougall, and contemporary psychologists like Hoffman and Krebs all claim that these egoistic accounts are not adequate to provide a full explanation of why people help. They claim that the two egoistic paths need to be supplemented by a third path, one based on the hypothesis that empathic emotion evokes altruistic motivation.

THE EMPATHY-ALTRUISM HYPOTHESIS:
PATH 3

The hypothesis that empathy evokes altruistic motivation can be made explicit and, as a result, empirically testable by detailing the psychological process involved in this third path, just as has been done for the two egoistic paths. This path appears as Path 3 of Fig. 6.1.

Perception of Another in Need

Like Paths 1 and 2, Path 3 begins with perception of another in need. The existence and magnitude of the perceived need are a function of the same factors specified for egoistic motivation. That is, existence of perceived need is a threshold function of (a) a perceptible discrepancy between the other's current and potential states on some dimension(s) of well-being, (b) sufficient salience of these states, and (c) the perceiver's attention being focused on the other. The magnitude of the perceived need is a function of (a) the number of dimensions of well-being on which discrepancies are perceived, (b) the size of each discrepancy, and (c) the perceived importance of each of these dimensions for the person in need.

On Path 3, however, perceiving the other's need is claimed to lead to a unique internal response: a feeling of empathy. Following the lead of Hoffman (1975, 1976), Krebs (1975), Ezra Stotland (1969), and, long before, of Adam Smith (1759/1853), it is proposed that this unique emotional response to perceived need is a result of the perceiver adopting the perspective of the person in need.

Adopting the Perspective of the Person in Need

Adopting another person's perspective involves more than simply focusing attention on the other. We may focus attention on another's need but maintain a relatively objective perspective, dispassionately observing that person's plight. In contrast, adopting the needy person's perspective involves imagining how that person is affected by his or her situation (Stotland, 1969).

Recollection of our own or others' reactions in similar situations, as well as imagining ourselves in the need situation, often provides information that facilitates adopting a needy person's perspective. There are, however, limits to this facilitation. We may get so wrapped up in reminiscences or in our own possible reactions to the situation that we fail to consider the specific way the situation is affecting the person in need (Hygge, 1976; Karniol, 1982). Considering the effect on the person in need is the essence of perspective taking, and it is perspective taking—in combination with a perception of the other as in need—that Path 3 claims leads to empathic emotion.

Adam Smith, focusing on the effect of perspective taking on sympathy, which he considered a precursor of pity or compassion (i.e., empathy), presented a subtle and graphic description of what perspective taking involves:

> Sympathy is very properly said to arise from an imaginary change of situations with the person principally concerned, yet this imaginary change is not supposed to happen to me in my own person and character, but in that of the person with whom I sympathize. When I condole with you for the loss of your only son, in order to enter into your grief I do not consider what I, a person of such a character and profession, should suffer, if I had a son, and if that son was unfortunately to die: but I consider what I should suffer if I was really you, and I not only change circumstances with you, but I change persons and characters. My grief, therefore, is entirely upon your account, and not in the least upon my own. (1759, VII. iii. 1. 4)

Taking the perspective of a needy person in this way appears to be a threshold function of two factors: (a) the ability to take another's perspective (Hoffman, 1976, 1981b; Krebs & Russell, 1981) and (b) a perspective-taking set, that is, a set to imagine how the person in need is affected by his or her situation (Stotland, 1969). A perspective-taking set may be induced by prior experience in similar situations, by instructions, or by a feeling of attachment to the other. In the psychological research laboratory, perspective taking has often been induced by instructions (e.g., Coke, Batson, & McDavis, 1978; Stotland, 1969; Toi & Batson, 1982). In the natural stream of behavior also, perspective taking may be the result of instructions, including self-instructions (e.g., "I should walk a mile in his moccasins"), but it is more often the result either of prior similar experience ("I know just how you must feel") or of attachment.

Attachment

Our attachment to certain other people seems quite important in social relations, yet attachment remains poorly understood. It is not possible even to specify the defining features of what I mean by attachment, only to provide some general clues and examples.

First, some general clues. When attachment exists—for example, a mother's attachment to her child—there is a general feeling of heartache and sadness at separation, and a feeling of warmth and joy at reuniting (Ainsworth, Blehar, Waters, & Wall, 1978; Bowlby, 1969). Cognitive processes such as perceived similarity and attractiveness can contribute to attachment, but its basic character seems to be affective and valuative. Some attachments—such as the parent's attachment to the child and the child's to the parent—probably have a genetic base (see Batson, Darley, & Coke, 1978; Bowlby, 1969; Hoffman, 1981a). Yet this genetic base is clearly subject to broad cognitive generalization, as in cases of adoption (Batson, 1983). Like the related, more general concepts of attitude and sentiment, attachment involves a relatively enduring predisposition or orientation toward the other person. Attachments can, of course, end.

The prototype for what I mean by attachment is the parent's attachment to the child (not the child's attachment to the parent, as in Bowlby's, 1969, work). Attachments can also occur in a variety of other interpersonal relationships, including other family relationships, friendships, love relationships, relationships with pets, and so on. Typically, attachments are based on personal contact. They may also be based on cognitive generalization from personal contact, as seems to be the case with similarity-based attachments. Attachments tend to be reciprocated, though they need not be. They may vary in strength. Attachments based on cognitive generalization are usually weaker than those based on personal contact. Extended intimate contact and dependency relations seem to produce particularly strong attachments. Other names for the phenomenon I am calling attachment might be love, caring, feeling close, we-feeling, or bonding.

Internal Response of Empathic Emotion

The arousal of empathic emotion is affected by attachment in two ways. First, the stronger the attachment to the person in need, the greater the likelihood of adopting that person's perspective. And, as already discussed, adopting the needy person's perspective seems to be a necessary precondition for arousal of empathic emotion. Second, strength of attachment can affect the magnitude of empathic emotion. If the perceiver adopts the perspective of a person in need, then the magnitude of empathic emotion is proposed to be a function of two factors: (a) magnitude of the perceived need and (b) strength of the attachment. Thus, the arrows of influence at the beginning of Path 3 represent two types of functions. Some represent threshold functions: Perception of the other as in need and perspective taking are both necessary for empathy to occur at all. Others represent continuous functions: Magnitude of the other's need and strength of attachment (not included in Fig. 6.1) combine to determine magnitude of the empathic emotion.

Research indicates that at least two different types of vicarious emotion are evoked by perceiving someone in need (Batson, Fultz, & Schoenrade,

1987). One, *personal distress,* has already been discussed. It includes feeling anxious, upset, disturbed, distressed, perturbed, and the like, and evokes egoistic motivation to have the distress reduced (Path 2). The other, *empathy,* remains to be discussed. It includes feeling sympathetic, compassionate, warm, softhearted, tender, and the like, and according to the empathy-altruism hypothesis, it evokes altruistic motivation.

Defining Empathy.   Let me explain as clearly as I can what I mean by the term empathy because, although empathy is a relatively new word, it has a number of meanings. The term was apparently coined by Titchener in 1909 to translate the German *Einfühlung,* which was used by Lipps in a perceptual context to refer to the process of intuiting one's way into an object or event to "see" it from the inside (Wispé, 1968, 1986, 1987). By the 1950s, empathy had taken on a more cognitive meaning in clinical discussions: It referred to understanding accurately and dispassionately the client's point of view concerning his or her situation (Dymond, 1949; Hogan 1969). Used in this way, empathy is often treated as synonymous with role taking or perspective taking (Borke, 1971; Krebs & Russell, 1981; Underwood & Moore, 1982).

Since about 1960, empathy has been given a less cognitive and more emotional meaning, especially when used by developmental and social psychologists. Empathy has been defined emotionally in at least three different ways: (a) as feeling any vicarious emotion, (b) as feeling the same emotion that another person is feeling, or (c) as feeling a vicarious emotion that is congruent with but not necessarily identical to the emotion of another (Batson & Coke, 1981; Eisenberg & Strayer, 1987; Krebs, 1975; Stotland, 1969). When empathy is defined in one of these ways, then adopting the needy person's point of view (i.e., perspective taking) is usually considered a prerequisite for feeling empathy, but is not considered the same as empathy (Coke et al., 1978).

Since the late 1970s, empathy has been defined in an even more specific emotional sense. It has been used to refer to one particular set of congruent vicarious emotions, those that are more other-focused than self-focused, including feelings of sympathy, compassion, tenderness, and the like (Batson et al., 1981, 1983; Coke et al., 1978; Toi & Batson, 1982). Defined in this way, empathy is distinct from feelings of personal distress (McDougall's sympathetic pain, Hoffman's empathic distress), but it is indistinguishable from what many philosophers and early psychologists called pity (Aquinas, Hume, Smith), compassion (Hume, Smith), or tenderness (McDougall).

Several psychologists have recently suggested using the term *sympathy* rather than *empathy* to refer to these other-oriented feelings evoked by seeing another in need (Eisenberg & Strayer, 1987; Hoffman, 1975; Lenrow, 1965; Wispé, 1986, 1987). Using the term *empathy* is not problem-free, but using *sympathy* seems even more problematic. First, as we have seen, sympathy has long had a different meaning in Western thought, referring to the transmission of what one person is feeling to another person, a sort of emotional resonance (see, e.g., the use of sympathy by Hume, Smith, and McDougall sketched in chapters 2 and 3). Second, as Allport (1968) notes, sympathy—like the classic terms *pity, compassion,* and *tenderness*—has become tinged with a paternalistic, moralistic cast. Given these problems with sympathy, I prefer the term *empathy*. Ultimately, of course, the phenomenon being described is more important than the specific term used to describe it.

Is Feeling Empathy Unpleasant?   Empathy felt for someone who is suffering will likely be an unpleasant, aversive emotion (people may, however, be pleased that they are experiencing it). Yet, even though empathy is aversive, the empathy-altruism hypothesis claims that it—unlike personal distress—does not evoke Path 2 egoistic motivation to have this aversive arousal reduced. This hypothesis claims that empathy evokes altruistic motivation directed toward the ultimate goal of reducing the needy person's suffering.

Altruistic Motivation

According to the empathy-altruism hypothesis, magnitude of the altruistic motivation evoked by empathy is a direct function of magnitude of the empathic emotion. The more empathy felt for a person in need, the more altruistic motivation to have that need reduced.

Reducing the need of a person for whom one feels empathy is likely to enable the helper to gain social and self-rewards (Path 1a), avoid social and self-punishments (Path 1b), and reduce feelings of personal distress (Path 2). The empathy-altruism hypothesis claims, however, that feeling empathy for the person in need evokes motivation to help in which these benefits to self are not the ultimate goal of helping; they are unintended consequences.

Note that the three-path model in Fig. 6.1 presents a strong form of the empathy-altruism hypothesis. The single arrow leading from internal response of empathy to altruistic motivation indicates not only that empathic emotion evokes altruistic motivation but also that all motivation to help evoked by empathy is altruistic. As presented, empathy evokes no motivation to help directed toward the egoistic goals of gaining rewards, avoiding punishments, or reducing aversive arousal. It is easy to imagine a weaker form of the empathy-altruism hypothesis, in which empathic emotion evokes both egoistic and altruistic motivation. Arrows would then extend from empathy to one or more of the egoistic motives as well.

The reason for presenting the strong form in Fig. 6.1 is not because it is logically or psychologically superior; the reason is strategic. The weak form has more overlap with egoistic explanations of the motivation to help evoked by empathy, making it more difficult to differentiate empirically from these egoistic explanations. So, lacking a good reason to prefer one form over the other, it seems wise to begin empirical inquiry by attempting to test the strong form against the egoistic explanations. If empirical evidence supports the strong form, then we have no need for the more complicated procedures and more sensitive measures required to test the weak form.

At the same time that the three-path model hypothesizes that the motivation evoked by empathy is exclusively altruistic, the model also emphasizes that the instigating conditions that arouse empathic emotion and, as a result, Path 3 altruistic motivation, are also likely to arouse Path 1 and Path 2 egoistic motives. Thus, to claim that empathic emotion evokes altruistic motivation and only altruistic motivation, as the strong form of the empathy-altruism hypothesis does, is not to claim that the empathically aroused individual is experiencing only altruistic motivation. He or she may also be experiencing egoistic motives arising from sources other than empathy. These egoistic motives and the altruistic motive are assumed to be distinct, but to the extent that the goals of these motives are compatible, their magnitudes should sum.

Hedonic Calculus

If the magnitude of the altruistic motivation or the summed egoistic and altruistic motivation is above some minimal threshold, then the individual will proceed to consider behavioral means of reaching the goal(s). As on the egoistic paths, the altruistically motivated individual will perform a hedonic calculus before acting, seeking the least costly means to the goal.

To suggest a hedonic calculus for altruistic motivation may seem contradictory, because the goal of this calculus is clearly egoistic: to reach the desired altruistic goal while incurring minimal costs to self. Yet the existence of this egoistic goal does not mean that the motivation to have the other's need reduced has now become egoistic; it only means that the impulse to act on this altruistic motivation is likely to evoke an egoistic motive as well. The existence of the latter motive need not negate or contaminate the former, although it may well complicate the relationship between the altruistic motive and behavior.

The magnitude of the benefit in the hedonic calculus is, as on the egoistic paths, a function of the magnitude of the motivational force, because the benefit is to reach the goal(s). The magnitude of the cost is the sum of the various costs associated with the behavior, including physical harm or risk, discomfort, exertion, mental strain, time, and monetary expense.

The hedonic calculus on Path 3 should be restricted to consideration of helping or having someone else help; no consideration should be given to escaping. This is because escape is not a viable behavioral means of reaching the altruistic goal of increasing the other's welfare. Moreover, the helping must be effective if the altruistic goal is to be reached. Finally, having someone else help effectively should be as viable, but no more viable, a means of reaching the altruistic goal as is being the helper oneself. There should be no bandwagon effect.

As with egoistic motivation, it seems likely that problem-solving heuristics will be used when conducting the hedonic calculus on Path 3, and that the sophistication of these heuristics varies widely. If the magnitude of the altruistic motivation increases very rapidly, then one may expect a rapid response based on a relatively crude heuristic. As on the egoistic paths, the potential helper may focus exclusively on the benefits of reaching the altruistic goal, failing to give weight to the associated cost. This would result in impulsive altruistic helping. Alternatively, the potential helper may focus on costs, giving little weight to the altruistic motive, producing an impulsive failure to act. Impulsiveness per se does not distinguish altruistic from egoistic motives in the present analysis; either type of motivation could lead to impulsive or to well thought-out responses.

Enacting a Behavior to Reach the Altruistic Goal

The altruistically motivated individual will help if (a) helping is possible; (b) the relative benefit of helping is perceived to be positive; and (c) the relative benefit of helping is perceived to be more positive than the relative benefit of having someone else help (assuming someone else is available to help). If the relative benefit is negative, that is, if the cost of helping exceeds the benefit, then the individual will not help. In this case, the force of the altruistic motivation should slowly dissipate as the empathic emotion dissipates. Alternatively, the individual could deny the person's need, break the attachment by derogating the needy individual (Lerner, 1970), or change other factors leading to adoption of that person's perspective. These responses do not enable the individual to reach the altruistic goal; they eliminate the empathic emotion and, hence, the altruistic motivation.

Summary

The proposed argument for the existence of altruism outlined on Path 3 is, then, as follows: Empathy is an other-oriented vicarious emotion produced by taking the perspective of a person perceived to be in need. It is distinct from personal distress. The magnitude of empathic emotion is a function of the magnitude of the perceived need and the strength of the perceiver's attachment to the person in need. These statements about the nature and origin of empathy provide the necessary background for the central proposition, the empathy-altruism hypothesis: Empathic emotion evokes altruistic motivation to have the other's need reduced. Consistent with the definition of altruism in chapter 1, the ultimate goal of this motivation is to increase the other's welfare, not one's own.

Even though empathic emotion is the only source of altruistic motivation specified on Path 3, we should not assume that feeling empathy is the only possible source of altruistic motivation. There may be other sources, such as one or another personality characteristic, including perhaps a disposition to feel empathy. These other possible sources of altruism lie outside the scope of the three-path model in Fig. 6.1 and are set aside until chapter 11.

In its general form, the proposal that empathic emotion evokes altruistic motivation is certainly not original. Our historical review in Part I uncovered similar proposals by Hoffman and Krebs, and much earlier, by Hume, Smith, Darwin, and McDougall. What is original, I think, is embedding the proposal in a more general framework that explicitly compares and contrasts empathy-evoked altruistic motivation with egoistic motives for helping. As we see in the next chapter, this embedding renders the empathy-altruism hypothesis empirically testable, whereas the earlier proposals were not.

CHAPTER 7

Three Egoistic Alternatives
to the Empathy-Altruism
Hypothesis

There is little argument that feeling empathy for a suffering person increases the likelihood of helping that person. There is much argument, however, about the nature of the underlying motivation: Is it altruistic, as the empathy-altruism hypothesis claims, or is it egoistic? This is the question we try to answer in Part III. Taking a second conceptual step toward this goal, in the present chapter we first review evidence that empathy increases helping. Then we use the model from the preceding chapter to identify three major egoistic explanations for this empathy-helping relationship. Finally, we specify how these explanations might be empirically tested against the empathy-altruism hypothesis.

EVIDENCE FOR AN EMPATHY–HELPING
RELATIONSHIP

We have heard claims that empathic emotion can motivate helping at least since the 13th century, when Aquinas (1270/1917) contended that "mercy is heartfelt sympathy for another's distress, impelling us to succour him if we can" (II-II, 30, 3). Recent psychological research has produced much empirical support for such a claim.

Evidence that Empathy Exists

Not wanting to take anything for granted, in the 1960s several psychologists sought to demonstrate that empathic emotions actually exist. Berger (1962) had people observe a target person performing a task and led them to believe that following the onset of a visual signal the target person either was receiving electric shock (electric shock condition) or was not (no shock condition). Further, the target person either jerked his arm following the visual signal (movement condition) or did not (no movement condition). All research participants were told that they themselves would not be shocked during the experiment.

Berger reasoned, first, that both a painful stimulus in the environment (shock) and a distress response (movement) were necessary for an observer to infer that the target person was experiencing pain. He reasoned, second, that if participants in his experiment were feeling empathy for the target, as opposed to feeling fear or anxiety about the shock itself, then they should display a physiological reaction to watching the target person only when they inferred that he was experiencing pain. Therefore, Berger predicted that participants in the shock/movement condition would display the most physiological arousal, because only they would infer that the target person was experiencing pain and so only they would feel empathy. For participants in each of the other three conditions, some information necessary for empathy was missing.

Results followed the predicted pattern. Consistent with the assumption that people experience empathy when attending to another perceived to be in need, participants in the shock/movement condition were more physiologically aroused while observing the target person than were participants in the other three conditions. Berger concluded that empathic arousal does occur. Subsequent research (Bandura & Rosenthal, 1966; Craig & Lowery, 1969; Craig & Wood, 1969) has provided further support for this conclusion.

Stotland (1969) reported a series of experiments supporting the more specific proposal that taking the perspective of a person in need increases feelings of empathy. He had research participants watch a target person undergo what they believed was a painful diathermy treatment. Participants previously instructed to imagine how the target person felt (imagine-him condition) tended to show more physiological arousal and to report more empathic feelings than participants instructed to watch the target person's movements (observe condition). Participants instructed to imagine the target's feelings also showed more physiological arousal and reported more empathic feelings than participants in a control condition, who were given the imagine-him instructions but were not led to believe that the diathermy treatment caused pain.

Evidence that Empathy Increases Helping

In the late 1960s and the 1970s, attention shifted from demonstrating that empathy exists to demonstrating that it leads to increased helping. Aronfreed and Paskal (cited in Aronfreed, 1968) and Aderman and Berkowitz (1970) each set up experimental conditions designed to encourage or inhibit empathic response to the distress of a target person. Participants were then given an opportunity to help. In the Aronfreed and Paskal study, they could help the target person; in the Aderman and Berkowitz study, they could help the experimenter. In each study, more helping occurred in the experimental conditions designed to encourage empathy, and both pairs of authors concluded that empathy increased helping.

As mentioned in chapter 4, Krebs (1975) also conducted an experiment designed to demonstrate an empathy–helping relationship. In Krebs's experiment, participants observed a peer undergo both positive (reward) and negative (shock) experiences. Krebs measured participants' physiological arousal, self-reports of empathy, and helping. He found that a high-empathy condition (a similar other undergoing a negative experience) created the greatest physiological arousal, highest reports of empathic feelings, and the most help.

Krebs's experiment demonstrated that both empathy and helping occurred under the same circumstances and were highly correlated, but it did not demonstrate that the empathic emotions caused the helping. A study by Harris and Huang (1973) provided evidence that the emotional arousal evoked by seeing someone in need can play a causal role in helping. In their study, as participants performed a mathematics task, a confederate with bandaged knee limped into the experimental room, tripped over a chair, fell to the floor, and cried out in pain. Some participants were induced to misattribute any emotional arousal they felt after witnessing this incident to aversive noise being broadcast during the math task; others were not. Harris and Huang based their predictions on Schachter's (1964) two-factor theory of emotion, which states that in order for an emotion to be experienced a person must (a) experience physiological arousal and (b) cognitively label this arousal as reflecting that emotion. Harris and Huang reasoned that if experiencing empathic emotion increases helping, then the emotional arousal produced by seeing the person fall should increase helping only when attributed to the victim's plight. As predicted, participants induced to misattribute their arousal to the aversive noise offered less help to the confederate than did those not so induced.

Unfortunately, it was not clear that the emotional arousal experienced by participants in the Harris and Huang study was empathic. The confederate's fall may instead have led participants to experience an unpleasantly high level of personal distress, which they then sought to reduce by helping.

Coke et al. (1978, Experiment 1), using a misattribution of arousal procedure similar to that used by Harris and Huang, provided clearer evidence that
empathy increases helping. They had undergraduates listen to a taped radio
newscast (actually fictitious) that presented the situation of a young college
senior, Katie Banks, who had recently lost her parents in a tragic automobile
wreck. Katie's parents did not have life insurance, and she was struggling to
support her surviving younger brother and sister while finishing her last
semester of college. Katie badly needed money, but she also needed transportation to the grocery store and laundry, and sitters to stay with her
younger brother and sister while she attended her two night classes. The
announcer then interviewed Katie. In a grief-stricken voice, she explained
that her major concern was graduating so that she could find a job that would
enable her to support her brother and sister. Without a good job, she would
have to give her brother and sister up for adoption.

Employing Stotland's (1969) technique for manipulating empathy through
perspective taking, Coke et al. instructed participants either to imagine how
Katie felt about her situation (imagine-her condition) or to observe the
broadcasting techniques used to make the newscast impactful (observe condition). Just before participants heard the newscast, in the context of another
experiment they were given a capsule ostensibly containing the drug Norephren (actually a powdered milk placebo). All participants were told that
Norephren had a side effect. Half were told that it would relax them (relaxation side-effect condition); the rest, that it would arouse them (arousal
side-effect condition). After hearing the newscast, all participants were unexpectedly given an opportunity to help Katie by offering to run errands, care
for her brother and sister, and so on.

Coke et al. (1978) assumed that perspective taking would increase empathic feelings, so people in the imagine condition would be more empathically aroused by the newscast than people in the observe condition. People in
the imagine/arousal side-effect cell, however, would have a salient alternative explanation for this arousal: They had just taken a Norephren capsule
that was causing their arousal. Only people in the imagine/relaxation side-
effect cell should both experience empathic arousal and label that arousal as
a response to Katie's plight. Therefore, following Schachter's (1964) two-
factor theory of emotion, only those participants should experience empathic
emotion. And if empathy increases helping, then those participants should
help more than participants in each of the other three cells. Helping responses
patterned as predicted; participants in the imagine/relaxation side-effect cell
offered significantly more help to Katie than did participants in any of the
other three cells.

In a second experiment, Coke et al. (1978) used a different strategy to
manipulate empathic emotion; they artificially increased perceived empathy
by providing false arousal feedback to participants listening to a (bogus) radio

broadcast. The need situation presented in the broadcast was designed to be intrinsically unarousing: A graduate student in Education was having a hard time finding volunteers to participate in her master's thesis research because she could offer neither payment nor course credit. All participants were instructed, while listening to the broadcast, to imagine how the graduate student felt about her situation. As they listened, some participants received false galvanic skin response (GSR) feedback indicating that they were not aroused (low-arousal condition); others received false feedback indicating that they were highly aroused (high-arousal condition). All participants were then unexpectedly given an opportunity to help the graduate student by volunteering to be in her research. Prior to this opportunity to help, participants were asked to indicate the degree to which they had experienced a number of emotions while listening to the broadcast.

Coke et al. (1978) predicted that people in the high-arousal condition would perceive themselves to be experiencing more empathy than people in the low-arousal condition and, moreover, that this empathy would lead to more helping. Results supported this prediction. Participants in the high-arousal condition (a) indicated that they felt more empathic emotion than participants in the low-arousal condition while listening to the broadcast, and (b) helped the graduate student more. Further, a path analysis indicated that the effect of the false-feedback manipulation on helping was mediated by self-reported empathy.

Finally, an experiment by Dovidio, Allen, and Schroeder (1990) revealed that inducing empathy does not simply activate a general disposition to help; it increases the motivation to help relieve the specific need for which empathy is felt. Using a perspective-taking manipulation much like the one used by Coke et al. (1978, Experiment 1), Dovidio et al. induced either low or high empathy for Tracy, a young woman with one of two specific problems: recruiting students to help with her senior honors project or finding volunteers to help gather information for a university committee. Participants in the experiment were then given a chance to help Tracy either with the problem for which empathy had been induced or with the other problem.

Regardless of the problem for which empathy had been induced, results were the same. When given a chance to help with the problem for which empathy had been induced, those in the high-empathy condition were more likely to help than those in the low-empathy condition. When given a chance to help with the other problem, those in the high-empathy condition were no more likely to help than those in the low-empathy condition. The increase in helping evoked by empathy was specific to the need for which empathy was felt.

The combined evidence from these studies indicates that there is indeed an empathy–helping relationship; feeling empathy for a person in need increases the likelihood of helping to relieve that need. (See Eisenberg & Miller,

1987, for a far more extensive meta-analytic review reaching the same conclusion.) To conclude that there is an empathy–helping relationship tells us nothing, however, about the nature of the motivation that underlies this relationship. It gives us a phenomenon to explain, not an explanation. The strong form of the empathy-altruism hypothesis presented in the previous chapter claims that the motivation is altruistic and exclusively so, but this hypothesis may be wrong. Just as in chapter 5 Frank had to entertain the possibility that Suzie's ultimate goal was the concert and not him, we must entertain the possibility that the ultimate goal of an empathically aroused helper is not to benefit the person who is helped but some form of egoistic self-benefit. What egoistic possibilities exist?

EGOISTIC ALTERNATIVES
TO THE EMPATHY-ALTRUISM HYPOTHESIS

The three-path model outlined in Fig. 6.1 directs our attention to three general classes of self-benefit that might be the ultimate goal of empathy-induced helping. The ultimate goal might be to gain material, social, or self-rewards (Path 1a); to avoid material, social, or self-punishments (Path 1b); or to reduce a state of aversive arousal (Path 2). Each of these egoistic possibilities has been proposed as an explanation for the empathy–helping relationship. Let us consider each in turn.

Empathy-Specific Rewards

The first egoistic possibility claims that the motivation to help associated with empathy does not introduce a third, altruistic path from perception of the other as in need to helping, as the empathy-altruism hypothesis claims; instead, the motivation follows Path 1a. According to this explanation, an arrow should be drawn in Fig. 6.1 from the internal response of empathy on Path 3 to the motivational state of gaining rewards for helping on Path 1a, and the rest of Path 3 should be erased. We help more when feeling empathy not because of altruistic concern for the other's welfare but because we know that when we feel empathy there are special rewards in the form of praise, honor, and pride that are attendant on helping.

We heard a precursor of such an argument in La Rouchefoucauld's maxim: "The most disinterested love is, after all, but a kind of bargain, in which the dear love of our own selves always proposes to be the gainer some way or other" (1691, Maxim 82). Recall also Mandeville's assertion that, "The humblest man alive must confess that the reward of a virtuous action, which is the satisfaction that ensues upon it, consists in a certain pleasure he procures to himself by contemplating on his own worth" (1714/1732, p. 43).

Each of these statements points to the role of social and self-rewards as general motivators of helping. To account for the empathy–helping relationship, however, it is necessary to postulate a source of motivation specific to empathy. It is not enough to appeal to general rewards associated with helping; we must assume that helping is especially rewarding when the helper feels empathy for the person in need, that empathy introduces a motivational additive along Path 1a. In recent years, two different versions of an *empathy-specific reward hypothesis* have been proposed.

One version claims that we learn through socialization that *additional rewards* follow helping someone for whom we feel empathy; these rewards most often take the form of extra praise from others or a special feeling of pride in ourselves. When we feel empathy, we think of these additional rewards, and we help in order to get them. Variations on this theme have been suggested by Thompson, Cowan, and Rosenhan (1980); Batson (1987); and Smith, Keating, and Stotland (1989; see also Meindl & Lerner, 1983).

A second version of the empathy-specific reward hypothesis claims that rather than being associated with additional rewards, empathy evokes *additional need* for the general rewards associated with helping. Just as a starving person values food more than a person comfortably replete, the additional need evoked by empathy makes helping more rewarding. This possibility was suggested by Cialdini, Schaller, Houlihan, Arps, Fultz, and Beaman (1987). They claimed that individuals who experience empathy for someone who is suffering find themselves in a negative affective state, a state of temporary sadness or sorrow. This negative state creates a need to feel better, which leads the empathically aroused individual to help "because helping contains a rewarding component for most normally socialized adults . . . [and] can be used instrumentally to restore mood" (p. 750).

According to each version of the empathy-specific reward hypothesis, then, empathy does not lead to increased helping because of an increased desire to relieve the suffering of the person for whom empathy is felt, as the empathy-altruism hypothesis claims. Rather, it leads to increased helping because of a purely egoistic desire to gain social or self-rewards.

Empathy-Specific Punishments

A second egoistic alternative to the empathy–altruism hypothesis claims that the increased motivation to help associated with empathy follows Path 1b. According to this explanation, an arrow should be drawn in Fig. 6.1 from the internal response of empathy on Path 3 to the motivational state of avoiding punishment for not helping on Path 1b, and the rest of Path 3 erased. We help more when feeling empathy not because of altruistic concern for the other's welfare but because we know that additional punishments in the form of guilt, shame, and censure follow failing to help someone for whom we feel empathy.

As precursors to such a view, recall Mandeville's claim that "There is no merit in saving an innocent babe ready to drop into the fire: The action is neither good nor bad, and what benefit soever the infant received, we only obliged our selves; for to have seen it fall, and not strove to hinder it, would have caused a pain, which self-preservation compelled us to prevent" (1714/1732, p. 42). Recall also Mill's suggestion that we act on our feeling for others lest we suffer either external sanction, "the hope of favor and the fear of displeasure, from our fellow-creatures or from the Ruler of the Universe," or internal sanction, "a pain, . . . the essence of Conscience, . . . derived from sympathy, from love, and still more from fear" (1861, Chapter 3, paragraphs 3–4).

Once again, if anticipated punishments are to account for the increased motivation to help associated with empathy, then these punishments cannot be general; they must be empathy specific. Empathy must introduce a motivational additive along Path 1b. In recent years, two versions of an *empathy-specific punishment hypothesis* have been proposed.

One version, introduced by Archer, Diaz-Loving, Gollwitzer, Davis, and Foushee (1981; see also Archer, 1984), focuses on *additional socially administered punishments*. According to this version, empathy leads to increased helping because the empathic individual anticipates negative social evaluation if he or she fails to act in a manner consistent with previously expressed empathic feelings for the person in need.

A second version, proposed by Dovidio (1984), Batson (1987), and Schaller and Cialdini (1988), focuses on *additional self-punishments*. This version claims that we learn through socialization that empathy carries with it a special obligation to help and, as a result, an extra dose of self-administered shame or guilt if we do not. When we feel empathy we think of the impending additional self-punishments and help in order to avoid them. It is as though we ask ourselves, what kind of person would not help when feeling like this? To dodge having to answer in a way that reflects badly on ourselves, we help.

According to each version of the empathy-specific punishment hypothesis, then, empathy does not lead to increased helping because of an increased desire to relieve the suffering of the person for whom empathy is felt, as the empathy–altruism hypothesis claims. Rather, it leads to increased helping because of a purely egoistic desire to avoid social or self-punishments.

Aversive-Arousal Reduction

By far the most popular egoistic explanation of the motivation to help associated with empathy, both in classical philosophy and in contemporary psychology, is that the motivation is directed toward the goal of aversive-arousal reduction (Path 2). According to this explanation, an arrow should be drawn in Fig. 6.1 from the internal response of empathy on Path 3 to the motivational state of arousal reduction on Path 2, and the rest of Path 3 erased. We help more when feeling empathy not because of altruistic concern for the other's welfare but because feeling empathy for someone who is suffering makes us feel bad, and helping removes the cause of the empathic arousal. Helping benefits us by turning off this aversive stimulus.

At first glance, this explanation may look very much like the second version of the empathy-specific reward hypothesis, the one based on negative-state relief. In fact, it is quite different. Both explanations begin with the proposition that feeling empathy for someone in need is unpleasant, a negative affective state. From this common starting point, the two explanations diverge. The negative-state relief explanation claims that the resulting motivation is directed toward the goal of adding the mood-enhancing rewards that we have learned are associated with helping; the aversive-arousal reduction explanation claims that the motivation is directed toward the goal of eliminating the mood-depressing stimulus.

Aquinas gave early expression to an aversive-arousal reduction explanation of the empathy–helping relationship when he argued: "From the very fact that a person takes pity on anyone, it follows that another's distress grieves him. And since sorrow or grief is about one's own ills, one grieves or sorrows for another's distress, in so far as one looks upon another's distress as one's own" (1270/1917, II-II, 30, 2).

In recent years, a similar *aversive-arousal reduction hypothesis* has been invoked to account for the motivation to help associated with empathy by Dovidio (1984), Hoffman (1981a), Hornstein (1978), Karylowski (1982), Krebs (1975), and Piliavin and Piliavin (1973). Each has suggested that when we feel empathy for someone who is suffering, we also suffer; we then act to relieve his or her suffering as an instrumental means to relieve our own. Hoffman (1981b) put it succinctly: "Empathic distress is unpleasant and helping the victim is usually the best way to get rid of the source" (p. 52).

According to the aversive-arousal reduction hypothesis, then, empathy does not lead to increased helping because of an increased desire to relieve the suffering of the person for whom empathy is felt, as the empathy-altruism hypothesis claims. Rather, it leads to increased helping because of a purely egoistic desire to be free of the unpleasant and upsetting empathic feelings.

CONCRETIZING THE EGOISM-ALTRUISM DEBATE

Each of these three egoistic alternatives implies that Fig. 6.1 should be redrawn to eliminate the altruistic motivation on Path 3. Each allows that (a) perception of the other as in need and (b) taking the other's perspective may combine to produce (c) empathic emotion. But each contends that the arrow from empathic emotion does not go to altruistic motivation; it goes to one of the three possible egoistic internal responses, and relieving the suffering of a person for whom empathy is felt is only an instrumental goal on the way to this egoistic ultimate goal. Each is thus in direct disagreement with the empathy-altruism hypothesis, which claims that relieving the person's suffering is the ultimate goal of empathy-induced motivation to help and that the rewards gained, punishments avoided, and aversive arousal reduced are unintended consequences. If one or more of the egoistic alternatives is valid, then we have no reason to accept the empathy-altruism hypothesis—at least not in the strong form presented in chapter 6.

Is one or more of these alternatives valid? This question returns us to the problem represented in Table 5.1, the problem of determining which benefits of helping are instrumental goals, which are ultimate goals, and which are unintended consequences. The problem however, is no longer as abstract as it was. We now have a conceptual framework that, on the one hand, specifies the source of the motivation to be explained—feeling empathy for the person in need—and, on the other, specifies possible egoistic goals of this motivation—gaining rewards, avoiding punishments, or reducing aversive arousal.

The question before us is not whether these various egoistic goals can motivate helping. As noted in chapter 6, there is already considerable empirical evidence that each can. Rather, the question before us is the nature of the motivation to help evoked by empathy. Given that empathy evokes some motivation to help, is this motivation directed toward one or more of these egoistic goals, or is it directed toward the altruistic goal of relieving the needy individual's suffering? That is the question.

To answer this question, our task is to determine whether any of the proposed forms of self-benefit are ultimate goals of empathically aroused helping, or whether they are only unintended consequences. To aid us in this task, we have the three-path model in Fig. 6.1. This model provides a sufficiently detailed sketch of the psychological processes involved in each of the proposed motives that we can make explicit empirical predictions that discriminate among the different proposed motives. Let us derive some of these empirical predictions.

VARIABLES THAT PERMIT DIFFERENT EMPIRICAL PREDICTIONS FOR THE EMPATHY-ALTRUISM HYPOTHESIS AND ITS EGOISTIC ALTERNATIVES

As discussed in chapter 5, we can determine whether a given behavioral outcome is an ultimate goal by observing the pattern of behavior across situations that systematically vary the relationship between the behavior and the outcome. Table 7.1 offers a taxonomy of variables that systematically vary the relationship between behavior and the different outcomes that could be ultimate goals of empathy-induced helping. These variables do not change the goal(s); they change the attractiveness or availability of different behavioral routes to the goal(s). As a result, each variable listed allows us to make different empirical predictions for the empathy-altruism hypothesis and at least one of the egoistic alternatives. By testing these predictions, we can assess the validity of the different hypotheses.

Also discussed in chapter 5, there is an asymmetry between the proposed altruistic and egoistic goals; the self-benefits of helping necessarily follow the attempt to benefit the person in need. Because of this asymmetry, our tests focus on the three proposed egoistic hypotheses. Only if empirical observations fail to pattern as predicted by any of these hypotheses, and instead pattern consistently as predicted by the empathy-altruism hypothesis, can we conclude that the latter hypothesis in its strong form is valid. Even then, we can accept the empathy-altruism hypothesis as valid only so long as no new plausible egoistic explanation can be proposed that accounts for the empirical observations.

Empathy-Specific Reward versus the Empathy-Altruism Hypothesis

Table 7.1 lists four variables that produce different empirical predictions for the empathy-specific reward hypothesis and the empathy-altruism hypothesis. These variables suggest ways we might test the relative merits of these two hypotheses.

First, as noted in chapter 6, only one's own helping makes one eligible for the rewards of helping; someone else's helping does not. Therefore, the empathy-specific reward hypothesis predicts that, when helping involves negligible costs to self, empathically aroused individuals should be more pleased if the suffering person's need is removed as a result of their own action than as a result of someone else's action. If someone else helps, the rewards are lost. In contrast, the empathy-altruism hypothesis predicts equal pleasure, regardless of whose action relieves the person's suffering, because the goal of altruistic motivation is to have the other person's need relieved.

To test these competing predictions, one might measure the mood of empathically aroused individuals after they learn that someone else, or fate, has beaten them to the punch and relieved the victim's distress. If these individuals are seeking rewards for helping, their mood should not be enhanced by this information; it might even grow worse. If these individuals are altruistically motivated, they should feel better.

Second, consider the effect of providing empathically aroused individuals

TABLE 7.1

Variables That Should Differentiate Between Egoistic and Altruistic Motivation to Help

Variable	Reward-seeking (Path 1a)	Punishment-avoiding (Path 1b)	Arousal-reducing (Path 2)	Altruistic motivation (Path 3)
1. *Acceptable helpers*: Whose help can attain the goal?	Only oneself	Oneself; others	Oneself; others	Oneself; others
2. *Necessity of one's help being effective*: Must one's help be effective to reach the goal?	Not necessary (if ineffectiveness justified)	Not necessary (if ineffectiveness justified)	Necessary	Necessary
3. *Viability of escape*: Can the goal be reach by escape without helping?	Escape not viable	Escape viable (from own shame, guilt)	Escape viable (from victim's distress)	Escape not viable
4. *Salient cognitions*: What cognitions are salient when deciding whether to help?	Anticipated rewards; costs of helping	Anticipated punishments; costs of helping	Aversive arousal; costs of helping	Victim's welfare; costs of helping
5. *Need for rewards of helping*: What is effect of increased need for rewards of helping?	Increased motivation	No effect	No effect	No effect

Note: From Batson (1987).

with information about the effectiveness of their helping. Because the rewards for helping are available to those who sincerely try to help even if their efforts fail, the empathy-specific reward hypothesis predicts that empathically aroused individuals should not be especially concerned if a sincere attempt to help does not succeed. The empathy-altruism hypothesis predicts that an unsuccessful attempt to help, even if sincere, will be disappointing.

Third, when deciding whether to help, the empathy-specific reward hypothesis predicts that empathically aroused helpers will be thinking about the rewards of helping (e.g., praise, pride) because getting these rewards is their ultimate goal. The empathy-altruism hypothesis predicts these helpers will be thinking about the needy other's welfare rather than about rewards because the other's welfare is their ultimate goal. There are various techniques for measuring salient thoughts, such as a Stroop task (Stroop, 1938) or incidental learning procedure (Hull & Levy, 1979; Smith, Ingram, & Brehm, 1983). One of these techniques might be used to assess the salience for empathically aroused helpers of thoughts about rewards and thoughts about the victim.

Finally, the empathy-specific reward hypothesis predicts that introducing any factor that increases or decreases an empathically aroused individual's need for the rewards associated with helping will increase or decrease the rate of helping accordingly; the empathy-altruism hypothesis predicts no effect for such factors. To compare these predictions, some need-increasing factor, such as a threat to one's self-concept as a helpful person (Steele, 1975), might be introduced and the effect on helping assessed. Alternatively, empathically aroused individuals might be led either to anticipate or not to anticipate a rewarding experience even if they decide not to help. Anticipating such an experience should reduce helping if these individuals are helping because they have a special need for the resulting rewards; it should have no effect if they are helping out of an altruistic desire to benefit the person in need.

Empathy-Specific Punishment versus the Empathy-Altruism Hypothesis

Table 7.1 lists three variables that produce different empirical predictions for the empathy-specific punishment and the empathy-altruism hypothesis. These variables suggest ways to test the relative merits of these two hypotheses.

Two of the variables are ones already discussed: effectiveness of helping and salient cognitions. Paralleling the methods just proposed for testing the empathy-specific reward hypothesis, each of these variables could be used to test the empathy-specific punishment hypothesis. Concerning effectiveness, as was true for gaining rewards, one's help need not be effective to avoid punishments for not helping; as noted in chapter 6, "It's the thought that counts." So, if one's ultimate goal is to avoid these punishments, then learning that a sincere attempt failed should not prove disappointing. Concerning salient cognitions, the empathy-specific punishment hypothesis predicts that empathically aroused helpers will be thinking about the punishments for not helping (e.g., guilt, shame), because avoiding these punishments is their ultimate goal. A Stroop task or incidental learning procedure might be used to assess the salience of thoughts about punishments.

In addition to the effectiveness of helping and salient-cognitions variables used to test the empathy-specific reward hypothesis, the empathy-specific punishment hypothesis can also be tested by varying ease of escape from the obligation to help. The empathy-specific punishment hypothesis predicts that any circumstance that permits empathically aroused individuals to escape from the anticipated social and self-censure for failure to help should reduce the rate of helping; the empathy-altruism hypothesis predicts no reduction. To test these predictions, one might make the anticipated punishment associated with empathy easier to escape by making individuals' helping decisions anonymous or by providing them with a face-saving excuse for not helping. Anonymity should reduce the threat of social censure; a face-saving excuse should reduce the threat of self-censure and guilt.

Aversive-Arousal Reduction Versus the Empathy-Altruism Hypothesis

Only two of the variables in Table 7.1 produce different empirical predictions for the aversive-arousal reduction hypothesis and the empathy-altruism hypothesis: salient cognitions and escape. The logic for salient cognitions is the same as for the empathy-specific reward and empathy-specific punishment hypotheses, except that here the cognitions concern aversive-arousal reduction. Specifying cognitions clearly relevant to aversive-arousal reduction seems much more difficult than specifying cognitions relevant to seeking rewards or avoiding punishments. Therefore, to test the aversive-arousal reduction hypothesis, it seems best to use the escape variable.

The type of escape necessary to test the aversive-arousal reduction hypothesis is different from that necessary to test the empathy-specific punishment hypothesis; it is escape from perception of the needy person's suffering rather than escape from one's own shame and guilt. The aversive-arousal reduction hypothesis predicts that if helping is at least moderately costly, and empathically aroused individuals can easily escape continued exposure to the person's suffering, then they will do that instead of helping; either of these responses can reduce their aversive empathic arousal. Helping removes the source of the aversive arousal; escaping removes contact with the source. In contrast, the empathy-altruism hypothesis predicts no reduction of empathically aroused helping when escape is made easy. Escape does not enable one to reach the altruistic goal of relieving the victim's suffering; only helping (or someone else helping) does that.

The relative merits of these two hypotheses might be tested, then, by presenting some empathically aroused individuals with an opportunity to help in a situation where escape from continued exposure to the needy person's suffering is easy, and others with the same opportunity in a situation where escape is difficult. The aversive-arousal reduction hypothesis predicts less helping by empathically aroused individuals in the former situation than in the latter; the empathy-altruism hypothesis does not.

INTO THE LABORATORY

Armed with the explicit empirical predictions just derived for the empathy-altruism hypothesis and the three egoistic alternatives, we are now ready to follow Galileo and Lewin into the laboratory. Not surprisingly, no single variable listed in Table 7.1 allows a clear test of the empathy-altruism hypothesis against all three egoistic alternatives. So it will be necessary either to conduct an experiment in which a number of the variables are manipulated at once—which seems unwieldy and unwise—or to conduct a series of experiments in which the egoistic alternatives are tested one after another. Following the latter strategy, care must be taken that, when moving from testing the empathy-altruism hypothesis against one egoistic alternative to testing it against another, conditions are not created in which the first egoistic alternative could produce the pattern of empirical observations now predicted by the empathy-altruism hypothesis.

Part III summarizes the predictions, procedures, and results of over 20 experiments conducted in the past 15 years to test the empathy-altruism hypothesis against one or more of the egoistic alternatives. In reviewing these experiments, we consider the three egoistic alternatives in reverse order to the way they were presented in this chapter, because reverse order is how they have come to the fore. Chapter 8 reviews research designed to test the aversive-arousal reduction hypothesis; chapter 9, the empathy-specific punishment hypothesis; and chapter 10, the empathy-specific reward hypothesis. The terrain of Part III is quite different from that traversed thus far. We leave behind the steady climb of conceptual analysis and plunge into a tangled thicket of experimental design and empirical observation.

PART
III

TESTING THE EGOISTIC ALTERNATIVES TO THE EMPATHY-ALTRUISM HYPOTHESIS

CHAPTER 8

Aversive-Arousal
Reduction

As noted in the previous chapter, the aversive-arousal reduction hypothesis has long been the most popular egoistic explanation of the empathy–helping relationship. Classic expressions were offered by Aquinas and Hobbes; contemporary expressions, by Hoffman (1981a), Hornstein (1978), Krebs (1975), Piliavin and Piliavin (1973), and Piliavin, Dovidio, Gaertner, and Clark (1981, 1982).

According to this hypothesis, becoming empathically aroused by witnessing someone in need is aversive and evokes motivation to reduce this aversive arousal. Rather than empathy evoking altruistic motivation directed toward the ultimate goal of relieving the victim's distress, as the empathy-altruism hypothesis claims (Path 3 of the three-path model presented in Fig. 6.1), the motivation to help evoked by empathy is directed toward the ultimate goal of relieving the helper's own empathic distress (Path 2). Because relieving the other's need removes the stimulus causing this aversive arousal, helping enables one to reach this egoistic goal.

One can easily understand why this explanation has been so popular. It is simple, direct, and intuitively plausible. Yet is it true? Is the reason empathy leads to increased helping because the empathically aroused individual is motivated to turn off this arousal?

TESTING THE AVERSIVE-AROUSAL
REDUCTION HYPOTHESIS

Beginning around 1980, a series of studies was conducted to test the aversive-arousal reduction hypothesis. The intent was to determine whether the ultimate goal of empathy-induced motivation to help is to increase the helper's own welfare by reducing his or her empathic emotional arousal, as the aversive-arousal reduction hypothesis claims, or is to increase the welfare of the person in need, as the empathy–altruism hypothesis claims.

As suggested in chapter 7, the best way to test the relative merits of these two hypotheses seems to be to vary the ease of escaping exposure to a needy individual's suffering without having to help. Escape is a viable means of reaching the egoistic goal of reducing one's own aversive empathic arousal because, although it does not remove the stimulus causing the aversive arousal, it terminates exposure to the stimulus. Escape is not, however, a viable means of reaching the altruistic goal of relieving the suffering individual's distress; it does nothing to promote this end. The difference in viability of escape as a means to these two goals produces competing predictions for the two hypotheses.

Predictions

Consider the effect of making it either difficult or easy to escape exposure to a needy person's suffering on the rate of offering help by individuals feeling high empathy for that person. When escape is difficult, both hypotheses predict a relatively high rate because helping is the best way to reach either goal, aversive-arousal reduction or relief of the victim's distress. When escape is easy, predictions differ. The aversive-arousal reduction hypothesis predicts that the rate of helping will drop; the empathy–altruism hypothesis predicts that it will remain high. This is because aversive-arousal reduction can now be achieved without having to help; relieving the victim's distress cannot.

For potential helpers feeling little empathy for the person in need, predictions of the two hypotheses do not differ. The three-path model presented in chapter 6 suggests that, even if little empathy is felt, an emotionally gripping need situation will likely produce feelings of personal distress, which will in turn evoke Path 2 egoistic motivation to reduce this distress. Neither hypothesis disputes this suggestion. Therefore, if helping is at least moderately costly, then among potential helpers feeling little empathy, both hypotheses predict higher helping when escape is difficult than when it is easy.

Tables 8.1 and 8.2 summarize these predictions. Table 8.1 presents predic-

TABLE 8.1
Predictions from Aversive-Arousal Reduction Hypothesis for Rate of
Helping in an Escape × Empathy Design

	Empathy	
Escape	Low	High
Easy	Low	Low
Difficult	High	High/Very High

TABLE 8.2
Predictions from Empathy-Altruism Hypothesis for Rate of Helping in
an Escape × Empathy Design

	Empathy	
Escape	Low	High
Easy	Low	High
Difficult	High	High

tions of the aversive-arousal reduction hypothesis for the rate of helping in the four cells of a 2 (easy vs. difficult escape) × 2 (low vs. high empathy) factorial design. As can be seen, this hypothesis predicts more helping in the difficult-escape condition than in the easy for both low- and high-empathy individuals. If observed, this pattern would provide evidence that motivation to help of high-empathy individuals is directed toward the egoistic goal of reducing their own aversive empathic arousal. Less theoretically relevant but also likely is an effect of empathy in the difficult-escape condition; helping will likely be higher among high-empathy individuals than among low. This secondary prediction is based on the assumption that there is more Path 2 egoistic motivation for high-empathy individuals than for low because, for them, empathic arousal is added to whatever other aversive arousal (distress, disgust) is evoked by witnessing the person in need. In the easy-escape condition, the added aversive arousal can be relieved without helping; hence, there is no reason to expect it to produce increased helping in this condition.

Table 8.2 presents predictions of the empathy-altruism hypothesis in the same 2 × 2 design. This hypothesis predicts more helping in the difficult-escape condition than in the easy only for low-empathy individuals; it predicts a high rate of helping even in the easy-escape condition for individuals experiencing high empathy for the person in need because helping is the only way to relieve the victim's distress. Across the four cells of the 2 × 2 design, then, the empathy-altruism hypothesis predicts a 1-versus-3 pattern: low helping in the easy-escape/low-empathy cell and high helping in the other three cells. If observed, this pattern would provide evidence that the motivation of high-empathy individuals is *not* directed toward the egoistic goal of reducing their own aversive empathic arousal, contradicting the aversive-arousal reduction hypothesis. It would be entirely consistent with the claim of the empathy-altruism hypothesis that the motivation to help evoked by empathy is directed toward the altruistic goal of relieving the victim's distress. As noted in the previous chapter, this pattern would also be consistent with the empathy-specific reward and empathy-specific punishment hypotheses. Escape from the victim's distress does not allow one to gain rewards, nor does it necessarily allow one to escape shame and guilt. Further research would be required to test the empathy-altruism hypothesis against these egoistic alternatives.

Importance of the Pattern of Behavior

Note that to test the competing predictions of the aversive-arousal reduction and the empathy-altruism hypotheses, the pattern of helping across all four cells of the Escape × Empathy design is important. If we were to compare helping under easy- and difficult-escape conditions only for high-empathy individuals, then the empathy-altruism hypothesis would predict no difference. Such a result could occur simply because the escape manipulation was too weak, or the behavioral measure of helping was insensitive. If, however, the escape manipulation has a significant effect on the helping of low- but not high-empathy individuals, then the lack of difference for high-empathy individuals cannot be attributed to a weak escape manipulation or insensitive measure.

It is also clear that one must guard against a possible ceiling effect. If the rate of helping by high-empathy individuals is extremely high in both escape conditions, then the difference among high-empathy individuals predicted by the aversive-arousal reduction hypothesis may not appear simply because the rate of helping in the difficult-escape/high-empathy cell can go no higher. One way to guard against a ceiling effect is to make helping at least moderately costly, so the rate is not too high.

EMPIRICAL EVIDENCE

To test the competing predictions of the aversive-arousal reduction and the empathy-altruism hypotheses in an Escape × Empathy design, it is necessary to have some individuals experience low empathy and others experience high empathy in response to exactly the same need situation. Then it is necessary that they all be given a chance to help, some from each empathy group under conditions of easy escape, others under conditions of difficult escape. This procedure has been followed in six different studies.

A Shocking Situation: Observing Elaine Perform under Aversive Conditions (Batson et al., 1981)

In the first two studies, female undergraduates observed a young woman named Elaine, whom they believed was receiving uncomfortable electric shocks. They were then given an unanticipated chance to help by volunteering to take the shocks in her stead. Both ease of escape and empathy were experimentally manipulated.

To manipulate ease of escape, participants in each experiment were informed that if they did not take Elaine's place, either they would continue to observe her take the shocks (difficult-escape condition) or they would not (easy-escape condition). Level of empathic emotional response to Elaine's suffering (low vs. high) was manipulated differently in the two experiments. In the first, similarity information was used to manipulate empathy; in the second, an emotion-specific misattribution technique was used.

Procedure for Experiment 1

The shock procedure employed in this experiment has been used in a number of subsequent experiments, so it is worth describing in some detail. When participants (all female undergraduates because the person in need was female) arrived at the laboratory, they were given an introduction to read, which explained the supposed rationale and procedure for the experiment:

> In this experiment we are studying task performance and impression projection under stressful conditions. We are investigating, as well, whether any inefficiency that might result from working under aversive conditions increases proportionately with the amount of time spent working under such conditions.
>
> Since this study requires the assistance of two participants, there will be a drawing to determine which role will be yours. One participant will perform a task (consisting of up to, but not more than, ten trials) under aversive conditions; the aversive conditions will be created by the presentation of electric shock at random intervals during the work period. The other participant will observe the individual working under aversive conditions. This role involves the formation and report of general attitudes towards the "worker" so that we may better assess what effect, if any, working under aversive conditions has upon how that individual is perceived.

After reading the introduction and signing a consent form, which reminded them that participation in the experiment was entirely voluntary and that they were free to withdraw at any time, participants drew lots for their role. The drawing was rigged so that they always drew the observer role; the other participant, Elaine, was to be the worker.

Observer Role. Participants were then escorted to the observation room and given written instructions for the observer role. They learned that they would not actually meet Elaine but would instead observe her over closed-circuit television as she performed up to ten 2-minute digit-recall trials. At random intervals during each trial, Elaine would receive moderately uncomfortable electric shocks (two to three times the strength of static electricity).

Ease of Escape Manipulation. To manipulate ease of escape without helping, the last line of the instructions varied the number of trials that participants expected to observe. In the *easy-escape condition,* participants read, "Although the worker will be completing between two and ten trials, it will be necessary for you to observe only the first two." In the *difficult-escape condition* participants read, "The worker will be completing between two and ten trials, all of which you will observe." All participants were later to learn that Elaine agreed to complete all 10 trials, and they were given the chance to help her by trading places after the second trial. Therefore, in the easy-escape condition, participants who did not help would not anticipate having to watch Elaine take any more shocks; in the difficult-escape condition, they would.

Similarity Manipulation of Empathy. Once participants finished reading these instructions, the experimenter handed them a copy of a 14-item personal values and interest questionnaire, like one they had completed several weeks earlier at a screening session. The experimenter explained that this copy had been filled out by Elaine and would provide information about her that might help in forming an impression. In fact, Elaine's questionnaire had been prepared in advance so that it reflected values and interests that were either very similar (*high-empathy condition*) or very dissimilar (*low-empathy condition*) to those that participants had expressed on their own questionnaires. Both Stotland (1969) and Krebs (1975) had found this kind of similarity information effective in manipulating empathy.

Need Situation. After participants looked over Elaine's questionnaire, the experimenter turned on a video monitor, allowing them to see Elaine. (Unknown to participants, what they saw was actually a videotape.) The experimenter then left participants alone to observe and form an impression of Elaine. As the trials progressed, Elaine's facial expression and body movements indicated that she was finding the shocks extremely uncomfortable. By the end of the second trial, her reactions were so strong that Martha, the assistant administering the shocks on the videotape, interrupted the procedure to ask Elaine if she was all right. A conversation ensued that led to Elaine confessing that as a child she had been thrown from a horse onto an electric fence. The doctor at the time said that she had suffered a trauma and in the future might react strongly to even mild shocks. (This information was provided to ensure that participants would view Elaine's extreme reaction to the shocks as atypical and would not expect to find the shocks as unpleasant if they chose to take her place.) Hearing this, Martha said that she did not think Elaine should continue with the trials. Elaine replied that even though she found the shocks very unpleasant, she wanted to go on: "I started; I want to finish. I'll go on . . . I know your experiment is important, and I want to do it."

At this point, Martha hit upon an idea: Since the observer was also an introductory psychology student, maybe she would be willing to help Elaine out by taking her place. With a mixture of reluctance and relief, Elaine consented to Martha's checking on this possibility. Martha said that she would shut off the equipment and go talk with the experimenter about it. Shortly thereafter, the video screen went blank.

Helping Measure: Taking Shocks for Elaine.   About 30 seconds later, the experimenter entered the participant's room and said:

> I guess you saw, Elaine's finding the aversive conditions pretty uncomfortable. Martha was wondering if maybe you'd like to help Elaine out by taking her place. Now, before you decide anything, let me explain just what that would involve.
>
> First of all, let me say that you're under no obligation to take Elaine's place. I mean, if you would like to continue in your role as observer that's fine; you did happen to draw the observer role.

What the experimenter said next depended on the participant's ease of escape condition. To participants in the *easy-escape condition,* the experimenter said, "If you decide to continue as the observer, you've finished observing the two trials, so all you need to do is answer a few questions about your impression of Elaine and you'll be free to go." To participants in the *difficult-escape condition,* the experimenter said, "If you decide to continue as the observer, I'll need you to observe Elaine's remaining eight trials. After you've done that and answered a few questions about your impression of Elaine, you'll be free to go." For participants in both escape conditions, the experimenter then continued, "If you decide to help Elaine out by taking her place, then what will happen is that she'll come in here and observe you, and you will go in and perform the recall trials while receiving the shocks. Once you have completed the trials, you'll be free to go. What would you like to do?" Response to this question provided the measure of helping.

Debriefing.   After responding, participants were given a brief reaction questionnaire to complete, while the experimenter ostensibly went to tell Martha what had been decided. As soon as participants completed this questionnaire, they were fully debriefed. Care was taken to explain all deceptive aspects of the experiment and the reasons for using deception. Participants were encouraged to express and discuss their reactions to the situation. All participants seemed to readily understand the necessity for the deception involved, and none appeared upset by it. Most said that they found the experiment quite interesting and were glad to have participated. Similar debriefing procedures followed each of the experiments described in chapters 8–10.

Results of Experiment 1

The proportion of participants in each experimental condition who offered to help Elaine by taking her place is presented in Table 8.3. As can be seen, the rate of helping conformed closely to the 1-versus-3 pattern predicted by the empathy-altruism hypothesis; there was no evidence of the effect of the escape manipulation in the high-empathy (similar-victim) condition predicted by the aversive-arousal reduction hypothesis. A planned comparison contrasting the rate of helping in the easy-escape/low-empathy cell with the rate in the other three cells was highly reliable, $\chi^2 (1, N = 44) = 14.62, p < .001$; residual variance across the other three cells was not reliable, $\chi^2 (2) = 2.60$, $p > .25$. (Statistical tests of predictions for these and other proportional data reported in this book are by analysis of variance after using an arcsin transformation to produce a normal approximation—see Langer & Abelson, 1972; Winer, 1971.)

Clearly, in the low-empathy (dissimilar-victim) condition, where, according to both the aversive-arousal reduction hypothesis and the empathy-altruism hypothesis, the motivation to help was expected to be egoistic, the ease of escape manipulation had a dramatic effect on helping. When escape

TABLE 8.3
Proportion of Subjects Agreeing to Take Shocks for Elaine
(Batson et. al., 1981, Experiment 1)

	Empathy Condition	
Escape Condition	Low (Dissimilar Victim)	High (Similar Victim)
Easy	.18	.91
Difficult	.64	.82

Note: $n = 11$ in each cell.

Copyright 1981 by the American Psychological Association. Adapted by permission of the publisher.

was easy, participants were not likely to help, presumably because (a) they felt little empathy for Elaine and (b) the least costly way to reduce the personal distress caused by watching her suffer was simply to answer the experimenter's final questions and leave. When escape was difficult, participants were quite likely to help, presumably because, even though they felt little empathy for Elaine, to take the remaining shocks themselves was less personally costly than to sit and watch her take more.

In the high-empathy (similar-victim) condition, however, where, according to the empathy-altruism hypothesis the motivation to help should be at least in part altruistic, making escape easy did not reduce participants' readiness to help. They were very likely to help even when escape was easy. Across the four cells of the Escape × Empathy (Similarity) design, then, helping patterned as predicted by the empathy–altruism hypothesis (see Table 8.2), not as predicted by the aversive-arousal reduction hypothesis (see Table 8.1).

The proportion of participants helping in the difficult-escape/high-empathy condition of this experiment was quite high. This raised the possibility of a ceiling effect. Moreover, even though Stotland (1969) and Krebs (1975) provided rather strong evidence that a similarity manipulation like the one used in this experiment affected empathic feelings, a similarity manipulation of empathy is indirect. Therefore, Batson et al. (1981) conducted a second experiment using the same shock procedure to test the relative merits of the aversive-arousal reduction and empathy-altruism hypotheses. In Experiment 2, they manipulated empathy more directly by use of an emotion-specific misattribution technique.

Procedure of Experiment 2

As discussed in chapter 6, two qualitatively distinct emotional states may be elicited by witnessing another person in distress: *empathy,* made up of other-oriented feelings for the victim such as sympathy, compassion, tenderness, warmth, and softheartedness, and *personal distress,* made up of more self-oriented feelings such as upset, alarm, anxiety, and distress. In the absence of a similarity manipulation, it seemed likely that watching Elaine react badly to the shocks would elicit a reasonably high degree of each of these emotional states. Extending the misattribution technique used by Coke et al. (1978) and described in the previous chapter, if individuals could be induced to misattribute one of these emotions to some extraneous source, such as a placebo, then these individuals should perceive their emotional reaction to Elaine's suffering to be predominantly the other emotion. That is, if they attributed their feelings of empathy to the placebo, they should perceive their response to Elaine to be predominantly personal distress. If they attributed their feelings of personal distress to the placebo, they should perceive their response to Elaine to be predominantly empathy.

Following this logic, the manipulation of empathy in Experiment 2 involved having participants take a drug, Millentana (actually a cornstarch placebo), as part of another study just prior to observing Elaine. All participants were informed that Millentana had a side effect. Those in the *personal-distress condition* were told: "Millentana produces a clear feeling of warmth and sensitivity, a feeling similar to that you might experience while reading a particularly touching novel." Those in the *empathy condition* were told: "Millentana produces a clear feeling of uneasiness and discomfort, a feeling similar to that you might experience while reading a particularly distressing novel." It was assumed that participants in the personal-distress condition, who were led to misattribute feelings of empathy to Millentana, would perceive their emotional response to watching Elaine to be primarily personal distress, whereas those in the empathy condition, who were led to misattribute feelings of personal distress to Millentana, would perceive their emotional response to Elaine to be primarily empathy.

Combining this emotion-specific misattribution manipulation with the ease of escape manipulation used in Experiment 1 produced a 2 (easy vs. difficult escape) × 2 (personal distress vs. empathy as the response attributed to watching Elaine) design. Predictions were as before: If empathy evokes egoistic motivation to reduce one's empathic arousal, as the aversive-arousal reduction hypothesis claims, then across the four cells of this 2 × 2 design, helping should pattern as depicted in Table 8.1 (with the columns relabeled *personal distress* and *empathy* instead of *low* and *high empathy*). If, on the other hand, empathy evokes altruistic motivation to relieve the suffering victim's distress, as the empathy-altruism hypothesis claims, then helping should pattern as depicted in Table 8.2.

Results of Experiment 2

The proportion of participants offering to help Elaine in each experimental condition is presented in Table 8.4. As can be seen, the rate of helping again

TABLE 8.4
Proportion of Subjects Agreeing to Take Shocks for Elaine
(Batson et. al., 1981, Experiment 2)

Escape Condition	Predominant Emotional Response	
	Personal Distress	Empathy
Easy	.33	.83
Difficult	.75	.58

Note: $n = 12$ in each cell.
Copyright 1981 by the American Psychological Association. Adapted by permission of the publisher.

conformed closely to the 1-versus-3 pattern predicted by the empathy-altruism hypothesis; there was no evidence of the effect of the escape manipulation in the empathy condition predicted by the aversive-arousal reduction hypothesis. A planned comparison contrasting the rate of helping in the easy-escape/distress cell with the rate in the other three cells was highly reliable, $\chi^2 (1, N = 48) = 5.96, p < .02,$; residual variance across the other three cells was not reliable, $\chi^2 (2) = 1.94, p > .40$. In this experiment there seemed to be little possibility of a ceiling effect in the difficult-escape/empathy cell, because the rate of helping in that cell was only slightly above 50%.

Moreover, results on two sets of ancillary measures indicated that the emotion-specific misattribution manipulation of empathy was successful. First, participants in the empathy condition, who were told that Millentana produced feelings of uneasiness and discomfort, reported experiencing more distress and less empathy as a result of taking Millentana than did participants in the personal-distress condition, who were told that Millentana produced feelings of warmth and sensitivity, $F (1, 44) = 14.82, p < .001$. Second, participants in the empathy condition reported more warmth and sensitivity and less uneasiness as a result of observing Elaine than did participants in the personal-distress condition, $F (1, 44) = 5.92, p < .02$.

In summary, these two experiments provided no support for the aversive-arousal reduction hypothesis; the results of each were instead as predicted by the empathy-altruism hypothesis. These experiments raised serious doubts about the validity of the aversive-arousal reduction hypothesis. Still, the results of two experiments using the same need situation did not seem sufficient to justify rejecting so popular a view. Therefore, Toi and Batson (1982) conducted a third experiment comparing the rates of helping across the four cells of a 2 (easy vs. difficult escape) $\times$ 2 (low vs. high empathy) design. They used a different method of manipulating empathy and a different need situation than had been used in the previous two experiments. Predictions were the same as before.

Bad News: Consequences of Carol's Car Crash (Toi & Batson, 1982)

Procedure

The best-known procedure for experimentally manipulating empathy is the perspective-taking manipulation introduced by Stotland (1969). As noted in the previous chapter, Stotland demonstrated that the perspective from which persons observe someone in distress can influence their feelings of empathy. Persons instructed to imagine how a distressed target person feels (an imagine set) become more physiologically aroused and report feeling more empathy than persons instructed to observe the target's movements (an observe set).

Following Stotland's lead, empathy was manipulated in this experiment by varying the perspective participants took as they listened to an audiotape describing the plight of another introductory psychology student. The audiotape was supposedly a pilot for a new, more personalized news program being considered by the local university radio station. On the tape Carol Marcy, a freshman at the university, was interviewed. Both Carol's legs had been broken in an automobile accident, and she had spent the last month in the hospital. Now she was out, but because she had missed so many classes, she was faced with having to drop introductory psychology, which would put her a whole year behind in her program in Elementary Education. After listening to the tape, participants were given an unexpected chance to help Carol by volunteering to spend time going over their introductory psychology class notes with her, enabling her to remain in the course.

Manipulating Empathy and Ease of Escape.   To manipulate empathy, some participants were instructed to attend carefully to the information presented on the tape (*low-empathy condition*); others were instructed to imagine how the person interviewed felt about what had happened (*high-empathy condition*). Ease of escape was manipulated by varying whether participants anticipated seeing Carol in the future. In the *easy-escape condition,* participants learned that because both her legs were still in casts, Carol was studying at home but could easily arrange transportation if the participant wished to help. Participants in this condition who did not help had no reason to expect to see or hear of Carol ever again. In the *difficult-escape condition,* participants learned that Carol was in the same discussion section of introductory psychology as they (discussion sections contained about 25–30 students) and that she would be back in class next week, easily recognizable in her wheelchair and casts. If participants in the difficult-escape condition did not help, they could anticipate being reminded in the future of Carol's unmet need. (Carol did not know that she was in the same section, so the participant did not have to fear verbal recriminations or knowing stares, only recollection of Carol's unmet need and knowledge that she would probably have to drop the course.)

Results

The proportion of participants in each cell of the Escape × Empathy design of this experiment who volunteered to help Carol by going over lecture notes is presented in Table 8.5. As can be seen, the rate of helping once again conformed closely to the 1-versus-3 pattern predicted by the

TABLE 8.5
Proportion of Subjects Volunteering to Help Carol
(Toi & Batson, 1982)

Escape Condition	Empathy Condition	
	Low (Observe set)	High (Imagine set)
Easy	.33	.71
Difficult	.76	.81

Note: n = 21 in each cell.
Copyright 1982 by the American Psychological Association. Adapted by permission of the publisher.

empathy-altruism hypothesis; there was no evidence of the effect of the escape manipulation in the high-empathy condition predicted by the aversive-arousal reduction hypothesis. A planned comparison contrasting the rate of helping in the easy-escape/low-empathy cell with the rate in the other three cells was highly reliable, $\chi^2 (1, N = 84) = 12.58, p < .001$; residual variance across the other three cells did not approach statistical significance, $\chi^2 (2) = .53$. Once again, this was precisely the pattern predicted by the empathy-altruism hypothesis (Table 8.2); it was not the pattern predicted by the aversive-arousal reduction hypothesis (Table 8.1).

Examining the Role of Self-Reported Empathy on Helping in the Shock Situation (Batson et al., 1983)

The three experiments reported thus far each employed a different experimental manipulation of empathy. Batson, O'Quin, Fultz, Vanderplas, and Isen (1983) conducted a series of three studies that examined the pattern of helping in easy- and difficult-escape conditions associated with naturally occurring rather than experimentally manipulated empathic feelings.

Assessing the effects of naturally occurring empathy had both strengths and weaknesses. The major strength was that naturally occurring empathic responses are less subject to experimental demand (Orne, 1962) than are responses following an experimental manipulation. The major weakness was that individuals reporting more or less empathy for someone in need might differ in other ways, and one of these other differences might be the actual cause of any observed effects. This weakness was, however, not as serious in the present case as it often is, because there were already three experiments assessing helping in an Escape × Empathy design. If naturally occurring empathy produced the same 1-versus-3 pattern predicted by the empathy-altruism hypothesis (Table 8.2), then in combination with the results of the previous experiments, there would be even stronger evidence that the motivation underlying the empathy-helping relationship is not directed toward the egoistic goal of aversive-arousal reduction. If, on the other hand, naturally occurring empathy produced the pattern predicted by the aversive-arousal reduction hypothesis (Table 8.1), then it would be necessary to question the meaning of the earlier experimental results.

Procedure of Study 1

To examine the nature of the motivation to help associated with naturally occurring empathy, Batson et al. (1983, Study 1) employed the same shock procedure and ease of escape manipulation used in the first experiment described in this chapter, with two changes. First, empathy was not manipulated, only measured. Before hearing about the opportunity to help, participants were asked to report their emotional response to observing the worker perform under the aversive conditions. Based on these reports, participants in both the easy- and difficult-escape conditions were divided into two groups, those who reported feeling a relative predominance of empathy and those who reported feeling a relative predominance of personal distress.

Second, a videotape of a male worker, Charlie, was created, paralleling the videotape of Elaine. This new videotape permitted use of both men and women participants, whereas the three previous experiments had used only women. To avoid any effects of a cross-sex interaction, such as attempts at chivalry or at impressing a member of the opposite sex, the person in need, the assistant administering the shocks, and the experimenter were always the same sex as the participant.

Across the four cells of the 2 (easy vs. difficult escape) × 2 (self-reported distress vs. empathy) design, the aversive-arousal reduction hypothesis again predicted the pattern of helping depicted in Table 8.1 (with the columns relabeled *predominant personal distress* and *predominant empathy* instead of *low* and *high empathy*). The empathy-altruism hypothesis again predicted the pattern depicted in Table 8.2.

Results of Study 1

The proportion of participants in each cell of this 2 × 2 design who offered to help Elaine (Charlie) is presented in Table 8.6. (The unequal cell sizes were due to a few participants failing to finish the emotional response questionnaire used to measure self-reported distress and empathy.) As can be seen, helping responses once again conformed to the 1-versus-3 pattern predicted by the empathy-altruism hypothesis; there was no evidence of the reduced helping under easy escape among high-empathy participants predicted by the aversive-arousal reduction hypothesis. A planned comparison contrasting the rate of helping in the easy-escape/predominant-distress cell with the rate in the other three cells was marginally significant, $\chi^2 (1, N = 37) =$

TABLE 8.6
Proportion of Subjects Agreeing to Take Shocks for Elaine or Charlie
(Batson et. al., 1983, Study 1)

Escape Condition	Predominant Emotional Response	
	Distress	Empathy
Easy	.40	.70
n	10	10
Difficult	.89	.63
n	9	8

Note: Coyright 1983 by the American Psychological Association. Adapted by permission of the publisher.

3.56, $p < .06$; residual variance across the other three cells did not approach significance, $\chi^2 (2) = 2.04, p > .30$.

The major reservation about the results of this study was that the observed 1-versus-3 pattern predicted by the empathy–altruism hypothesis was not especially strong; it attained only marginal statistical significance. Therefore, to check the reliability of this pattern, Batson et al. (1983) conducted a second, replication study, making three methodological improvements.

Procedure of Study 2

First, in the written introduction to Study 2, participants were provided with additional information about the electric shocks to be used during the work period. Four different shock levels were described: 1 = minimally uncomfortable (minimum level of shock perceived as at all aversive); 2 = moderately uncomfortable; 3 = minimally painful; 4 = moderately painful (maximum level of shock; clearly painful but not harmful). The shock level used was to be randomly selected; the worker would be informed of the level, but the observer would not.

This additional information permitted the experimenter later to specify with more precision the severity of the shocks that participants would receive if they chose to help. In Study 2, participants were always informed at the time they were given the chance to help that the shock level was minimally uncomfortable (Level 1). This change clarified the costs of helping for participants; it also provided an opportunity in Study 3 to examine the effect on helping of very high cost, simply by specifying that the shocks were at the highest level.

Second, in the previous study participants drew the observer role; in this study the experimenter assigned them to that role, ostensibly by a random procedure. This change eliminated any chance that participants would feel responsible for the worker's plight.

Third, instead of being given a chance to trade places with the worker, as had been done in the previous study and in both of the Batson et al. (1981) experiments, participants were given a chance to "take Elaine's (Charlie's) place." No mention was made of having the worker watch the subsequent trials if the participant decided to help. This change eliminated any chance that participants would help in order to be seen and appreciated by the worker. The remainder of the procedure was identical to that used in the previous study.

Results of Study 2

The proportion of participants in each cell of the 2 (easy vs. difficult escape) × 2 (self-reported distress vs. empathy) design in Study 2 who offered to help Elaine (Charlie) is presented in Table 8.7. As can be seen, helping responses conformed even more closely to the 1-versus-3 pattern predicted by the empathy-altruism hypothesis (Table 8.2) than they had in the previous study; once again, there was no evidence of the reduced helping under easy escape among high-empathy participants predicted by the aversive-arousal reduction hypothesis (Table 8.1). A planned comparison contrasting the rate of helping in the easy-escape/predominant-distress cell with the rate in the other three cells was highly significant, χ^2 (1, $N = 33$) = 8.15, $p < .005$; residual variance across the other three cells did not approach significance, χ^2 (2) = 1.88.

Procedure of Study 3

The final study in this series sought to test the limits of the 1-versus-3 pattern predicted by the empathy-altruism hypothesis. The procedure was identical to that of the previous study, except that at the point participants were given the opportunity to help by taking Elaine's (Charlie's) place, they were informed that the shock level being used was at the highest level,

TABLE 8.7
Proportion of Subjects Agreeing to Take Shocks for Elaine or Charlie
(Batson et. al., 1983, Study 2)

Escape Condition	Predominant Emotional Response	
	Distress	Empathy
Easy	.25	.86
n	8	7
Difficult	.89	.63
n	9	8

Note: Copyright 1983 by the American Psychological Association. Adapted by permission of the publisher.

Level 4: "Clearly painful but not harmful." It was expected that this information would increase the cost of helping and so might direct attention away from the worker's need and toward the participant's own need to avoid pain. The attention even of participants experiencing a predominance of empathy for the worker might be refocused on their own need, increasing feelings of personal distress. This increase would, in turn, shift the relative emotional response in the direction of distress, producing a predominance of aversive-arousal reduction (Path 2) egoistic motivation and so a lower rate of helping in the easy-escape condition than in the difficult—even among participants who had previously reported feeling a predominance of empathy.

Results of Study 3

The proportion of participants in each cell of the 2 (easy vs. difficult escape) × 2 (self-reported distress vs. empathy) design in Study 3 who offered to help Elaine (Charlie) is presented in Table 8.8. Clearly, these data do not follow the 1-versus-3 pattern expected if the helping of participants who had reported a predominance of empathy before knowing about the high level of shock were still altruistically motivated (Table 8.2); instead, the data show the effect of ease of escape expected if these participants' motivation was redirected toward the egoistic goal of aversive-arousal reduction (Table 8.1). A planned comparison contrasting the rate of helping in the easy-escape/predominant-distress cell with the rate in the other three cells was not reliable, χ^2 (1, $N = 34$) < 1.0; the residual variance across the other three cells was, χ^2 (2) = 6.40, $p < .04$. This significant residual was due to a reliable difference between the rate of helping in the easy- and difficult-escape conditions by participants who had reported a predominance of empathy before learning of the opportunity to help and the high cost of doing so, $z = 2.04$, $p < .05$.

Results of this study, considered in the context of results of the other five studies reviewed in this chapter, suggest that any altruistic motivation that blossoms from feeling empathy may be a fragile flower, easily crushed by

TABLE 8.8
Proportion of Subjects Agreeing to Take Shocks for Elaine or Charlie
(Batson et. al., 1983, Study 3)

Escape Condition	Predominant Emotional Response	
	Distress	Empathy
Easy	.50	.14
n	8	7
Difficult	.67	.60
n	9	10

Note: Copyright 1983 by the American Psychological Association. Adapted by permission of the publisher.

overriding egoistic concerns. Not only did increasing the cost of helping in this study reduce the overall level of helping (from 73% in Study 2 using Level 1 shocks to 41% in this study), but it also appeared to change the nature of the underlying motivation. Even among participants who had reported a predominance of empathy over personal distress while watching Elaine (Charlie) suffer, the motivation appeared to be directed toward the egoistic goal of minimizing their own distress.

Presumably, when these empathically aroused participants learned about the high shock level being used—and therefore the high cost of helping—their attention shifted away from seeing the situation from the worker's point of view toward seeing it more from their own. The resulting increase in feelings of personal distress overrode their empathic concern for the worker with Path 2 egoistic motivation.

GENERAL CONCLUSION

Each of the six studies reported in this chapter used an Escape × Empathy design to test the relative merits of the aversive-arousal reduction and empathy-altruism hypotheses. The results of the first five studies were remarkably consistent. In not one was there the effect of ease of escape on the helping of high-empathy individuals depicted in Table 8.1 and predicted by the aversive-arousal reduction hypothesis. Instead, each produced the 1-versus-3 pattern depicted in Table 8.2 and predicted by the empathy-altruism hypothesis. Treating these five studies as independent tests of the same hypothesis, the probability that the evidence for this 1-versus-3 pattern occurred by chance is infinitesimally small, well below one in a million.

The consistency of the 1-versus-3 pattern across these five studies is all the more impressive because the studies differed from one another in a number of ways. Low- and high-empathy conditions were created by four different techniques: a similarity manipulation, an emotion-specific misattribution manipulation, a perspective-taking manipulation, and participants' self-reports. Ease of escape was manipulated in two ways: In four of the five studies, participants believed that if they did not help they either would or would not continue to watch another introductory psychology student endure electric shocks; in the other study, participants believed that they either would or would not see the needy person next week in their introductory psychology class. Finally, two different need situations were used: Watching a peer react with increasing discomfort to a series of electric shocks, and hearing about a peer who might have to give up her career aspirations as a result of an auto accident.

Results of the final study reviewed, in which the costs of helping were extremely high, did not conform to the 1-versus-3 pattern. Any altruistic motivation felt by high-empathy participants in this study seems to have been overridden by increased self-concern introduced by awareness of the high cost of helping. To find that altruistic motivation can be overridden by egoistic concerns does not, of course, contradict the claim of the empathy–altruism hypothesis that feeling empathy for a person in need evokes altruistic motivation to help that person. It only suggests that there are limits on the maintenance and expression of that motivation.

Aversive-arousal reduction has long been the most popular egoistic explanation of the empathy–helping relationship. In light of the empirical evidence reviewed in this chapter, it appears that this explanation is almost certainly wrong. The evidence indicates that aversive-arousal reduction is an important motive for helping when feelings of empathy are low relative to feelings of distress. When feelings of empathy are high, however, helping does not pattern as we would expect if the goal were aversive-arousal reduction.

Of course, to conclude that the aversive-arousal reduction explanation of the empathy–helping relationship is wrong does not mean that the empathy–altruism hypothesis is right, even though the studies reviewed in this chapter provide considerable evidence consistent with that hypothesis. We must also test the empathy-specific punishment and the empathy-specific reward hypotheses. Each of these egoistic alternatives claims that it can account for the apparent evidence for the empathy-altruism hypothesis reported in this chapter.

CHAPTER 9

Empathy-Specific Punishment

As outlined in chapter 7, the empathy-specific punishment hypothesis claims that we learn through socialization that we incur an additional obligation to help a person for whom we feel empathy, and with it additional guilt and shame for failure to help. Thereafter, when we feel empathy, we are faced with impending social or self-censure above and beyond any general punishment associated with not helping. We say to ourselves, "What will others think—or what will I think of myself—if I don't help when I feel like this?" And we help out of an egoistic desire to avoid these empathy-specific punishments. Two versions of this hypothesis have been tested.

VERSION 1: SOCIALLY ADMINISTERED
EMPATHY-SPECIFIC PUNISHMENTS

The first version, proposed by Archer et al. (1981; see also, Archer, 1984), claims that empathy-specific punishments are socially administered. According to this version, empathy leads to increased helping only when empathic individuals anticipate negative social evaluation for failing to act in a manner consistent with their expressed feelings of concern.

The social-evaluation version of the empathy-specific punishment hypothesis does not question the validity of the 1-versus-3 pattern of helping found in the Escape × Empathy studies reviewed in the previous chapter. It simply claims that this pattern is the result of high-empathy individuals seeking to avoid negative social evaluation.

Archer (1984) pointed out how, in each of the studies reviewed in chapter 8, social-evaluation concerns may have been aroused: In the Toi and Batson (1982) study, participants may have felt that the researchers were encouraging help by writing a letter presenting the opportunity. In each of the studies using the shock procedure (Batson et al., 1981, 1983), an experimenter was face-to-face with the participant when presenting the opportunity to help. These factors, suggested Archer (1984), may have led participants to feel pressure to help in order to avoid negative social evaluation. Even though any pressure that existed would be present for participants in all conditions, high-empathy participants may have been especially sensitive to the pressure. They may have felt a special need to act in a manner that was consistent with their expressed feelings of empathy.

If this is what occurred, then none of the studies reported in the previous chapter provides evidence that empathy evokes altruistic motivation. Each provides evidence that the empathy–helping relationship is motivated by a purely egoistic desire to avoid looking bad in the eyes of others. Yet is this what occurred?

Loneliness of the Long-Distance Student (Fultz et al., 1986)

Fultz, Batson, Fortenbach, McCarthy, and Varney (1986) conducted two studies to test the social-evaluation version of the empathy-specific punishment hypothesis. In each, individuals feeling either low or high empathy for a person in need were confronted with an opportunity to help in a situation in which no one else—not even the person in need—would ever know if they decided not to help. If socially evaluative circumstances are a necessary condition for the empathy–helping relationship, as the social-evaluation version of the empathy-specific punishment hypothesis proposes, then in such a situation the empathy–helping relationship observed in past studies should disappear. On the other hand, if empathy evokes motivation to reduce the victim's need, as the empathy-altruism hypothesis proposes, then even in this situation the relationship should remain.

How is it possible to confront individuals with an opportunity to help in which they believe that no one else will know if they decide not to help? The answer, suggested Fultz et al., is to have these individuals receive information about the victim's need and desire for help from one source, and information about the opportunity to help from a second, independent source. Using these two independent sources, potential helpers should believe that only they know about both the need and the opportunity to help.

Procedure for Study 1

Fultz et al. first employed this strategy in a simple correlational study, in which self-reported empathy was correlated with helping when the chance for negative social evaluation was low. Ostensibly as part of an impression-formation study, participants (all female undergraduates because the person in need was female) assumed the role of listener, reading two confidential notes from another introductory psychology student, Janet Arnold, assigned to the role of communicator. Janet was an out-of-state freshman, and her notes reveal that she was quite lonely and seeking a friend:

> I guess I just feel kind of out of it because I don't really have any friends. . . . I'll bet there are some days I don't say more than a couple dozen words to anyone. . . . I don't know, if I had someone I could count on, someone I knew I could get together with every day or so—that would sure help—just to talk or spend some time together. Sitting here, I've even wondered if maybe you could help me out. . . .

After reading Janet's notes, participants completed an emotional response questionnaire that measured self-reported empathy and distress. They were then given a letter from the professor in charge of the research. This letter presented an unexpected opportunity to be a friend for Janet. Participants could volunteer to take part in a study concerning long-term relationships, receiving no compensation or course credit. The relationship study would involve an initial meeting with the communicator (i.e., Janet), as well as periodic telephone interviews about the development of their friendship.

The letter made it clear, however, that the communicator would be contacted about the relationship study only if the listener agreed to participate: "We will contact the communicator to see if he or she wants to meet you *only* if you want a meeting; if you do not, then we will not contact the communicator, and he or she will not know that you were ever asked about actually meeting." Responses to the professor's letter provided the measure of desire to help Janet overcome her loneliness. Participants were asked to indicate whether they wished to participate in the long-term relationship study with Janet and, if so, how much time they wished to spend with her during the next month (1–3 hours, 4–6 hours, 7–9 hours, over 10 hours).

Results of Study 1

The overall level of help offered in this study was fairly low; only 12 of the 22 participants (55%) indicated a desire to spend any time with Janet during the next month. Correlations of self-reported empathy and distress with both a dichotomous (0 = no help; 1 = help) and a scaled measure of desire to help, as well as partial correlations (empathy partialing distress; distress partialing empathy), are presented in Table 9.1.

TABLE 9.1
Correlations of Self-Reported Empathy and Distress with Help Offered
Janet (Fultz et al., 1986, Study 1)

Self-Reported Emotion Index	Partialing	Measure of Helping	
		Dichotomous	Scaled
Empathy	----	.68**	.70**
Empathy	Distress	.62**	.67**
Distress	----	.42*	.40
Distress	Empathy	−.24	−.31

Note: N = 22.
*p < .05; **p < .001, one-tailed.
Copyright 1986 by the American Psychological Association. Adapted by permission of the publisher.

As can be seen, correlations between helping and empathy were positive and highly significant, rs (20) = .68 and .70, for the dichotomous and scaled measures, respectively (ps < .001). This relationship remained even when the association with distress was controlled, $rs_{partial}$ (19) = .62 and .67, ps < .001. Correlations between helping and distress were also positive, rs (20) = .42, p < .05, and .40, p < .06, for the dichotomous and scaled measures, but these correlations became nonsignificantly negative when the association with empathy was controlled, $rs_{partial}$ (19) = −.24 and −.31.

Results of this small correlational study suggested that the empathy–helping relationship persists even in the absence of socially evaluative circumstances. Because empathy was measured not manipulated in this study, however, the evidence was inconclusive. Differences in participants' empathy for Janet might have been a result of other, hypothesis-irrelevant individual differences. Participants reporting more empathy might be more sociable or more lonely themselves. More sociable or more lonely individuals might want to participate in the long-term relationship study for reasons other than a desire to satisfy Janet's need for a friend. If so, then the empathy–helping relationship could be an artifact, and Archer's (1984) claim that some form of social evaluation is necessary for empathy to lead to helping would remain untested.

Predictions and Procedure for Study 2

To provide a more conclusive test of the social-evaluation version of the empathy-specific punishment hypothesis, Fultz et al. ran a second study, in which they employed an experimental version of the research procedure used in their first study. Both potential for negative social evaluation for not helping (low vs. high) and empathy (low vs. high) were experimentally manipulated.

The social-evaluation version of the empathy-specific punishment hypothesis predicted a 1-versus-3 pattern of helping across the four cells of this 2 × 2 design. If empathy leads to increased helping only under socially evaluative circumstances, then when the potential for negative social evaluation is high, there should be more helping in the high-empathy condition than in the low. When the potential for negative social evaluation is low, there should be low helping in both empathy conditions. Thus, helping should be higher in the high-potential/high-empathy cell than in each of the other three cells.

The empathy-altruism hypothesis predicted that even when potential for negative social evaluation was low, high empathy would lead to more help being offered than would low empathy. Thus, it predicted a main effect for empathy across both potential for negative evaluation conditions.

Empathy Manipulation.   Perspective-taking instructions that participants were given prior to reading Janet's notes provided the manipulation of empathy. Participants in the *low-empathy condition* were instructed to: "Read the information in the communicator's notes carefully, trying to be as objective as possible. Try to focus on the techniques used to get the communicator's message across." Participants in the *high-empathy condition* were instructed to: "Read the information in the communicator's notes carefully, trying to take the perspective of the individual writing the notes. Try to imagine how this individual feels about what he or she writes."

Manipulation of Potential for Negative Social Evaluation.   Potential for negative social evaluation for not helping was manipulated by simultaneously varying (a) whether participants had reason to believe that the experimenter knew that Janet needed a friend, (b) whether participants believed the experimenter could compare their emotional and helping responses, and (c) whether participants thought that Janet would know if they declined to participate in the long-term relationship study with her. In the *low-potential condition*, the procedure was essentially the same as for the previous study. The written introduction explained that the listener would be the only person ever to read the communicator's notes, and Janet's notes were delivered in sealed envelopes. Participants in this condition were assured that their responses to all questionnaires would be anonymous. Moreover, they sealed the response form concerning the long-term relationship study in an envelope addressed to the professor, so no one would know if they did not want to help Janet (the professor, of course, would not know of Janet's special need for a friend). Finally, as in the first study, these participants were informed in the professor's letter that Janet would be contacted about meeting "*only* if you want a meeting; if you do not, then we will not contact the communicator, and he or she will not know that you were ever asked about actually meeting."

In the *high-potential condition,* the situation was quite different. First, the written introduction explained that both the experimenter and the listener would read the communicator's notes. Moreover, the experimenter would personally collect all questionnaires as the listener completed them, comparing the content of the notes with the impression the listener formed. No envelopes were provided for Janet's notes, for the completed questionnaires, or for the response to the professor's letter. Thus, participants in this condition could infer that the experimenter knew of Janet's need for a friend and could compare their emotional and helping responses. In addition, the letter from the professor was changed to make it clear that Janet would know if the participant decided not to help. Participants read in the letter that both the communicator and the listener were being asked about participating in the long-term relationship study, and they would actually participate only if both agreed: "We would like to invite you and the communicator to participate. . . . The communicator has also received a letter mentioning this possibility. . . . If both you and the communicator would like to meet each other, then we will make arrangements for an initial meeting time and place." Procedures in this condition were designed to highlight the possibility of negative social evaluation if the participant decided not to volunteer to spend time with Janet.

Results of Study 2

The overall percentage of participants offering help was somewhat higher in this study (23 of 32, or 72%) than in the previous one (12 of 22, or 55%). This may have been because of minor changes made in Janet's notes or because of the time in the semester when the two studies were run (late in the semester for the first study, early for the second). Whatever the cause, the higher rate of helping in Study 2 resulted in a more normal distribution of responses on the scaled measure and introduced the possibility of a ceiling effect on a dichotomous measure, so it seemed most appropriate to focus analyses on the scaled measure. (Analyses paralleling those reported were also performed on the dichotomous measure and proved quite similar). The mean helping response in each cell of the 2 (low vs. high potential for negative evaluation) × 2 (low vs. high empathy) design is presented in Table 9.2.

The social-evaluation version of the empathy-specific punishment hypothesis predicted a 1-versus-3 pattern: Helping should be greater in the high-potential/high-empathy cell than in the other three cells. As can be seen, there was no sign of this pattern. Instead, there was a significant main effect for empathy, $F(1, 28) = 7.67$, $p < .01$; more help was offered in the high-empathy condition ($M = 2.13$) than in the low ($M = .94$). This was the effect predicted by the empathy-altruism hypothesis. The main effect for the potential for negative social evaluation manipulation was not significant, $F(1,$

TABLE 9.2
Amount of Help Offered Janet in Potential for Negative Social
Evaluation × Empathy Design (Fultz et al., 1986, Study 2)

Potential for Negative	Empathy Condition	
Social Evaluation Condition	Low	High
High	.67	1.71
n	9	7
Low	1.29	2.44
n	7	9

Note: Copyright 1986 by the American Psychological Association. Adapted by permission of the publisher.

28) $= 2.86$, *ns*, although somewhat more help was offered in the low-potential condition ($M = 1.94$) than in the high ($M = 1.12$). This was just the opposite of what would be expected if potential for negative social evaluation led to increased pressure to help. Correlations between self-reported empathy and helping produced a pattern of effects that were the same as the pattern for the empathy manipulation and for correlations in the previous study.

Conclusion

Contrary to what the social-evaluation version of the empathy-specific punishment hypothesis predicted, eliminating anticipated negative social evaluation in these two studies clearly did not eliminate the empathy–helping relationship. Rather than high empathy leading to more help only under high social evaluation, it led to more helping under both low and high social evaluation. This pattern of results is not consistent with what would be expected if empathically aroused individuals are egoistically motivated to avoid looking bad in the eyes of others; it is quite consistent with what would be expected if empathy evokes altruistic motivation to reduce the victim's need.

VERSION 2: SELF-ADMINISTERED
EMPATHY-SPECIFIC PUNISHMENTS

The Fultz et al. (1986) results clearly count against a version of the empathy-specific punishment hypothesis that assumes the relevant punishments are socially administered. They do not, however, rule out the second version of the empathy-specific punishment hypothesis, that high-empathy individuals are motivated to help to avoid self-administered punishments and negative self-evaluation. To test whether self-punishments underlie the empathy–

helping relationship, high-empathy individuals must anticipate being able to escape not only from negative social evaluation for not helping but also from negative self-evaluation.

How can potential helpers escape the expectation of self-punishment for not helping? Clearly, this problem is more difficult than the problem of providing escape from social punishment; one cannot simply separate the sources of information about the need and the opportunity to help. The potential helper must know about both.

Indeed, if expectations of self-punishment have been internalized to the degree that they are automatic and invariant across all helping situations, then providing escape seems impossible. It seems unlikely, however, that many people—if any—have internalized procedures for self-punishment to such a degree. Even those who reflexively slap themselves with guilt and self-recrimination whenever they do wrong are likely to be sensitive to situational cues in determining when they have done wrong. Doing another person even serious harm may not be seen as wrong if the situation demands it, as Milgram (1963, 1974) has shown. And, given the discomfort produced by guilt and self-recrimination, one suspects that most people will not reflexively self-punish but will, if possible, overlook their failures to help. They will dole out self-punishments only in situations in which such failures are salient and inescapable.

If there is this kind of leeway in interpreting failure to help as unjustified and hence deserving of self-punishment, then expectation of self-punishment may be reduced by providing some individuals with information that justifies not helping in some particular situation. The justifying information probably cannot be provided directly by telling individuals not to feel guilty about not helping. Calling direct attention to the failure may have the reverse effect; it may highlight the associated punishments. The information needs to be provided in a more subtle, indirect way.

Following this logic, Batson et al. (1988) reported three studies designed to test the self-punishment version of the empathy-specific punishment hypothesis. Each study used a different technique to provide indirect justification for not helping.

1. Justifying Not Helping Through the Inaction of Others (Batson et al., 1988, Study 2)

Research on social influence and norms (Moscovici, 1985; Sherif, 1936) suggested using information about the inaction of other potential helpers to provide justification for not helping. If most people asked have said no to a request for help, then one should feel more justified saying no as well. Employing this justification technique, Batson et al. (1988, Study 2) conducted a study using the broadcast paradigm developed by Coke et al. (1978), in which individuals feeling either low or high empathy for the young woman in need, Katie Banks, were given an opportunity to pledge time to help her. Some participants received no information about how other participants had responded to this opportunity to help (replication condition). Others received information on the pledge form indicating either that most previously asked peers had pledged (low-justification condition) or that most had not (high-justification condition). Katie's need was such that others' responses did not affect her need for help.

Predictions

In the replication condition, both the empathy-specific punishment hypothesis and the empathy-altruism hypothesis predicted more overall helping by high-empathy individuals than by low, because both assumed that increased empathy leads to increased helping. The two hypotheses differed, however, in their predictions for the effects of the justification manipulation. Paralleling the predicted effects for ease of physical escape in Table 8.1, the empathy-specific punishment hypothesis predicted less helping in the high-justification condition than in the low for individuals feeling either low or high empathy. Low-empathy individuals should be egoistically motivated to avoid general shame and guilt associated with a failure to help (Path 1b); high-empathy individuals should be even more highly motivated to avoid shame and guilt because of the added empathy-specific punishments. For each group, it should be easier to avoid shame and guilt without having to help in the high-justification condition than in the low.

Paralleling the predictions in Table 8.2, the empathy-altruism hypothesis predicted less helping in the high-justification condition than in the low for individuals feeling low empathy, because it accepted that they would be egoistically motivated to avoid self-punishment. It predicted high helping in both justification conditions for individuals feeling high empathy; only by helping could they relieve Katie's need. Across the four cells of the 2 (low vs. high justification) × 2 (low vs. high empathy) design, then, the pattern of results most consistent with the empathy-altruism hypothesis would be a 1-versus-3 pattern; the rate of helping in the high-justification/low-empathy cell should be lower than the rate in the other three cells.

Procedure

Empathy Manipulation. Before listening to the pilot broadcast tape that presented Katie Banks and her need, participants were given one of two listening perspectives. Participants in the *low-empathy condition* were instructed to: "Try to *focus on the technical aspects of the broadcast.* Try to concentrate on those techniques and devices that are used to make the broadcast have an impact on the listener." Participants in the *high-empathy condition* were instructed to: "Try to *imagine how the person who is being interviewed feels* about what has happened and how the events have affected her life. Try to feel the full impact of what this person has been through and how she feels as a result." All participants were led to believe that previous research participants had been given the same listening-perspective instructions they received. This ensured that, when interpreting the justification information, they would perceive other participants to have been responding to the same helping situation as themselves.

Manipulation of Justification for Not Helping. Enclosed with the letters presenting the opportunity to help Katie was a response form. In both justification conditions, this form had spaces for the responses of eight people. The first seven spaces were already filled with the handwritten names of same-sex individuals (actually fictitious). In the *low-justification condition,* five of the seven previous participants had volunteered to help Katie. In the *high-justification condition,* only two of the seven had helped. (Participants in both justification conditions filled in the last blank on the form so that they could be assured that the form with their name on it would not be seen by later participants. This avoided concern over praise or censure from friends or acquaintances who might learn of their response.) In the *replication condition,* the form provided exactly the same response options but was designed for only one person's response; participants in this condition received no information about the action of their peers. To ensure that participants did not feel they were Katie's last chance for help, it was made clear that theirs was not the only response form and that Katie's request would be presented to a number of other research participants.

Results

The proportion of participants helping in each cell of this study is presented in Table 9.3. As expected, the empathy–helping relationship was found in the replication cells, in which participants received no information about others' response to the request for help; helping was higher in the high-empathy condition (.70) than in the low (.35) $z = 2.26, p < .02$.

Effects of the justification manipulation on helping can be seen in the last two rows of Table 9.3. The pattern of helping across the four cells of the 2 (low vs. high justification for not helping) $\times$ 2 (low vs. high empathy) design was very much as predicted by the empathy-altruism hypothesis: lower helping in the high-justification/low-empathy cell than in the other three cells. A planned comparison testing this 1-versus-3 pattern was highly significant, $\chi^2 (1, N = 80) = 15.39, p < .001$, and accounted for all reliable between-cell

TABLE 9.3
Proportion of Participants Volunteering to Help Katie
(Batson et al., 1988, Study 2)

Justification Condition	Empathy Condition	
	Low	High
Replication (no justification information)	.35	.70
Low justification for not helping	.55	.70
High justification for not helping	.15	.60

Note: $N = 20$ (10 men, 10 women) per cell.

Copyright 1988 by the American Psychological Association. Adapted by permission of the publisher.

variance, residual χ^2 (2, $N = 80$) $= 1.35$. There was no evidence of the significant effect of the justification manipulation in the high-empathy condition predicted by the self-punishment version of the empathy-specific punishment hypothesis ($z < 1.0$).

2. Justifying Not Helping Through Attributional Ambiguity (Batson et al., 1988, Study 3)

Research by Snyder, Kleck, Strenta, and Mentzer (1979) suggested a second technique for providing justification for not helping: attributional ambiguity. If individuals can attribute a decision not to help to helping-irrelevant features of the decision, such as features of the helping task itself, then they should be less likely to anticipate self-punishment for not helping.

Procedure and Predictions

Employing this technique, Batson et al. (1988, Study 3) gave research participants a chance to work on either or both of two task options during a 120-second work period. For each correct response on Option A, participants would receive one raffle ticket for a $30 prize for themselves; for each correct response on Option B, they would reduce by one the shocks a peer was to receive. Spending time working on Option B rather than Option A constituted helping.

Justification for not helping was manipulated by varying information about helping-irrelevant attributes of the two task options. In the *low-justification condition*, the two tasks were equivalent; both involved circling combinations either of letters or of numbers. In the *high-justification condition*, the two tasks were different—one involved circling numbers, the other involved letters, and participants were told that most people preferred to work on the numbers (letters), whichever was the Option A task. Thus, participants in the high-justification condition could attribute choosing to work on the nonhelpful Option A to the type of task rather than to selfishness, reducing anticipated self-punishment. Participants in the low-justification condition could not justify choosing to work on Option A in this way.

An attempt to manipulate empathy by varying similarity to the person in need proved ineffective in this study; the similarity information had no reliable effect on either reports of empathy or helping. Therefore, participants' self-reports of empathy for the peer who was to receive shock were used to define low- and high-empathy groups, producing a Justification (low vs. high) × Empathy (low vs. high) design.

Predictions were essentially the same as for the previous study. The empathy-specific punishment hypothesis predicted less helping in the high-justification condition than in the low for both low- and high-empathy participants. The empathy-altruism hypothesis predicted less helping in the high-justification condition than in the low for low-empathy participants, but it predicted high helping in both justification conditions for high-empathy participants. Across the four cells of the 2 × 2 design, the pattern of results most consistent with the empathy-altruism hypothesis was a 1-versus-3 pattern: The rate of helping in the high-justification/low-empathy cell should be lower than the rate in the other three cells.

Results

Helping scores could range in value from 0.0 if all the combinations circled were on Option A, the option that would earn participants raffle tickets for themselves, to 1.0 if all combinations circled were on Option B, the option that would reduce the number of shocks for the peer. The mean helping score for each cell is presented in Table 9.4.

Once again, the pattern of helping was very much as predicted by the

TABLE 9.4
Proporation of Combinations Circled to Help Peer
(Batson et al., 1988, Study 3)

Justification Condition	Self-Reported Empathy	
	Low	High
Low justification for not helping	.65	.61
n	21	22
High justification for not helping	.28	.50
n	23	22

Note: Copyright 1988 by the American Psychological Association. Adapted by permission of the publisher.

empathy-altruism hypothesis; lower helping in the high-justification/low-empathy cell than in the other three cells. A planned comparison testing this 1-versus-3 pattern was highly significant, $F(1, 84) = 12.69$, $p < .001$, and accounted for all reliable between-cell variance, residual $F(2, 84) < 1.0$. There was clear evidence of the significant effect of the justification manipulation on the helping of low-empathy participants predicted by both the empathy-specific punishment hypothesis and the empathy-altruism hypothesis, $t(84) = 3.51$, $p < .001$. Presumably, this effect was due to egoistic motivation to avoid general—not empathy-induced—shame and guilt associated with a failure to help. There was no evidence of the significant effect of the justification manipulation on the helping of high-empathy participants predicted by the empathy-specific punishment hypothesis ($t < 1.0$).

3. Justifying Not Helping By Making Qualifying to Help Difficult (Batson et al., 1988, Study 4)

A third technique for providing justification for not helping is to make qualifying to help difficult. Imagine that potential helpers must perform a task requiring effort in order to qualify to help. In such a situation, how hard potential helpers try on the qualifying task should indicate whether they are motivated to reduce the needy individual's suffering (which requires qualifying) or to avoid self-punishment (which does not). This should be true, however, only if poor performance can be justified, which it can if the performance standard on the qualifying task is so difficult that most people fail. If the standard is this difficult, then potential helpers cannot be blamed for not qualifying—either by themselves or by others.

Procedure and Predictions

To test the relative merits of the empathy-specific punishment and the empathy-altruism hypotheses using this technique, Batson et al. (1988, Study 4) introduced a qualifying task into the shock paradigm developed by Batson et al. (1981) and described in chapter 8. The study was presented as an examination of auditory numeric facility—measured by a digit recall task—of individuals who display a certain level of visual numeric facility—measured by a digit scan task. Thus, even if participants (all female) were willing to help Elaine by performing the digit recall task and receiving the shocks in her stead, they would be allowed to do so only if they met a certain performance standard on the digit-scan task.

The experimental manipulation of qualifying-standard difficulty was introduced by information provided about the performance standard set for the digit-scan task. In the *easy qualifying-standard condition,* participants were told: "A moderately stringent standard has been adopted for performance on the digit-scan task. On the average, about 7 of 10 college students meet the standard." In the *difficult qualifying-standard condition,* participants were told: "An extremely difficult standard has been adopted for performance on the digit-scan task. On the average, only 1 of 5 college students meet the standard, so do not be surprised or disturbed if you do not."

As in the Batson et al. (1983) studies, a median split was performed on participants' scores on an index of predominant emotional response to watching Elaine suffer. This split produced two groups, one experiencing a relative predominance of personal distress, the other a relative predominance of empathy.

All participants were told that if they chose not to help, they would watch Elaine's remaining eight trials. In previous studies, reviewed in chapter 8, this difficult-escape information had produced a high rate of helping among participants reporting a predominance of distress, as well as among those reporting a predominance of empathy. To examine the effects of difficulty of the performance standard both on whether participants would offer to help and, if they offered, on their performance on the qualifying task, it seemed best to make escape without helping difficult.

The empathy-specific punishment hypothesis predicted that the difficulty of the qualifying standard would have much the same effect on the behavior of participants feeling a relative predominance of empathy as on the behavior of those feeling a relative predominance of distress. Because the motivation to help for both groups would be egoistic, either the rate of helping or performance on the qualifying task, or both, should be lower when the qualifying standard was difficult than when it was easy.

The empathy-altruism hypothesis made this prediction only for participants feeling a relative predominance of distress. For those feeling a relative predominance of empathy, it predicted that (a) the rate of helping should be high regardless of the difficulty of the qualifying standard and (b) performance on the qualifying task should be higher when the qualifying standard was difficult than when it was easy. Only by both volunteering to help and qualifying could these participants reach the altruistic goal of relieving Elaine's suffering.

Results

Helping Response. The proportion of participants who offered to help Elaine in each cell of the 2 (easy vs difficult qualifying standard) × 2 (predominant distress vs. empathy) design of this study is presented in Table 9.5. As in the previous two studies, the pattern of helping was very much as predicted by the empathy-altruism hypothesis: less helping in the difficult-standard/distress cell (.28) than in the other three cells (.65 or higher). A planned comparison testing this 1-versus-3 pattern was highly significant, χ^2 $(1, N = 60) = 10.47, p < .001$, and accounted for all reliable between-cell variance; residual $\chi^2 (2, N = 60) = 1.84$.

TABLE 9.5
Proportion of Participants Agreeing to Take Shocks for Elaine
(Batson et al., 1988, Study 4)

Qualifying Standard	Predominant Emotional Response	
	Distress	Empathy
Easy	.73	.86
n	11	14
Difficult	.28	.65
n	18	17

Note: Copyright 1988 by the American Psychological Association. Adapted by permission of the publisher.

Performance on the Qualifying Task. All participants who agreed to help performed the qualifying task. The empathy-specific punishment hypothesis predicted a main effect for difficulty of the qualifying standard on performance of this task; performance should be better in the easy-standard condition than the difficult both for helpers reporting a predominance of distress and for those reporting a predominance of empathy. In contrast, the empathy-altruism hypothesis predicted a Difficulty of Standard × Predominant Emotional Response interaction: performance should be better in the easy-standard condition than in the difficult for helpers reporting a predominance of distress; it should be better in the difficult-standard condition than in the easy for helpers reporting a predominance of empathy.

The digit-scan task was the same number-circling task used in the previous study; as before, performance was measured by the number of combinations correctly circled. Mean performance in each cell of the 2 × 2 design of this study is presented in Table 9.6. Analysis of variance revealed no evidence of the main effect for the qualifying-standard manipulation predicted by the empathy-specific punishment hypothesis ($F < 1.0$). The Difficulty of Standard

TABLE 9.6
Mean Performance on Qualifying Task by Participants Agreeing
to Help Elaine (Batson et al., 1988, Study 4)

Qualifying Standard	Predominant Emotional Response	
	Distress	Empathy
Easy	11.30	9.90
n	10	10
Difficult	8.25	13.00
n	8	8

Note: Copyright 1988 by the American Psychological Association. Adapted by permission of the publisher.

$\times$ Predominant Emotional Response interaction predicted by the empathy-altruism hypothesis was, however, highly significant, $F(1, 32) = 10.17, p < .003$.

Conclusion from the Three Justification-for-Not-Helping Studies

Across these three studies conducted to test the self-evaluation version of the empathy-specific punishment hypothesis, justification for not helping—whether provided by the inaction of others, by introducing attributional ambiguity, or by making it difficult to qualify to help—dramatically reduced the helping of low-empathy individuals. It had very little effect on the helping of high-empathy individuals. This pattern of results suggests that, although the helping of low-empathy individuals is motivated at least in part by a desire to avoid the self-punishment associated with failing to do the right thing, the helping of high-empathy individuals is not. The relatively high rate of helping by high-empathy individuals, even when justification for not helping was high, is precisely what we would expect if feeling empathy for the person in need evoked altruistic motivation to have that person's need reduced. It is not what we would expect if feeling empathy evoked increased egoistic motivation to avoid anticipated self-punishment.

Still, all three of these studies relied on some form of a justification manipulation. In a final attempt to find evidence for the empathy-specific punishment hypothesis, Batson et al. (1988, Study 5) tried a very different strategy. They examined goal-relevant cognitions associated with empathy-induced helping.

Goal-Relevant Cognitions Associated With Empathy-Induced Helping (Batson et al., 1988, Study 5)

The empathy-specific punishment hypothesis and the empathy-altruism hypothesis each postulate a different goal for the helping associated with feeling empathy: The goal is avoiding punishment for the former; the goal is relieving the victim's need for the latter. Each hypothesis assumes that the empathically aroused individual, when deciding to help, has one of these goals in mind. If this is true, then cognitions relevant to one of these goals should be associated with empathy-induced helping. Specifically, if the goal is to avoid punishment, then punishment-relevant cognitions—thoughts of shame and guilt—should be associated with this helping; if the goal is to relieve the victim's need, then victim-relevant cognitions—thoughts of his or her need and suffering—should be associated with it.

To ask empathically aroused helpers to tell us their goal-relevant thoughts is, of course, problematic; it assumes that they know and will report these thoughts. Fortunately, Stroop (1938) has provided a less reactive means of determining what someone is thinking; it involves having the person name as quickly as possible the color of the ink in which words or other visual stimuli appear. As Geller and Shaver (1976, p. 101) have observed concerning the Stroop procedure: "In general, it appears that latency of color naming for a particular word will increase whenever a subject has been thinking about something related to that word." Employing a Stroop procedure, it should be possible to assess the goal or goals associated with the empathy–helping relationship by examining the association between empathy-induced helping and color-naming latency for words related to the different possible goals of this helping.

Predictions

If the motivation to help associated with feeling empathy is directed toward the egoistic goal of avoiding social or self-punishments, as the empathy-specific punishment hypothesis claims, then the increased helping associated with empathic emotion should be positively correlated with color-naming latency for punishment-relevant words. If the motivation to help associated with feeling empathy is directed toward the altruistic goal of reducing the victim's suffering, as the empathy–altruism hypothesis claims, then the increased helping associated with empathic emotion should be positively correlated with color-naming latency for victim-relevant words.

Preliminary Test of These Predictions

In a preliminary attempt to test these predictions, Batson, Orendain, Shetrompf, and Templeton (Batson et al., 1988) conducted a pilot study in which female undergraduates read about Sandy, a lonely, disadvantaged 12-year-old girl seeking a surrogate grandparent to be an adult friend and guide. After reading about Sandy, participants were informed that they would soon be given a chance to volunteer time to write letters to prospective "grandparents" on her behalf. First, however, ostensibly as a baseline control for a measure of cognitive reactions to the information about Sandy, participants were asked to name as quickly as possible the color (red, blue, green, or brown) in which each word in a series appeared.

Some of the words were punishment-relevant (DUTY, GUILT, SHAME, SHOULD); some were victim-relevant (HOPE, CHILD, NEEDY, FRIEND); some were neutral (LEFT, RAPID, LARGE, BREATH). Using a millisecond timer and voice-operated relay, it was possible to assess color-naming latencies for the different types of words by repeated measures within participants.

After completing this Stroop task, helping was measured by the amount of time, if any, participants volunteered to spend writing letters for Sandy.

In an attempt to manipulate empathy, written instructions directed some participants to focus on technical aspects of the information about Sandy (low empathy) and others to imagine how she felt (high empathy). This manipulation proved unsuccessful. The amount of help offered did not differ reliably between the low- and high-empathy conditions, $t(21) < 1.0$, and in debriefing, participants assigned to the low-empathy condition consistently reported that they had been unable to keep from imagining how Sandy felt. Because it appeared that all participants either were placed or placed themselves in a high-empathy condition, correlations between the amount of helping and color-naming latencies were computed for all participants combined.

The correlations revealed a significant positive relation between amount of help volunteered and color-naming latency for the victim-relevant words (averaged and adjusted for individual differences in reaction time by subtracting the average latency to the neutral words), $r(21) = .53$, $p < .004$, one-tailed. The correlation between amount of helping and adjusted average latencies for the punishment-relevant words was $-.10$.

These results were as predicted by the empathy-altruism hypothesis, not the empathy-specific punishment hypothesis. Because the sample in this pilot study was small and the empathy manipulation failed, however, results were far from conclusive. So Batson et al. (1988, Study 5) conducted another Stroop study, using a need situation and empathy manipulation known to produce the customary empathy–helping relationship: They used the need situation and empathy manipulation introduced by Coke et al. (1978), in which participants adopt a particular perspective while listening to a (bogus) radio broadcast that informs them of the need of Katie Banks.

Procedure

Reaction-Time (Stroop) Task. In a written introduction, the Stroop task was presented as a reaction-time measure of the effect of radio broadcasts on thoughts. Participants would be shown a series of words after each of two broadcasts. Some of the words would be relevant to possible thoughts after hearing the broadcast, others would not. Different words would appear in different colors. For each word, participants assigned to the test group would say as quickly as possible whether it was relevant to their thoughts; participants assigned to the control group would say as quickly as possible the color in which the word was printed. The introduction explained, "Responses of people in the control group will provide a baseline needed to interpret the responses of people in the test group. Therefore it is important that you do your best no matter to which group you have been assigned." Once participants read this information, the experimenter consulted a chart and informed participants that they had (ostensibly randomly) been assigned to the control group; their task would be to name the color (red, blue, green, or brown) in which each word appeared. (Mention of the test group made it plausible not only that the reaction-time measure be taken but also that some of the words be relevant to thoughts evoked by the broadcast.)

Empathy Manipulation.   Before listening to the pilot broadcast tape that presented Katie Banks's need, participants were instructed to adopt one of two listening perspectives. The perspective instructions were identical to the observe and imagine instructions described earlier in this chapter for creating low- and high-empathy conditions, as was the broadcast about Katie's need: Her parents had been killed in an automobile accident, and she was struggling to support her younger brother and sister, lest she have to put them up for adoption.

Measurement of Color-Naming Latencies for Punishment- and Victim-Relevant Words, and Measurement of Helping.   After the broadcast, participants were informed of their opportunity to help Katie but were given no response form. It was explained that they should think about the possibility of helping for a few minutes before deciding; a response form would be provided later. The experimenter then administered the Stroop slides, which included four punishment-relevant words (DUTY, GUILT, SHAME, OBLIGE), four victim-relevant words (LOSS, NEEDY, ADOPT, TRAGIC), and four neutral words (PAIR, CLEAN, EXTRA, SMOOTH). Participants as quickly as possible named the color of the ink in which each word appeared. (Appropriateness of the words selected to represent each type was verified by ratings of five independent judges. Punishment-relevant and victim-relevant words were correctly classified 100% of the time by the five judges; neutral words were correctly classified 85% of the time.) When participants completed the Stroop task, the experimenter gave them a brief form on which to indicate how many hours, if any, they wished to volunteer to help Katie.

Results

Helping was coded using the same scale employed by Coke et al. (1978): 0 = no help volunteered; 1 = 1 hour volunteered; 2 = 2–3 hours; 3 = 4–5 hours; 4 = more than 5 hours. Consistent with previous research demonstrating the empathy–helping relationship, participants volunteered more help in the high-empathy condition ($M = 1.50$) than in the low ($M = 0.50$), $t(46) = 2.94, p < .005$. Similarly, a dichotomous measure (0 = *no help*, 1 = *help*) revealed that more subjects helped in the high-empathy condition (.63; 15 of 24) than in the low (.29; 7 of 24), $z = 2.36, p < .02$. These results indicated successful replication of the empathy–helping relationship.

The nature of the goal-relevant cognitions associated with this empathy-induced helping was assessed by the same kind of color-naming latency measure used in the pilot study. Beta coefficients from regressing amount of help offered on adjusted average color-naming latency for punishment- and victim-relevant words are presented in Table 9.7.

As can be seen from the table, the only positive association in the high-empathy condition was a correlation between helping and color-naming latency for the victim-relevant words, $\beta = .62$, $p < .01$. This was the correlation predicted by the empathy-altruism hypothesis. Contrary to the prediction of the empathy-specific punishment hypothesis, there was no evidence of a positive correlation in the high-empathy condition between helping and color-naming latency for the punishment-relevant words.

In the low-empathy condition, in which empathic feelings had not been explicitly aroused, there was not a positive correlation between helping and latency for the victim-relevant words. This finding suggested that the positive correlation for victim-relevant words in the high-empathy condition was not due to some general characteristic of these words or their association with helping. The relationship seemed to be empathy specific.

GENERAL CONCLUSION

When the results of all seven studies reviewed in this chapter are considered together, a remarkably consistent pattern emerges. Using different need situations, different techniques for operationalizing empathy, and different dependent measures, results consistently conform to the pattern predicted by the empathy-altruism hypothesis. In no study do the results pattern as predicted by the empathy-specific punishment hypothesis. We find much evi-

TABLE 9.7
Betas from Regressing Amount of Help Offered Katie on Adjusted
Average Color-Naming Latency for Punishment- and Victim-Relevant
Words (Batson et al., 1988, Study 5)

| | | Empathy Condition | |
| | Overall | Low | High |
Type of Word	($N = 48$)	($N = 24$)	($N = 24$)
Punishment-relevant	$-.20$	$-.29$	$-.30$
Victim-relevant	$.48^*$	$-.06$	$.62^*$

$^*p < .01$, one-tailed.

dence that the helping of individuals experiencing low empathy for someone in need is motivated, at least in part, by a desire to avoid punishment. We find no evidence that the helping of individuals experiencing high empathy is so motivated. Having looked hard in a number of likely places to find empirical support for an empathy-specific punishment explanation of the empathy–helping relationship, we have found none.

Given these results, the claim that the motivation to help evoked by empathy is directed toward the egoistic goal of avoiding empathy-specific punishments must, it seems, be rejected. Two of the three egoistic alternatives to the empathy-altruism hypothesis have been ruled out, and the evidence supporting the empathy-altruism hypothesis continues to mount. One egoistic alternative remains.

CHAPTER 10

Empathy-Specific Reward

T he empathy-specific reward hypothesis claims that we learn through socialization that we are eligible for special praise from others or special self-rewards when we help a person for whom we feel empathy. Thereafter, when we feel empathy, we think of these social or self-rewards and help out of an egoistic desire to gain them. Two versions of this empathy-specific reward hypothesis have been tested.

VERSION 1: SOCIAL AND SELF-REWARDS ASSOCIATED WITH THE EMPATHY–HELPING RELATIONSHIP

The first version claims that we gain additional social and self-rewards when we help someone for whom we feel empathy. To test this version, Batson et al. (1988) used two strategies. The first involved assessing the effects on mood when individuals feeling empathy learn that, without their help, the victim is no longer in need. The second strategy employed the Stroop procedure (described in the preceding chapter) to assess the association between reward-relevant cognitions and empathy-induced helping.

One That Got Away: Effect on Mood of Not Being Allowed to Help (Batson et al., 1988, Study 1)

Procedure and Predictions

As discussed in chapter 7, one way to test the first version of the empathy-specific reward hypothesis is to compare (a) the mood of individuals who believe that the need of a person for whom they feel empathy has been relieved due to their help with (b) the mood of individuals who believe that the person's need has been relieved, but not as a result of their own action. Employing this logic, Batson et al. (1988, Study 1) told research participants that they would likely have a chance to perform a simple task (number-combination circling) that would reduce the number of electric shocks a peer would receive. It was assumed that because participants knew they could help, their mood at this point would be somewhat positive. Later, half of the participants learned that, by chance, they would not perform the helping task after all, producing two experimental conditions (perform vs. not perform). Within each of these conditions, half of the participants learned that the peer was still to receive shocks, and half learned that by chance the peer would not receive shocks, producing two more experimental conditions (no prior relief vs. prior relief). A median split on a measure of self-reported empathy for the peer was combined with the two experimental manipulations to produce a 2 (low vs. high empathy) × 2 (no prior relief of peer's need vs. prior relief) × 2 (perform the helping task vs. not perform) factorial design.

The major dependent measure was change in self-reported mood after participants were or were not allowed to help the peer. Because the mood-enhancing rewards for helping are available only to a person who helps, the empathy-specific reward hypothesis predicted a 1-versus-3 pattern of mood change among high-empathy individuals: In the no prior-relief/perform cell, mood either should not change or should become more positive, whereas in each of the other three cells—in which in one way or another participants were deprived of the anticipated opportunity to obtain the empathy-specific rewards for helping—mood should become more negative. The empathy–altruism hypothesis also predicted a 1-versus-3 pattern of mood change among high-empathy individuals, but a very different one: In the no prior-relief/not-perform cell, mood should become more negative, whereas in each of the other three cells—in which in one way or another the peer's need had been relieved—mood either should not change or should become more positive.

Results

Mood Change. A mood-change score was created for each participant by subtracting the score on a pre-manipulation mood measure from the score on a post-manipulation mood measure. Mean mood-change for participants in each cell of the 2 × 2 × 2 design is reported in Table 10.1.

The empathy-specific reward hypothesis predicted that mood change among high-empathy individuals would be more positive in the one cell in which they were able to gain the empathy-specific rewards for helping (no prior-relief/perform) than in the other three cells. A planned comparison contrasting the mood change in this cell with the change in the other three high-empathy cells provided no support for this prediction, $F < 1.0$.

The empathy-altruism hypothesis predicted that mood change among high-empathy individuals would be more positive in the three cells in which the peer's need was relieved than in the one cell in which it was not (no prior-relief/not-perform). A planned comparison contrasting the mood change in this cell with the change in the other three high-empathy cells provided clear support for this prediction, $F(1, 72) = 7.09, p < .02$. Moreover, this effect appeared to be empathy-specific; the same comparison among low-empathy individuals did not approach statistical significance, $F < 1.0$. Indeed, the 1-versus-3 comparison among high-empathy individuals predicted by the empathy-altruism hypothesis accounted for all reliable between-cell variance in mood change across the entire $2 \times 2 \times 2$ design, residual $F(6, 72) = 1.17$. (The particularly high mean mood change in the prior-relief/not-perform cell probably reflected a combination of motives: pleasure that the peer's need was relieved and pleasure at relief from performance apprehension.)

Task Performance.   Further evidence that high-empathy individuals in this study were oriented toward relief of the peer's need, whereas low-empathy individuals were not, was provided by the differences in task performance in the perform condition. Performance was assessed by the number of combinations that participants correctly circled during the two minutes they

TABLE 10.1
Mean Mood Change for Participants Who Were or Were Not Allowed
to Help (Batson et al., 1988, Study 1)

State of Victim's Need	Low Empathy		High Empathy	
	Perform Helping Task	Not Perform Helping Task	Perform Helping Task	Not Perform Helping Task
No prior relief	.13	.10	.50	−.30
n	12	11	8	9
Prior relief	.27	.43	.31	1.36
n	10	10	10	10

Note: Positive mood-change scores indicate more positive mood after introduction of the experimental manipulations; negative scores indicate less positive mood after introduction of the experimental manipulations.

Copyright 1988 by the American Psychological Association. Adapted by permission of the publisher.

worked on the task. Mean performance scores for participants in each cell are reported in Table 10.2. As can be seen, high-empathy individuals circled more combinations when the peer's welfare was still dependent on their performance $(M = 12.38)$ than when it was not $(M = 10.20)$, $t(36) = 3.37$, $p < .001$. In contrast, low-empathy individuals actually circled more combinations when the peer's welfare was not dependent on their performance $(M = 12.40)$ than when it was $(M = 10.83)$, $t(36) = 2.43$, $p < .02$. An analysis of variance in these performance scores revealed that the Empathy $\times$ Prior-Relief interaction was highly significant, $F(1, 36) = 16.78$, $p < .001$.

Reward-Relevant Cognitions and Empathy-Induced Helping (Batson et al., 1988, Study 5)

The Stroop procedure described at the end of the previous chapter provided another way to test the first version of the empathy-specific reward hypothesis. Recall that Batson et al. (1988, Study 5) used the Stroop procedure to test the relative merits of the empathy-specific punishment and empathy-altruism hypotheses by assessing goal-relevant cognitions associated with empathy-induced helping. They found both in a preliminary study and in their main study that the helping of high-empathy individuals was correlated with increased color-naming latency for victim-relevant words, but not with increased latency for punishment-relevant words. These correlations suggested that high-empathy helpers were thinking more about the victim's welfare, as predicted by the empathy-altruism hypothesis, but were not thinking more about the relevant social and self-punishments, contrary to the predictions of the empathy-specific punishment hypothesis.

Procedure and Predictions

Although this was not mentioned in the previous chapter, both the preliminary and main Stroop studies also included, as part of the reaction-time

TABLE 10.2
Mean Number of Combinations Circled on Task by Participants
in Perform Condition (Batson et al., 1988, Study 1)

Status of Other's Need	Level of Self-Reported Empathy	
	Low	High
No prior relief	10.83	12.38
n	12	8
Prior relief	12.40	10.20
n	10	10

Note: Copyright 1988 by the American Psychological Association. Adapted by permission of the publisher.

measure, reward-relevant words (GOOD, MERIT, HONOR, and PRAISE in the preliminary study; NICE, PROUD, HONOR, and PRAISE in the main study). These words permitted a test of the empathy-specific reward hypothesis. If the motivation to help associated with feeling empathy was directed toward the egoistic goal of obtaining social and self-rewards, as the empathy-specific reward hypothesis claims, then the helping of high-empathy individuals should be positively correlated with color-naming latency for reward-relevant words.

Results

Results of the two studies provided no support for this prediction. The correlation between amount of helping and adjusted average latency for the reward-relevant words in the preliminary study was $-.06$. The betas from regressing the amount of help offered Katie on the adjusted average color-naming latency for the reward-relevant words in the main study were non-significantly negative in both low- and high-empathy conditions ($-.15$ and $-.30$, respectively).

Conclusion

The Stroop studies, like the mood change study, failed to provide any support for the first version of the empathy-specific reward hypothesis. Based on this evidence, it does not appear that empathically aroused helpers are motivated to gain whatever additional social and self-rewards follow their helping.

A VARIANT ON VERSION 1: EMPATHIC JOY

Smith, Keating, and Stotland (1989) recently proposed an interesting variant on the first version of the empathy-specific reward hypothesis. Rather than helping to gain the rewards of seeing oneself or being seen by others as helpful, Smith et al. suggested that empathically aroused individuals help to gain the good feeling of sharing vicariously in the needy person's joy at improvement: "It is proposed that the prospect of empathic joy, conveyed by feedback from the help recipient, is essential to the special tendency of empathic witnesses to help. . . . The empathically concerned witness to the distress of others helps in order to be happy" (1989, p. 641). Individuals experiencing empathy for a person in need are especially motivated to gain the rewards of vicarious joy because "empathic concern reflects a broad-based sensitivity to the emotional state of the victim, which includes an enhanced sensitivity to vicarious joy and relief at the resolution of the help recipient's needs" (p. 642). As a result, "empathically concerned witnesses may find empathic joy more accessible and more satisfying than do their self-focused counterparts, helping more frequently for that reason" (p. 642).

The assumed motive underlying this empathic-joy hypothesis is clearly egoistic. The ultimate goal is to gain the rewarding experience of empathic joy; relief of the victim's need is simply instrumental to this end. In contrast, although the empathy-altruism hypothesis also predicts that an empathically aroused individual will feel empathic joy at learning the victim's need has been relieved, the empathy-altruism hypothesis claims that this joy is a consequence, not the goal, of relieving the need.

The empathic-joy hypothesis is especially interesting because, unlike other forms of Version 1 of the empathy-specific reward hypothesis, the rewards described are contingent on the victim's need being relieved, not on the empathically aroused individual being the agent of this relief. The agent might be another person, time (which, it is said, heals all wounds), or chance, and the empathic joy would be as sweet. None of the evidence against Version 1 of the empathy-specific reward hypothesis reviewed thus far counts against the empathic-joy hypothesis; all of the preceding evidence deals with rewards from helping, not from knowing that the victim is feeling better.

Effect of Feedback on Answering a Stressed Student's Questions (Smith et al., 1989)

Predictions

To test their empathic-joy hypothesis against the empathy-altruism hypothesis, Smith et al. (1989) manipulated both empathy and expectation of feedback concerning the effect of one's helping efforts. They reasoned that if the empathic-joy hypothesis is correct, then the empathy–helping relationship should be found only when prospective helpers anticipate receiving feedback about the victim's improvement: "When feedback is assured, the empathic person can expect to move from a state of empathic concern to one of empathic joy by helping, and we would expect the familiar positive relation between empathic concern and helping" (pp. 642–643). When prospective helpers do not anticipate receiving feedback, "helping is a goal-irrelevant response, and we would expect empathic witnesses to refuse to help as often as their nonempathic counterparts" (p. 643). Thus, in a 2 (feedback vs. no feedback) × 2 (low vs. high empathy) design, the empathic-joy hypothesis predicts a 1-versus-3 pattern of helping: high helping in the feedback/high-empathy cell and low helping in each of the other three cells. If, on the other hand, the empathy-altruism hypothesis is correct, then the empathy–helping relationship should be found even in the no-feedback condition; helping can still relieve the victim's need.

Smith et al. (1989) recognized that removing feedback might, at least in some helping situations, increase the cost of helping. And, as discussed in chapter 6, an increase in the cost of helping should reduce the likelihood of either egoistically or altruistically motivated individuals helping. Thus, so long as helping rates in the low-empathy condition did not drop so low as to obscure differences, the empathy-altruism hypothesis predicted either an empathy main effect or both feedback and empathy main effects in a Feedback × Empathy design. The clearest competing predictions between the two hypotheses were in the no-feedback condition. In this condition, the empathy-altruism hypothesis predicted more helping in the high-empathy cell than in the low, whereas the empathic-joy hypothesis predicted relatively low helping by both low- and high-empathy individuals.

Procedure

Smith et al. (1989) tested these predictions in what was ostensibly a study of how students perceive other students' methods of coping with the stresses of the university environment. All research participants watched a videotaped interview (actually fictitious) with a young woman having difficulty adjusting to college life: She was feeling pressure from her father to do well, and was finding her courses harder than expected. In addition, she felt isolated and lonely, and living in a dormitory was proving difficult. The interview concluded with her saying that other people seemed to be adjusting better than she, and she often wondered if she was the only one feeling overwhelmed. Participants were led to believe that they were the only participant to see this particular videotape.

Empathy Manipulation. Before watching the tape, participants were given perspective-taking instructions adapted from Stotland (1969) and Toi and Batson (1982). These instructions were used to manipulate empathy. Participants in the *low-empathy condition* were asked to try to be as objective as possible; participants in the *high-empathy condition* were asked to try to imagine how the person interviewed on the tape felt.

Helping Opportunity. After watching the tape, participants were given a choice of how to spend the remainder of the session. One option was to write answers to questions that the young woman on the videotape had about problems for which she would most like another college student's advice; the answers would be given to the woman the next day. The other option was to watch and rate a videotape of another student. Which option participants chose was the measure of helping, with the former option coded 1 (help) and the latter 0 (no help).

Feedback Manipulation.   Before making their choice, participants received information about feedback. Those in the *feedback condition* were told that if they wrote answers, they would see another video of the young woman when they returned to the lab a week later for their second appointment (all participants expected a second appointment). This video would be made after the young woman had had time to read their answers and begin applying their advice in her life; it would focus on her reactions to their advice and the difference the advice had made in her adjustment. Those in the *no-feedback condition* were given no expectation of further information about the young woman, whether they wrote answers to her questions or not.

Results

Effectiveness of the Empathy Manipulation.   Although the instructional set manipulation of empathy had a significant effect on helping, with participants helping more in the high-empathy condition (.81) than in the low (.50), χ^2 (1) = 6.25, $p < .02$, (arcsin analysis adjusted for extremity), it did not have a significant effect on self-reported empathy for the young woman or on a difference measure of self-reported empathy minus distress. Contending that there was "no basis for interpreting the instructional set [manipulation of empathy] as the more accurate operationalization" (p. 647), Smith et al. (1989) chose to move away from their original experimental design and focus their analyses on a design using a median split on the difference measure of self-reported empathy minus distress to create low- and high-empathy conditions. They did, however, report the helping results for the low- and high-empathy conditions created by the experimental manipulation and for a median-split analysis using self-reported empathy alone rather than a difference measure. Because the comparison is instructive, their helping results are presented in Table 10.3 using each of these three ways of assessing empathy.

Effects of Feedback and Empathy on Helping.   As can be seen, when empathy condition (low vs. high) was based on the experimental manipulation (Column 1 of Table 10.3), helping results conformed to the predictions of the empathy-altruism hypothesis, not the empathic-joy hypothesis. Both the feedback and empathy main effects were significant, χ^2s (1) = 3.88 and 6.25, ps < .05 and .02, respectively, with no evidence of an interaction ($\chi^2 < 1.0$). In the no-feedback condition, helping was higher in the high-empathy cell (.69) than in the low (.38), $z = 1.79$, $p < .08$.

When empathy condition (low vs. high) was based on a median split on self-reported empathy (Column 2), helping results were very similar to those for the empathy manipulation, but they were weaker. Consistent with the

TABLE 10.3

Proportion of Participants Helping Based on Three Different Ways of
Assessing Empathy in the Smith et al. (1989) Experiment

	Technique for Assessing Empathy		
Feedback Condition	Perspective-Taking Manipulation of Empathy	Self-Reported Empathy	Self-Reported Empathy Minus Distress
Feedback			
Low empathy	.62[a]	.60	.62
High empathy	.93	.94	.93
No feedback			
Low empathy	.38	.44	.53
High empathy	.69	.62	.53

[a]The same 63 participants appear in each column.

Copyright 1989 by the American Psychological Association. Adapted by permission of the publisher.

empathy–altruism hypothesis, the empathy main effect was significant, χ^2 (1) = 4.45, $p < .04$, the feedback manipulation was marginally significant, χ^2 (1) = 3.65, $p < .06$, and there was no reliable interaction ($\chi^2 < 1.0$). The difference in helping in the no-feedback condition between the two levels of self-reported empathy (.62 vs. .44) did not, however, approach significance ($z = 1.06$).

When empathy condition was based on a median split on the difference measure of self-reported empathy minus distress (Column 3), helping results conformed to the pattern predicted by the empathic-joy hypothesis, not the empathy-altruism hypothesis. Helping was higher in the feedback/high-relative-empathy cell than in each of the other three cells ($zs > 2.05$, $ps < .04$), and there were no reliable differences among the other three cells ($zs < 1.0$). In the no-feedback condition the proportion helping was identical in the low- and high-relative-empathy cells (.53).

Which of these three ways of assessing empathy should we consider most valid? Smith et al. (1989) chose to dismiss the manipulation and the self-report empathy measure, and to conclude based on the results using the difference measure that their data supported the empathic-joy hypothesis. They justified this choice by appealing to the previous studies by Batson et al. (1981, 1983) and Toi and Batson (1982), reviewed in chapter 8, in which manipulated empathy and a difference measure produced parallel results.

This justification seems tenuous at best when one considers two differences between the need situation used in those previous studies and the situation used by Smith et al. First, in the previous studies, the victim's need was not one that participants shared; in the Smith et al. study, a number of participants—themselves university freshmen and sophomores—may have been experiencing at least some of the same problems adjusting to college as the young woman. It is easy to imagine that reports of empathy would be higher for participants who were themselves having similar problems, and that, moreover, these individuals would be especially interested to learn whether their advice produced beneficial effects. After all, this information might be useful in their own coping efforts. Participants could get this information only in the feedback condition. So at least some of the "helping" in the feedback/high-relative-empathy cell might actually have been directed toward self-help.

Second, as noted by Batson et al. (1988), in situations like the one used by Smith et al. (1989), in which participants are led to anticipate hearing about someone in need and are then presented with a rather stereotypic and not physically disturbing need situation, reports of empathic concern are apt to be contaminated by the desire to present oneself as empathic. Moreover, reports of distress are apt to reflect distress *for* the person in need (as opposed to being distressed *by* the need) and may be as appropriate—if not more appropriate—indicators of true empathic feeling than the self-presentation contaminated reports of empathy. In such situations, using a difference measure of self-reported empathy minus distress to assess empathy may be quite inappropriate. It may involve removing the empathy from the empathy index, leaving a relatively pure index of desire for positive self-presentation (Jones & Pittman, 1982). This desire could easily evoke an egoistic motive to look good that would lead to increased helping only in the presence of feedback, when the effectiveness of one's self-presentation is known, producing precisely the pattern of helping that Smith et al. found using their difference measure.

Given these problems with interpretation of the self-report measures, especially the difference measure, the experimental manipulation of empathy seems the best way of assessing empathy in this study. And if it is, then the results support the empathy-altruism hypothesis, not the empathic-joy hypothesis. In light of the interpretational ambiguities, however, we probably should not place much confidence in this conclusion. A more appropriate conclusion is that the empathic-joy hypothesis needs further testing. To this end, Batson et al. (in press) conducted three experiments. In the first, they used a Feedback × Empathy design much like the one Smith et al. (1989) used, but, to avoid the self-help problem, they used a different need situation.

Effect of Feedback on Helping Katie Banks (Batson et al., in press, Experiment 1)

Procedure and Predictions

To assess the effect of feedback on the empathy–helping relationship, Batson et al. (in press) turned to the broadcast paradigm developed by Coke et al. (1978). It seemed unlikely that Katie Banks's need for help taking care of her younger brother and sister after the tragic death of her parents was a need that participants would have themselves. Empathy was manipulated by perspective-taking instructions. To accommodate a feedback manipulation, the helping opportunity was changed to involve working at home stuffing and addressing envelopes for a fund drive for Katie.

Feedback was manipulated by whether or not participants expected to learn the results of their helping efforts. In the *no-feedback condition* participants were told: "It will not be possible for you to learn the results of your efforts on Katie's behalf." In the *feedback condition* participants were told: "She [Katie] has said she will be sure to provide anyone who helps with follow-up information on results of your efforts on her behalf."

In addition to the no-feedback and feedback conditions, Batson et al. included a no-information condition, in which participants received no information about feedback. This condition served two functions. It provided a replication condition in which to test the empathy-helping relationship in the absence of explicit information about feedback. It also provided a check on the Smith et al. (1989) assumption that, in the absence of explicit information about feedback, people assume they will receive feedback on the results of their helping efforts. Smith et al. used this assumption to explain why in previous research an empathy–helping relationship had been found when no explicit information about feedback was provided.

Both the empathic-joy hypothesis and the empathy-altruism hypothesis predicted more helping in the high-empathy cell than in the low when no information about feedback was provided (no information condition) and when subjects were explicitly led to expect feedback (feedback condition). The two hypotheses differed, however, in their predictions for the effect of the empathy manipulation when subjects were explicitly led to expect no feedback (no-feedback condition): The empathic-joy hypothesis predicted equally low helping in both low- and high-empathy cells; the empathy-altruism hypothesis predicted more helping in the high-empathy cell than in the low.

Results

Unlike in the Smith et al. (1989) experiment, there was consistent evidence that the empathy manipulation was effective in this experiment. Participants in the high-empathy condition of this experiment reported feeling significantly more empathy for Katie than did participants in the low-empathy condition, $F(1, 66) = 41.82, p < .0001$.

The proportion of subjects volunteering to help Katie in each cell of the 2 (low empathy, high empathy) × 3 (no information, no feedback, feedback) design is presented in Table 10.4. Analyses revealed a reliable empathy main

TABLE 10.4
Proportion of Participants Agreeing to Help Katie
(Batson et al., in press, Experiment 1)

Empathy Condition	No Information About Feedback (Replication Condition)	Information About Feedback	
		No Feedback	Feedback
Low	.42	.33	.67
High	.75	.83	.58

Note: $n = 12$ per cell.
Copyright by the American Psychological Association. Adapted by permission of the publisher.

effect, $\chi^2 (1) = 5.04$, $p < .025$. This main effect was, however, qualified by a marginally significant interaction, $\chi^2 (2) = 4.87$, $p < .10$. Inspection of cell means and tests for simple main effects revealed evidence of the empathy–helping relationship predicted by the empathy-altruism hypothesis in both the no-information (replication) condition, $z = 1.69$, $p < .10$, and the no-feedback condition, $z = 2.62$, $p < .01$. The significant difference in the no-feedback condition was contrary to the prediction of the empathic-joy hypothesis. There was no evidence of an empathy–helping relationship in the feedback condition.

The lack of an empathy–helping relationship in the feedback condition seemed to be due primarily to the relatively high helping among the low-empathy individuals led to anticipate feedback; there was a marginally significant increase in the proportion of low-empathy individuals helping in the feedback condition (.67) relative to the no-feedback condition (.33), $z = 1.66$, $p < .10$. There was a nonsignificant decrease in the proportion of high-empathy individuals helping in the feedback condition (.58) relative to the no-feedback condition (.83), $z = -1.38$. Thus, rather than the helping of high-empathy individuals dropping to the level of low-empathy individuals in the no-feedback condition, as predicted by the empathic-joy hypothesis, the helping of low-empathy individuals rose to the level of high-empathy individuals in the feedback condition. Low-empathy individuals, not high-empathy individuals, were the ones whose helping increased with anticipation of feedback.

In retrospect, this unpredicted increase seemed entirely reasonable. Low-empathy individuals, less concerned about Katie's welfare and more concerned about their own, may have been especially sensitive to the potential for vicarious pleasure in knowing Katie was better. They, rather than high-empathy individuals, may have, in Smith et al.'s (1989) words, "an enhanced sensitivity to vicarious joy" (p. 642) and so help "in order to be happy" (p. 641).

The pattern of helping in the no-information (replication) condition, although falling between the pattern in the no-feedback and feedback conditions, paralleled the former more closely than the latter. Contrary to the assumption of Smith et al. (1989), in the absence of explicit feedback information, participants' responses paralleled those of individuals explicitly told that they would not receive feedback more than those of individuals told that they would receive feedback.

In summary, this experiment, which was a conceptual replication of Smith et al.'s (1989) Feedback × Empathy design but was not complicated by possible failure of the empathy manipulation, produced no support for the empathic-joy hypothesis. Allowing for the increased helping in the feedback cell among participants in the low-empathy condition, which in retrospect seemed entirely reasonable, results conformed to the pattern predicted by the empathy-altruism hypothesis, not the empathic-joy hypothesis. Results in the key no-feedback condition replicated the results Smith et al. (1989) obtained in their experimental design, which were, once again, the results predicted by the empathy-altruism hypothesis, not the empathic-joy hypothesis.

Likelihood of Improvement and Desire for Further Exposure to a Person in Need (Batson et al., in press, Experiments 2 & 3)

Procedure and Predictions

In two other experiments, Batson et al. (in press) tested the relative merits of the empathic-joy and empathy-altruism hypotheses using a different technique. Research participants presented with a person in need were given no chance to help. Instead, they were given a choice between hearing update information about this person's condition or hearing about someone else. Before choosing, participants received information (ostensibly from experts) on the likelihood that the needy person's situation would be substantially improved by the time of the update. Some participants were told the likelihood was only 20%; some were told it was 50%; and some were told it was 80%. Perspective-taking instructions were used to manipulate empathy, producing a 2 (low empathy, high empathy) × 3 (20%, 50%, 80% likelihood of improvement) factorial design.

The two experiments used two different need situations. The first used a situation similar to that employed by Smith et al. (1989): Ostensibly as part of a study of peer evaluation of student stress, participants watched a videotape of a young woman who was having trouble adjusting to college. The second used Katie Banks once again.

Predictions were the same for both experiments. If feeling empathy for a person in need evokes egoistic motivation to gain empathic joy, then in the high-empathy condition there should be a linear relation between the likelihood the needy person would be better and choosing to hear about this person again: Few participants should make this choice in the 20% condition; more should make it in the 50% condition; and the most in the 80% condition. In the low-empathy condition, there should be little incentive to choose to hear from the needy person again, regardless of the likelihood of improvement.

If, on the other hand, empathically aroused individuals are altruistically concerned for the needy person's welfare, then, overall, there should be a main effect for empathy. Participants in the high-empathy condition should have more interest in hearing how this person is doing than participants in the low-empathy condition. The desire to hear more about the needy person's welfare should be relatively high in all three likelihood-of-improvement conditions, although it might well be highest in the 50% condition, where there would be maximum uncertainty about improvement. To the degree that participants in both the 20% and 80% conditions believe that they already know how the person will be faring, they should have less need to hear further. Thus, the pattern of choices in the high-empathy condition that would be most consistent with the empathy-altruism hypothesis would be either flat or curvilinear (with the highest proportion of participants choosing to hear from the needy person again in the 50% condition), not the linear increase predicted by the empathic-joy hypothesis.

Results

Results of these two experiments are presented in Table 10.5. As can be seen, in both experiments choices patterned as predicted by the empathy-altruism hypothesis, not the empathic-joy hypothesis. Participants in the

TABLE 10.5
Proportion of Participants Choosing to Hear Second Interview with
Person in Need (Batson et al., in press, Experiments 2 & 3)

	Need Situation			
	Difficulty Adjusting to College (Experiment 2)		Supporting Siblings After Loss of Parents (Experiment 3)	
Likelihood of Improvement	Low Empathy	High Empathy	Low Empathy	High Empathy
20%	.17	.33	.22	.50
50%	.17	.58	.33	.67
80%	.33	.42	.44	.44

Note: In Experiment 2, $n = 12$ in each cell; in Experiment 3, $n = 18$ in each cell.
Copyright by the American Psychological Association. Adapted by permission of the publisher.

high-empathy condition were more likely than participants in the low-empathy condition to choose to hear from the person in need again, .44 vs. .22, $\chi^2(1) = 4.26, p < .05$, in Experiment 2; .54 vs. .33, $\chi^2(1) = 4.84, p < .04$, in Experiment 3. In neither experiment was there the linear trend in the high-empathy condition predicted by the empathic-joy hypothesis (both χ^2s < 1.0). As in the previous experiment, there was more evidence of a linear trend in the low-empathy condition, especially in Experiment 3. Indeed, a test of this trend across all three of the Batson et al. (in press) experiments indicated that it was statistically reliable, $\chi^2(6) = 14.59, p < .025$. Apparently, if anyone was sensitive to the likelihood of hearing good or bad news, it was the participants who were feeling relatively little empathy for the person in need. Contrary to the empathic-joy hypothesis, this sensitivity was not apparent in the choices of participants who were feeling relatively high empathy.

Conclusion

Results of these three experiments were quite consistent with one another and with the results obtained by Smith et al. (1989) in their experimental design. In none of the three experiments, nor in the Smith et al. experiment, did results pattern as predicted by the empathic-joy hypothesis. Results consistently patterned as predicted by the empathy-altruism hypothesis. Only with the internal analysis using the difference measure did Smith et al. find any support for the empathic-joy hypothesis. And there are reasons to doubt the appropriateness of that analysis. Apparently, empathically aroused individuals are not motivated simply to gain the pleasure of sharing vicariously in the needy person's joy at relief. This interesting variation on the first version of the empathy-specific reward hypothesis, like the previously considered form of this version, does not appear capable of accounting for the empathy–helping relationship.

VERSION 2: NEGATIVE-STATE RELIEF AND THE EMPATHY–HELPING RELATIONSHIP

Even if we conclude that the first version of the empathy-specific reward hypothesis should be rejected, the second version still needs to be considered. Cialdini et al. (1987; see also Schaller & Cialdini, 1988) have argued that *need* for the reward of helping, not the reward itself, is empathy specific. They claim that feeling empathy for a person who is suffering involves a state of temporary sadness or depression, and empathic individuals are motivated to relieve this negative affective state. The negative state can be relieved by any mood-enhancing experience, including but not limited to obtaining the social and self-rewards that accompany helping. Desire for negative-state relief, not altruism, underlies the empathy–helping relationship.

As Cialdini et al. (1987) pointed out, the negative-state relief model can explain why more empathy leads to more helping even when escape is easy, a finding that has been taken as evidence for the empathy-altruism hypothesis (see chapter 8). According to the negative-state relief model, the empathy–helping relationship remains even under conditions of easy escape because empathically aroused individuals are in special need of a positive, mood-enhancing experience, and the self-rewards associated with helping are the only such experience available. Escape may reduce personal distress, but it does not satisfy the need for positive mood enhancement evoked by empathy. Personal distress and empathy are both negative feelings, but they are "functionally distinct in their relation to helping" (Cialdini et al., 1987, p. 750). Empathy-induced helping "is mediated by the increased sadness of high-empathy subjects witnessing a suffering other," and "the help is an egoistic response designed to dispel the temporary depression" (p. 750). In contrast, feelings of distress "are agitation or anxiety rather than sadness based"; these negative states "are normally not reduced through benevolence," and "consequently would not be expected to increase helping" (p. 750).

Evidence for the Negative-State Relief Explanation

Cialdini et al. (1987) tested their negative-state relief explanation of the empathy–helping relationship by conducting two experiments. In the first, they examined the effect of providing participants in a high-empathy condition with a mood-enhancing experience prior to the opportunity to help.

Introducing a Mood-Enhancing Experience into the Shock Paradigm (Cialdini et al., 1987, Experiment 1)

Procedure and Predictions.   The basic procedure of this experiment combined parts of the procedures used by Batson et al. (1981) and by Toi and Batson (1982) to provide evidence for the empathy-altruism hypothesis. (These procedures are described in chapter 8.) Female introductory psychology students were asked to adopt either an objective or an empathic perspective as they watched over closed-circuit TV while another female introductory psychology student, Elaine (actually a confederate), reacted with increasing discomfort to a series of electric shocks. Participants were then given an unexpected opportunity to help Elaine by taking the remaining shocks in her stead. For some participants, escape was easy; even if they did not help, they would see Elaine suffer no more. For others, escape was difficult; if they did not help, they would continue watching Elaine suffer. The four conditions described so far were intended as replication conditions.

To test the negative-state relief version of the empathy-specific reward hypothesis, four more conditions were added. In each escape condition, some participants in the high-empathy condition were given a mood-enhancing experience just before the opportunity to help; they were informed either that they would be paid one dollar for their participation in the study (payment) or that their performance on a previously completed questionnaire indicated that they had "fine social abilities" (praise). The negative-state relief explanation predicted that either of these mood-enhancing experiences would relieve the negative affective state associated with feeling empathy, thereby eliminating the increased motivation to help in the high-empathy condition. As a result, Cialdini et al. (1987) predicted that in the easy-escape/high-empathy condition those participants who received either payment or praise would help less than those who did not. The empathy-altruism hypothesis predicted high helping by all participants in the easy-escape/high-empathy condition; only by helping could they reach the altruistic goal of relieving Elaine's distress.

Results.   The proportion of participants helping in each cell of this experiment is presented in Table 10.6. (As in other experiments using the shock procedure, responses on a scaled measure of amount of helping were bimodally distributed, reflecting the decision whether to help. This bimodal distribution rendered parametric statistics inappropriate, so only the more interpretable proportional results are reported.) As can be seen, the proportions patterned somewhat as predicted by the negative-state relief explanation. In the easy-escape/high-empathy condition, participants who received payment or praise helped a bit less than those who did not. This difference did not, however, approach statistical significance, $z < 1.0$.

Other results rendered interpretation of this weak pattern even more difficult. First, although the rate of helping was somewhat lower for easy-escape/high-empathy participants who had an interposed mood-enhancing

TABLE 10.6
Proportion of Participants Agreeing to Take Shocks for Elaine
(Cialdini et al., 1987, Experiment 1)

Ease of Escape	Low-Empathy Set	High-Empathy Set		
	No Reward	No Reward	Praise	Money
Easy	.33	.50	.45	.29
n	12	10	11	7
Difficult	.40	.73	.56	.36
n	10	11	9	11

Note: Copyright 1987 by the American Psychological Association. Adapted by permission of the publisher.

experience, as predicted by the negative-state relief explanation, the decrease was clear only for those paid, not for those praised. Second, payment decreased the rate of helping in the difficult-escape condition as much as in the easy-escape condition, which suggested the presence of processes other than negative-state relief, such as reactance (Brehm & Cole, 1966). Clearly, this first experiment by Cialdini et al. (1987) raised more questions than it answered.

Introducing a Mood-Fixing Drug into the Carol Marcy Broadcast Paradigm (Cialdini et al., 1987, Experiment 2)

Procedure and Predictions. In their second experiment, Cialdini et al. (1987) did not interpose a mood-enhancing experience between exposure to another person's suffering and the opportunity to help; they interposed information designed to convince participants that helping would not enhance their mood. After learning that another female introductory psychology student, Carol Marcy, needed someone to help her go over class notes, participants were given a chance to volunteer. (These were the same need situation and helping response employed by Toi & Batson, 1982, and described in chapter 8.) Just before being given the chance to volunteer, however, some participants were informed that a drug they had previously taken had a mood-fixing effect and would keep them in their current mood for the next thirty minutes (fixed-mood condition); other participants were told nothing (labile-mood condition). A similar mood-fixing manipulation had been used to demonstrate negative-state relief by Manucia, Baumann, and Cialdini (1984). Perspective-taking instructions like those employed in the previous experiment were used to manipulate empathy. All participants were run under conditions of easy escape.

The negative-state relief explanation predicted that high-empathy participants would help more than low only in the labile-mood condition, because only then could they expect helping to enhance their negative empathic state. The empathy-altruism hypothesis predicted an empathy–helping relationship in both the labile- and the fixed-mood conditions, because the lability of participants' own mood was irrelevant to the altruistic goal of relieving the victim's distress.

Results. The proportion of participants helping and the mean amount of helping in each cell of this experiment are presented in Table 10.7. The mean amount of helping (the time participants agreed to spend going over class notes) patterned reliably as predicted by the negative-state relief model, $F(1, 31) = 6.96$, $p < .02$; the proportion of participants helping did not. The pattern of proportions fell somewhere between the pattern predicted by the negative-state relief model and the pattern predicted by the empathy-altruism hypothesis, both zs < 1.0.

TABLE 10.7
Proportion of Participants Helping and Mean Amount of Helping
(Cialdini et al., 1987, Experiment 2)

Mood-Lability Condition	Empathy Condition	
	Low	High
Labile	.63	.80
M	0.75	1.30
n	8	10
Fixed	.56	.63
M	0.56	0.63
n	9	8

Note: Copyright 1987 by the American Psychological Association. Adapted by permission of the publisher.

Cialdini et al. (1987) concluded that these two experiments "appear to support an egoistic (Negative-State Relief model) interpretation over a selfless (Empathy-Altruism model) interpretation of enhanced helping under conditions of high empathy" (p. 757). They were careful to point out, however, that their case was not airtight because distraction could have been a confound in each experiment: "The reward procedures of Experiment 1 or the placebo-drug procedures of Experiment 2 may have turned subjects' attention away from their empathic emotions" (p. 757). Cialdini et al. recognized that their results offered no strong disconfirmation of a distraction explanation, and they called for research to address this issue.

Could Distraction Account for the Apparent Support for the Negative State Relief Explanation?

Mood-Fixing Revisited (Schroeder et al., 1988)

Procedure. The possibility that distraction produced the apparent support for the empathy-specific reward hypothesis in the Cialdini et al. (1987) experiments is underscored by the results of an experiment by Schroeder, Dovidio, Sibicky, Matthews, and Allen (1988). Working at the same time but independently of Cialdini et al., Schroeder et al. also sought to test the relative merits of the negative-state relief and empathy-altruism explanations of the empathy–helping relationship. Moreover, like Cialdini et al. (1987, Experiment 2), they employed a perspective-taking manipulation of empathy and the Manucia et al. (1984) mood-fixing manipulation. They also employed a very similar need situation and helping response.

Results. As can be seen in Table 10.8, Schroeder et al. obtained quite different results from Cialdini et al. (1987). On their measure of amount of helping, Schroeder et al. failed to find the drop in the fixed-mood/high-

TABLE 10.8
Proportion of Participants Helping and Mean Amount of Helping
(Easy Escape Only) (Schroeder et al., 1988)

Mood-Lability Condition	Empathy Condition	
	Low	High
Labile	.53	.73
M	2.73	4.07
Fixed	.60	.60
M	3.67	4.40

Note: $n = 15$ in each cell.

empathy cell predicted by the negative-state relief model. Instead, they found more helping in the high-empathy condition than in the low under each mood-lability condition, as predicted by the empathy-altruism hypothesis, but the empathy main effect was not statistically reliable. Moreover, as had been true for Cialdini et al. (1987), the proportion of participants helping in each cell showed a weak and ambiguous pattern, $zs < 1.0$. Based largely on internal analyses comparing the helping of participants reporting a relative predominance of empathy with the helping of those reporting a relative predominance of distress, Schroeder et al. concluded that their results were more supportive of the empathy-altruism hypothesis than the negative-state relief explanation.

What could explain the apparently conflicting results on amount of helping between the Schroeder et al. experiment and Experiment 2 by Cialdini et al., which were so similar? Because the effects in neither study were especially strong, the difference might be due to chance. But another possibility exists. There was an important procedural difference between the two experiments. In the Schroeder et al. experiment, participants were informed of the drug's impending effect (not mood fixing vs. mood fixing) *before* they were exposed to the person in need. After exposure, participants in the fixed-mood condition were simply reminded that the drug should fix their present mood "for the next 20 minutes or so." In the Cialdini et al. experiment, the mood-fixing effect of the drug was introduced for the first time *after* participants had been exposed to the victim's need. The Schroeder et al. procedure seems far less likely to cause distraction.

Introducing Anticipation of Mood Enhancement (Schaller and Cialdini, 1988)

Procedure.   Schaller and Cialdini (1988), recognizing that both Cialdini et al. (1987) studies were subject to a distraction explanation, conducted a study in which they used the same need situation, empathy manipulation, and helping response used by Cialdini et al. in their Experiment 2. Rather than interposing mood-enhancing or mood-fixing information between the empathy induction and the opportunity to help, however, Schaller and Cialdini led some participants to expect that their mood would be enhanced shortly even if they chose not to help: They would be listening to an audiotape of comedy routines. Other participants did not expect a mood-enhancing experience. To keep distraction to a minimum, information about the upcoming comedy tape was presented at the beginning of the study; only a brief reminder was inserted between the empathy induction and the opportunity to help.

Results. The proportion of participants helping and mean amount of helping in each cell of this 2 (no mood enhancement vs. mood enhancement) × 2 (low vs. high empathy) design are presented in Table 10.9. As can be seen, these results do not provide unambiguous support for either the negative-state relief explanation or the empathy-altruism hypothesis. Results on the scaled measure of amount of helping seem more consistent with the former explanation, whereas results on the dichotomous proportions seem at least as consistent with the latter. On neither dependent measure was the pattern predicted by either hypothesis statistically reliable.

Schaller and Cialdini (1988) chose to interpret these results as more supportive of their negative-state relief explanation than of the empathy-altruism hypothesis. But they also counseled caution, for two reasons: First, they noted that effects were weak due to a great amount of error variance on their helping measure. In an attempt to reduce this error variance, they introduced a post hoc time-of-semester variable, which created 30 cells of small and unequal Ns (an average of 3 participants per cell) that were subject to unequal weighting in the least-squares analyses that Schaller and Cialdini performed. In these least-squares analyses, comparisons on the scaled mea-

TABLE 10.9
Proportion of Participants Helping and Mean Amount of Helping
(Schaller & Cialdini, 1988)

	Empathy Condition	
Anticipated Mood Enhancement	Low	High
No	.27	.73
M	0.40	1.13
Yes	.53	.60
M	0.80	0.73

Note: $n = 15$ in each cell.
Copyright 1988 by the American Psychological Association. Adapted by permission of the publisher.

sure predicted by the negative-state relief explanation were statistically reliable. Unfortunately, post hoc analyses of this kind run a high risk of capitalizing on chance.

Second, especially for the proportional data, the lack of difference in helping between the low- and high-empathy conditions for participants antici- pating mood-enhancement seemed due more to an unpredicted increase in helping in the low-empathy condition than to the predicted decrease in the high-empathy condition. This unpredicted increase in the low-empathy con- dition could easily account for the observed lack of association between empathy and helping in the mood-enhancement condition.

Another Look at the Negative-State Relief Explanation

Unpersuaded by the inconsistent and unclear results of the three studies that Cialdini and his colleagues claimed as support for the negative-state relief version of the empathy-specific reward hypothesis, but at the same time intrigued by the possibility that here at last was an egoistic explanation of the empathy–helping relationship that could withstand empirical test, Batson et al. (1989) undertook a series of three studies. To avoid the distraction con- found of earlier work, they used an anticipated mood-enhancement manipu- lation much like the one used by Schaller and Cialdini (1988). Participants were led to expect that if they chose not to help they would immediately watch a 5-minute video that either would not enhance their mood or would cause "strong feelings of happiness and pleasure." The first study in this series tested and confirmed the effectiveness of this anticipated mood-enhancement manipulation; Studies 2 and 3 then used this manipulation to test the com- peting predictions of the negative-state relief explanation and the empathy- altruism hypothesis.

Anticipated Mood Enhancement and Taking Shocks for a Peer (Batson et al., 1989, Study 2)

Procedure and Predictions.   In Study 2, female and male undergraduates were given an opportunity to help Elaine (Charlie) by taking electric shocks in her (his) stead. Some participants were led to expect that if they chose not to help they would immediately watch a video that would cause "strong feelings of happiness and pleasure" (anticipated mood-enhancement condition); others were led to expect a neutral video (no anticipated mood-enhancement condition). To minimize distraction, information about the nature of the upcoming video was presented at the beginning of the study; only a brief reminder was inserted between watching Elaine (Charlie) and the opportu- nity to help. Relative predominance of feelings of personal distress and empathy were measured through self-reports, as had Batson et al. (1983, Studies 1 & 2) when providing evidence for the empathy-altruism hypothesis using the shock procedure.

The negative-state relief explanation made two predictions for the pattern of helping across the four cells of a 2 (no anticipated mood enhancement vs. anticipated mood enhancement) × 2 (predominant distress vs. empathy) design (all easy escape). First, in the no anticipated mood-enhancement condition, the rate of helping by individuals reporting a predominance of empathy should be higher than the rate by individuals reporting a predominance of distress. This difference would replicate the difference observed previously by Batson et al. (1983, Studies 1 & 2; see chapter 8). Second, among individuals reporting a predominance of empathy, the rate of helping should be lower in the anticipated mood-enhancement condition than in the no anticipated mood-enhancement condition. This difference was predicted because individuals in the former condition could anticipate reaching the egoistic goal of having their negative empathic state relieved without having to help, whereas individuals in the latter condition could not.

In contrast, the empathy-altruism hypothesis predicted a main effect for predominant emotional response. The rate of helping should be relatively low for predominantly distressed individuals and high for predominantly empathic individuals, regardless of whether they anticipated mood enhancement. Relieving their own negative state would not enable empathic individuals to reach the altruistic goal of relieving Elaine's (Charlie's) distress.

Results. The proportion of participants who offered to help in each cell of the 2 × 2 design of Study 2 is presented in Table 10.10. Consistent with the predictions of the empathy-altruism hypothesis, there was only one reliable effect, a main effect for predominant emotional response, $\chi^2 (1, N = 40) = 3.91, p < .05$; the proportion helping was higher among individuals reporting a predominance of empathy (.70) than among individuals reporting a predominance of distress (.40). The anticipated mood-enhancement main effect and the interaction did not approach significance (χ^2s < 1.0).

Contrary to the predictions of the negative-state relief version of the

TABLE 10.10
Proportion of Participants Agreeing to Take Shocks for Elaine or
Charlie (Batson et al., 1989, Study 2)

	Predominant Emotional Response	
Anticipated Mood Enhancement	Distress	Empathy
No	.33	.70
n	9	10
Yes	.45	.70
n	11	10

Note: Copyright 1989 by the American Psychological Association. Adapted by permission of the publishers.

empathy-specific reward hypothesis, there was no evidence that anticipated mood enhancement reduced the rate of helping by individuals reporting a predominance of empathy. The proportion helping among these individuals was exactly the same in the two anticipated mood-enhancement conditions (.70).

Anticipated Mood Enhancement and Offering to Help Katie Banks (Batson et al., 1989, Study 3)

Procedure and Predictions. In their third study, Batson et al. (1989) gave participants a chance to help Katie Banks, the young woman struggling to support her younger brother and sister after her parents were killed in an automobile accident. Anticipated mood enhancement was manipulated as in the previous study; empathy was manipulated with perspective-taking instructions. Predictions were the same as for the previous study.

Results. The proportion of participants volunteering to help Katie and the mean amount of time volunteered in each cell of the 2 (no anticipated mood enhancement vs. anticipated mood enhancement) $\times$ 2 (low vs. high empathy) design of Study 3 are presented in Table 10.11. Consistent with the predictions of the empathy-altruism hypothesis, there was only one reliable effect, the main effect for empathy, χ^2 $(1, N = 60) = 10.46, p < .001$; the proportion helping was higher in the high-empathy condition (.77) than in the low (.37). The anticipated mood-enhancement main effect and the interaction did not approach significance (χ^2s < 1.0).

Contrary to predictions of the negative-state relief version of the empathy-specific reward hypothesis, there was no evidence that anticipated mood enhancement reduced the rate of helping in the high-empathy condition, $z < 1.0$. Analysis of the scaled measure of amount of time volunteered produced exactly the same pattern of significant effects.

TABLE 10.11
Proportion of Participants Volunteering to Help Katie and Mean
Amount of Time Volunteered (Batson et al., 1989, Study 3)

Anticipated Mood Enhancement	Empathy Condition	
	Low	High
No	.40	.80
M	0.67	1.33
Yes	.33	.73
M	0.53	1.33

Note: $n = 15$ in each cell. Means are for a scaled measure of amount of time volunteered (0 = no help; 1 = 1–2 hours; 2 = 3–5 hours; 3 = 6–8 hours; 4 = 9–10 hours). Copyright 1989 by the American Psychological Association. Adapted by permission of the publisher.

Conclusion

Results of these last two studies strongly suggest that something other than a desire for negative-state relief motivates the helping of high-empathy individuals. In both studies, an empathy–helping relationship was found even when anticipated mood enhancement provided the opportunity for negative-state relief without helping. Apparently, contrary to the claim of Cialdini and his colleagues, the empathy–helping relationship is not simply the product of an egoistic desire for negative-state relief. There is more to it than that. It is not that negative-state relief never motivates helping, but it does not seem to be the motive for empathy-induced helping.

GENERAL CONCLUSION

The research reviewed in this chapter provides little support for either version of the third major egoistic alternative to the empathy-altruism hypothesis—the empathy-specific reward hypothesis. The first version proposed that the motivation underlying the empathy–helping relationship is an egoistic desire for the additional rewards associated with helping when feeling empathy. Studies testing this version found no evidence for the predicted mood or cognitive effects.

A variation on this first version proposed that the motivation is an egoistic desire to experience vicarious empathic joy at seeing the suffering person's need relieved. Studies testing this variation again found no clear support. Smith et al. (1989) did obtain data that patterned as predicted by this empathic-joy hypothesis when they used a difference measure (self-reported empathy minus distress) to assess empathy. The appropriateness of using this difference measure in the need situation they employed was questionable, however, and their experimental manipulation produced data contrary to the predictions of the empathic-joy hypothesis. Three other experiments failed to provide support for the empathic-joy hypothesis. Results of each instead supported the empathy-altruism hypothesis.

The second version of the empathy-specific reward hypothesis proposed that the empathy–helping relationship is motivated by additional need for the mood-enhancing self-rewards generally associated with helping. Although Cialdini and his colleagues have claimed support for this version, other researchers using procedures less subject to interpretational ambiguity have not found support. There now seems to be clear evidence that an empathy–helping relationship can exist even among individuals anticipating a mood-enhancing experience. This finding is not consistent with the negative-state relief version of the empathy-specific reward hypothesis. It is entirely consistent with the empathy-altruism hypothesis.

Yet, in spite of the frequent failure to find support for the empathy-specific reward hypothesis, it may be premature to close the book firmly on this egoistic alternative. Evidence to date suggests that this third egoistic alternative to the empathy-altruism hypothesis is probably wrong, but the evidence is not as overwhelming or clear as evidence against the aversive-arousal reduction and empathy-specific punishment hypotheses. Further tests of the empathy-specific reward hypothesis, especially Version 2 of this hypothesis, are warranted.

AN AFFIRMATIVE ANSWER?

At the same time, it is worth noting that if we cast an eye back over the approximately 25 studies reported in this and the two preceding chapters, we find no clear support for any of the three egoistic alternatives to the empathy-altruism hypothesis proposed in chapter 7. In study after study, with no clear exceptions, we find results conforming to the pattern predicted by the empathy-altruism hypothesis, the hypothesis that empathic emotion evokes altruistic motivation. At present, there is no plausible egoistic explanation for the results of these studies.

Even though it plays serious havoc with our dominant views of human motivation and, indeed, of human nature, the consistent, varied evidence supporting the empathy-altruism hypothesis has become harder and harder to ignore. Sherlock Holmes stated: "When you have eliminated the impossible, whatever remains, *however improbable,* must be the truth." If we apply Holmes's dictum to our attempt to answer the altruism question, then I believe we must, tentatively, accept the truth of the empathy-altruism hypothesis. It is impossible for any of the three major egoistic explanations of the empathy–helping relationship—or any combination of these—to account for the evidence reviewed in the last three chapters. So what remains? The empathy-altruism hypothesis; it can account for the evidence. Pending new evidence or a plausible new egoistic explanation for the existing evidence, the empathy-altruism hypothesis, however improbable, seems to be true.

Our extensive review of the research designed to test this hypothesis against the egoistic alternatives appears to have borne fruit. For, if the empathy-altruism hypothesis is true, then we at last have an answer to the altruism question: Contrary to the beliefs of Hobbes, La Rouchefoucauld, Mandeville, and virtually all psychologists, altruistic concern for the welfare of others is within the human repertoire. The empirical evidence we have reviewed suggests that Adam Smith's (1759/1853) bold assertion was not just wishful thinking:

> How selfish soever man may be supposed, there are evidently some principles in his nature, which interest him in the fortune of others, and render their happiness necessary to him, though he derives nothing from it except the pleasure of seeing it. Of this kind is pity or compassion, the emotion which we feel for the misery of others, when we either see it, or are made to conceive it in a very lively manner. (I. i. 1. 1)

PART
IV

EXTENSIONS

CHAPTER 11

Other Possible Sources
of Altruistic Motivation:
The Altruistic Personality

Adam Smith (1759/1853) claimed that the empathic emotion of pity or compassion is among the principles in our nature that interest us in the welfare of others. The empirical evidence to date suggests that he was right, that empathic emotion does evoke altruistic motivation. Smith's claim, however, actually implies more. To say that pity or compassion is *among* the principles evoking altruism implies that there are other principles that evoke altruism as well.

In this chapter, we consider the empirical evidence, pro and con, for other possible sources of altruistic motivation. The sources that we consider by no means exhaust the possibilities. Our list is short because, for most potential sources, there has been no attempt to test the nature of the underlying motivation. Far too often, the mere fact that some potential source correlates with increased helping has been taken by advocates of altruism as evidence that it evokes altruistic motivation. By this criterion, the list of other sources of altruism would be quite long. It would encompass a wide range of characteristics of (a) helpers—including self-esteem, competence, the disposition to feel empathy, and internalization of moral standards, (b) persons helped—including innocence, attractiveness, dependence, age, and sex, (c) the relationship between helper and helped—including prior positive contact, anticipated future contact, friendship, kinship, and similarity, and (d) helping situations—including clarity of need, cost of helping, and availability of other helpers.

Yet, to find that these factors correlate with increased helping only allows us to ask the question of whether they evoke altruistic motivation; it does not provide an answer. In most cases, the research necessary to determine whether the underlying motivation is altruistic or egoistic—whether a given factor evokes motivation directed toward the ultimate goal of benefiting another or toward some more or less subtle form of self-benefit—has not even been started. Many potentially fertile research fields await tilling.

The research that does exist focuses on one general class of potential sources of altruistic motivation, personality attributes of helpers. It seeks to answer the question of whether there is an altruistic personality.

CLAIMS FOR THE EXISTENCE
OF AN ALTRUISTIC PERSONALITY

Oliner and Oliner (1988)

In an attempt to determine whether altruistic personality attributes exist, Samuel and Pearl Oliner (1988) conducted extensive interviews with 406 rescuers of Jews in Nazi Europe. Many of these rescuers risked their own lives, and the lives of their own family members, to help people marked for death, some of whom were total strangers. In some cases, a single dramatic, courageous act enabled one or more people to escape; in many cases, however, refuge and care was provided day after day for months, even years. Not only was this helping dangerous, but often it was quite costly in terms of scarce food supplies shared, inconvenience of living arrangements, and time spent ministering to the needs of the one or more "invisible" members of the household. These rescuers have justly been called heroes.

What led rescuers to provide this kind of aid, whereas others living in the same neighborhood did not? Some of the key differences between rescuers and nonrescuers identified by Oliner and Oliner are more situational than dispositional: Rescuers were more likely to have Jewish friends or co-workers, to be asked for help, and to have family members already involved in rescue work. Yet Oliner and Oliner identified some dispositional differences as well. Compared to nonrescuers, rescuers reported in the interviews that there was more emphasis in their childhood training on learning ethical values expressing care and responsibility for others, empathy, and generosity; but no more emphasis on learning values expressing fairness and reciprocity. Rescuers also reported that their training placed more emphasis on applying ethical values universally. Some rescuers reported that religion was important, especially religious training that emphasized the common humanity of all.

Here are some examples of the way rescuers spoke about their upbringing:

1. I learned to live honestly, to study well in school, to respect others, and to have compassion and generosity toward those who were less well treated by life.
2. I learned generosity, to be open, to help people.
3. My mother was a model of Christian faith and love of neighbor.
4. They taught me to respect all human beings.
5. He [my father] taught me to respect a man no matter what his origin.
6. He [my father] taught me to love my neighbor—to consider him my equal whatever his nationality or religion. He taught me especially to be tolerant. (Oliner & Oliner, 1988, pp. 164–165)

Such reports were less common in the interviews of a matched sample of nonrescuers.

How do we know the courageous and noble acts of the rescuers that Oliner and Oliner interviewed were altruistically motivated? We really do not. Oliner and Oliner used three major criteria to identify rescuers: (a) rescuers received no remuneration of any kind for their helping; (b) they risked their own lives, and (c) they were motivated purely by humanitarian considerations. The first two criteria seem possible to determine; the third, given the retrospective nature of the research, impossible. Judgments about the rescuers' motivation were based on the testimony of rescued survivors. Unfortunately, we cannot know the accuracy of these judgments.

The rescuers themselves claimed a wide range of motives for their actions. Some are altruistic, many egoistic:

1. I did it out of sympathy and kindness.
2. I did it out of a feeling of compassion for those who were weaker and who needed help.
3. It was unfair that I was safe simply because I was born a Protestant. That was the main reason for me. What I did was a question of justice. It was a very humble thing because I was in a privileged situation compared with other people who didn't deserve their situation at all.
4. The reason is that every man is equal. We all have the right to live. It was plain murder, and I couldn't stand that.
5. I knew they were taking them and they wouldn't come back. I didn't think I could live with that knowing that I could have done something.
6. When you see a need, you have to help. Our religion was part of us. We are our brother's keeper. It was very satisfying to us.
7. If you can save somebody's life, that's your duty. (Oliner & Oliner, 1988, pp. 166–169)

Of course, we have no way of knowing the accuracy of these judgments about motivation by the rescuers themselves either.

In *The Altruistic Personality* (1988), Oliner and Oliner presented a rich and valuable panoply of dramatic examples of helping. Yet their claims that this helping is an expression of an altruistic personality, and that they have identified attributes of this altruistic personality, seem unfounded. They presented no real evidence to back up these claims. We are offered ideas to be tested, not tested ideas.

Staub (1974)

Oliner and Oliner were not the first researchers to claim to have discovered altruistic personality attributes. In 1974, Ervin Staub reported that several moral personality variables were associated with a general predisposition to help. His report was based on responses of a number of young men to a series of opportunities to help a male confederate who appeared to be suffering from stomach cramps. Helping the confederate was associated with scores on the following personality measures: Berkowitz and Lutterman's (1968) Social Responsibility scale (sample item: "Every person should give some of his time for the good of his town or country."); Schwartz's (1968) Ascription of Responsibility scale (sample item: "If a good friend of mine wanted to injure an enemy of his, it would be my duty to try to stop him."); Rokeach's (1969) Value Survey rankings of *clean* (negative association) and *helpful;* Christie's (Christie & Geis, 1968) Machiavellianism scale (sample item: "The best way to handle people is to tell them what they want to hear."—negative association); and a short written version of Kohlberg's (1969) test of moral reasoning.

Staub (1974) created a prosocial orientation index by combining these various measures through factor analysis, and he found that scores on this index correlated with helping. Based on these correlations, Staub concluded: "People with a prosocial orientation may, under conditions which still need to be further specified, be willing to endure greater sacrifices and to give up more of their self-interest for the sake of others" (p. 36).

Rushton (1980)

Philippe Rushton (1980, 1981; see also Rushton, Chrisjohn, & Fekken, 1981) made even more explicit claims than Staub for the existence of an altruistic personality. On the basis of a careful review of the classic studies of moral behavior conducted by Hartshorne and May (1928; Hartshorne, May, & Maller, 1929; Hartshorne, May, & Shuttleworth, 1930), as well as more recent research, Rushton (1980) claimed: "There is a 'trait' of altruism. Some people are consistently more generous, helping, and kind than others. . . . There is an altruistic personality . . ." (pp. 66, 84).

Rushton sought to identify characteristics that reflect this trait of altruism. In addition to the personality variables cited by Staub (1974), on whose research Rushton heavily relied, he presented evidence for an association of helping with (a) personal efficacy or self-esteem and (b) dispositional empathy, including the tendency to take another's perspective. (Dispositional empathy should not be confused with the empathic feelings for a specific person in need in a specific situation that was the subject of the research reviewed in chapters 8–10. Dispositional empathy, including the tendency to take another's perspective, is assumed to be a trans-situational attribute varying in strength across individuals. It is typically assessed by self-reports of a general tendency to experience feelings of sympathy, compassion, and concern for others in need.)

Staub's claim that people with a prosocial orientation are willing to give up self-interest for the sake of others and Rushton's claim that there is an altruistic personality seem at once quite radical and quite important. These claims, like the empathy-altruism hypothesis, contradict the dominant assumption in psychology that we are so constituted that we care only for our own welfare.

When one looks more closely at their arguments, however, paying particular attention to what Staub and Rushton mean by altruism, their claims seem less radical. Both Staub and Rushton adopt the second of the pseudoaltruistic definitions of altruism discussed in chapter 4. For them, altruism is not an alternative to egoism; it is a particular form of egoism, one in which the rewards for acting prosocially are self rather than socially administered. Given this pseudoaltruistic use of the term, Staub's and Rushton's claim to have found empirical evidence for an altruistic dimension of personality seems far less newsworthy. The claim reduces to an assertion that some people are more likely than others to help without external rewards. Once again, this assertion does not answer the altruism question; it raises it. We are left wondering whether individuals possessing the "altruistic" personality attributes identified by Staub and Rushton—and by Oliner and Oliner—help more because they are seeking the welfare of at least some others as an ultimate goal, or whether they help more as an instrumental means of enhancing their own welfare by, for example, receiving self-rewards or avoiding self-punishments.

To answer this question of underlying motivation, we must move beyond the research procedures normally used in studies of personality and helping. Looking for correlations between personality variables and helping is not enough; nor is it enough to (a) map consistencies and variations in the personality–helping association across an array of need situations or (b) aggregate analyses across situations and helping measures (as Rushton,

Brainerd, & Pressley, 1983, propose). Associations revealed by these kinds of analyses are the starting point, not the end, of an inquiry into the nature of the underlying motivation. These associations provide the phenomena needing explanation, not the needed explanation. Using Lewin's (1935) distinction discussed in chapter 5, we must move beyond an Aristotelian to a Galilean approach if we wish to determine the nature of the motivation—altruistic or egoistic—associated with Oliner and Oliner's, Staub's, and Rushton's "altruistic" dimensions of personality.

EMPIRICAL TESTS

Taking advantage of the conceptual analysis and research strategies developed to test the empathy-altruism hypothesis, several studies have sought to assess the nature of the motivation underlying the associations between various "altruistic" personality dimensions and helping. As was true for research testing the empathy-altruism hypothesis, the first step in designing these studies was to identify possible egoistic motives for the increased helping associated with these personality dimensions.

Individuals who score high on "altruistic" personality dimensions report an especially strong sense of responsibility and concern for those in need; they report a more principled morality, and a highly positive self-image. Given these reports, the most likely egoistic motive for the helping of these individuals seems to be avoidance of self-punishment in the form of shame and guilt for failing to live up to their positive self-image as good, compassionate, caring, altruistic persons. As Abraham Lincoln is said to have responded after a friend accused him of altruism for saving a sow's pigs that were in danger of drowning, "Why, bless your soul, Ed, that was the very essence of selfishness. I should have had no peace of mind all day had I gone on and left that suffering old sow worrying over those pigs. I did it to get peace of mind, don't you see?" (Sharp, 1928, p. 75, originally from the Springfield, Illinois, *Monitor*). Or as one of Oliner and Oliner's (1988) rescuers put it, "I didn't think I could live with that knowing that I could have done something" (p. 168). Instead of reflecting altruistic motivation, the increased helpfulness associated with so-called "altruistic" personality dimensions may reflect an egoistic desire to avoid this shame and guilt, ensuring the peace of mind of which Lincoln spoke.

Predictions

How might we know if this egoistic motive, rather than an altruistic motive, lies behind the increased helpfulness associated with "altruistic" personality dimensions? What empirical observation can we predict if the motivation is actually directed toward the egoistic goal of avoiding anticipated shame and guilt? It was noted in chapter 9 that most individuals are likely to self-punish only when the failure to live up to their moral self-image is clear and inescapable. Applying this principle to high scorers on an "altruistic" personality dimension, if they are motivated by punishment avoidance, then not only helping but also any other means of escaping from the threat of shame and guilt should suffice, especially if helping is relatively costly. Empirically, this means that when potential helpers believe that it will be relatively difficult to escape from the threat of shame and guilt without helping, there should be a positive correlation between the so-called "altruistic" personality dimension and helping; this is because the personality dimension provides a source of egoistic motivation to help over and above any egoistic motivation arising from other sources. When escape from shame and guilt is relatively easy, there should be no correlation; this is because now those scoring high on the personality dimension have no more need to help than those scoring low. These predictions are summarized in the top half of Table 11.1.

What can we predict if the motivation of high scorers on some "altruistic" personality dimension is directed toward the altruistic goal of increasing the other's welfare? The correlation of this dimension with helping should be positive when escape from the threat of shame and guilt is easy. Those scoring high on the dimension should be able to reach their altruistic goal only by helping, whereas those scoring low, who would not have the altruistic motivation associated with the personality dimension, should be less likely to help. On the other hand, when escape is difficult, the correlation with helping should be no more positive than when escape is easy, and quite possibly less positive. In this case, even those having little of the altruistic personality attribute may help in order to satisfy other egoistic motives, such as aversive-arousal reduction (see chapter 8). Both high and low scorers on the attribute would be motivated to help (although for different reasons), which would diminish the correlation between the attribute and helping. These predictions are summarized in the bottom half of Table 11.1.

Given these competing predictions, if for an "altruistic" personality vari-

TABLE 11.1
Predicted Correlations Between Helping and
"Altruistic" Personality Dimension, Varying
Ease of Escape from Shame and Guilt

If Motivation Egoistic:	
Easy escape	0
Difficult escape	+
If Motivation Altruistic:	
Easy escape	+
Difficult escape	0/+

able we observe a positive correlation with helping when escape from anticipated self-recrimination is difficult but not when escape is easy, then we have evidence that the associated motivation to help is actually egoistic. If, however, we observe a positive correlation with helping when escape is easy, and this correlation is at least as strong as when escape is difficult, then we have evidence that the associated motivation may be altruistic.

A First Look for Altruism in the Altruistic Personality (Batson et al., 1986)

Procedure

To test these predictions, Batson, Bolen, Cross, and Neuringer-Benefiel (1986) conducted a study in which they first assessed participants (all female) on a number of the "altruistic" personality dimensions identified by Staub and Rushton. Then, at a second session several weeks later, participants were run through the shock procedure (described in detail in chapter 8), in which they observed Elaine reacting badly to electric shocks and were given a chance to help by taking her place. As before, ease of escape was manipulated by whether, if participants choose not to help, they expected to continue watching Elaine suffer (difficult escape) or not (easy escape).

One important change was introduced into the procedure of this study. The previous studies using this escape manipulation had been designed to test whether the motivation to help associated with empathic emotion was altruistic or was directed toward the egoistic goal of aversive-arousal reduction. Accordingly, those studies were designed to make it easy or difficult to escape from witnessing the peer's distress, the stimulus causing the aversive empathic arousal. In testing the nature of the motivation to help associated with "altruistic" personality attributes, the issue is not escape from the stimulus; the issue is escape from anticipated self-censure for failing to live up to one's altruistic self-image.

Still, following the old adage, "Out of sight, out of mind," it seemed likely that the escape manipulation used previously could be used to manipulate escape from anticipated self-censure, so long as evaluative cues were kept low in the easy-escape condition. To keep these cues low, the experimenter did not present participants with the opportunity to help face-to-face, as had been done in the previous studies. The opportunity was presented over an audio intercom, and participants were left alone until they had a chance to decide whether to help.

This procedural change did not fully eliminate evaluative cues in the easy-escape condition. Not only the participant but also the experimenter, the assistant administering the shocks, and the peer in need would eventually know what the participant decided to do. It was not, however, necessary to eliminate all evaluative cues, only to create a clear difference in the strength of these cues between the easy- and difficult-escape conditions. Not only were participants in the easy-escape condition alone at the crucial point of decision, but also they believed that if they decided not to help they would soon be free to leave the experimental setting altogether. In contrast, if participants in the difficult-escape condition did not help, then they would be reminded of their failure as they watched the peer continue to suffer.

Four "altruistic" personality variables were assessed at the initial session: self-esteem, social responsibility, ascription of responsibility, and dispositional empathy. Self-esteem was measured by Rosenberg's (1965) Self-Esteem scale (sample item: "I feel that I'm a person of worth, at least on an equal basis with others."); social responsibility was measured by Berkowitz and Lutterman's (1968) Social Responsibility scale; ascription of responsibility was measured by Schwartz's (1968) Ascription of Responsibility scale; and dispositional empathy was measured by Davis's (1983) Interpersonal Reactivity Index. Davis's index is a multidimensional empathy scale that includes four subscales: Perspective Taking (sample item: "I try to look at everybody's side of a disagreement before I make a decision."), Empathy Fantasy (sample item: "I really get involved with the feelings of the characters in a novel."), Personal Distress (sample item: "In emergency situations, I feel apprehensive and ill-at-ease."), and Empathic Concern (sample item: "I often have tender, concerned feelings for other people less fortunate than me."). Davis's four subscales provided a more differentiated measure of dispositional empathy than earlier empathy scales.

In addition to these four personality variables, Batson et al. (1986) also measured birth order, a background variable not considered by Staub or Rushton. Stotland (1969) had reported some evidence of a relationship between birth order and feeling empathy for persons in need (see also Stotland, Sherman, & Shaver, 1971). Later-borns, especially female later-borns, tended to empathize more with someone similar to themselves than did first-borns (including only children). Elaine, the person ostensibly in need in this study, was a female introductory psychology student, as were all research participants. Therefore, one might expect the later-born participants to be more empathic and, as a result, more altruistically motivated.

Results

Relation of Personality Measures to Helping.   Correlations (point biserials) between the eight personality measures (including the four measures of the Interpersonal Reactivity Index) and helping in each escape condition are reported in Table 11.2. As can be seen, none of the measures of the four personality attributes claimed by Staub (1974, 1978) or Rushton (1980, 1981) to reflect an altruistic personality produced the pattern of correlations expected if the scale were associated with altruistic motivation (bottom half of

TABLE 11.2
Point-Biserial Correlations Between Personality Measures and Helping
When Escape Is Easy or Difficult (Batson et al., 1986)

Personality Measures	Ease of Escape Without Helping	
	Easy	Difficult
Self-esteem	− .11	.43**
Social responsibility	.19	.18
Ascription of responsibility	− .04	.32*
Interpersonal reactivity		
Perspective taking	.21	.26
Empathy fantasy	.13	− .01
Personal distress	− .04	− .11
Empathic concern	− .04	.41**
Birth order[a]	.46***	− .15

Note: $n = 30$ for each escape condition.

[a]0 = first-born or only child; 1 = later-born.

*$p < .05$; **$p < .01$; ***$p < .001$, two-tailed.

Copyright 1986 by the American Psychological Association. Adapted by permission of the publisher.

Table 11.1). The Social Responsibility and Perspective Taking scales had the highest positive correlations in the easy-escape condition, but neither of the correlations was reliably different from zero.

Three of the personality scales—Self-Esteem, Ascription of Responsibility, and Empathic Concern—produced the pattern of correlations expected if the underlying motivation was egoistic. For each, there was a significant positive correlation with helping when escape was difficult (*r*s ranged from .32 to .43) and a correlation near zero when escape was easy. This pattern of correlations suggested that the prosocial motivation of participants scoring higher on these personality measures arose from an egoistic desire to avoid self-recrimination, not from an altruistic desire to relieve Elaine's distress. When it was difficult to escape self-censure for the contradiction between a failure to help Elaine and their self-concept as good, responsible, concerned individuals, high scorers were more likely to help than were low scorers. When it was easy to escape this self-censure without incurring the cost of helping, they were no more likely to help.

Only one measure produced the pattern of correlations that would be expected if the motivation was altruistic: birth order. When escape was easy, later-borns were significantly more likely to help than were first-borns (including only children); there was a nonsignificant trend in the opposite direction when escape was difficult.

A Closer Look at Birth Order.   To better illustrate this birth order effect, Table 11.3 presents the number of first-borns and later-borns who did and did not help in each escape condition. As is apparent from the table, the effect of

TABLE 11.3
Number of First-Borns and Later-Borns Helping and Not Helping
When Escape Is Easy or Difficult (Batson et al., 1986)

	First-Born		Later-Born	
Ease of Escape	Help	Not Help	Help	Not Help
Easy	0	10	9	11
Difficult	6	2	13	9

Note: Copyright 1986 by the American Psychological Association. Adapted by permission of the publisher.

the escape manipulation on the behavior of first-borns was dramatic: When escape was easy, 0 of 10 helped; when escape was difficult, 6 of 8 helped. This difference was highly reliable ($p < .002$, Fisher's exact test). For later-borns, there was a slight trend in the same direction, but it did not approach significance: When escape was easy, 9 of 20 helped; when escape was difficult, 13 of 22 helped. The interaction between birth order and escape was statistically reliable, $\chi^2 (1, N = 60) = 5.77, p < .02$.

It has been suggested that first-borns are more likely than later-borns to have thoroughly internalized a sense of moral obligation and, as a result, are more attuned to doing the right thing (MacDonald, 1969, 1971; Moran, 1967). The birth-order results appeared entirely consistent with this socialization explanation, so long as one adds that the first-borns seemed to be acting not to benefit Elaine but to protect themselves from the consequences of a failure to comply with their own internalized values. If they could easily escape these consequences without helping, they did; if they could not, they helped.

Compared with the pattern of helping for first-borns, the pattern for later-borns appeared to reflect more responsiveness to Elaine's needs. Later-borns were only a little less likely to help when escape was easy than when it was difficult. This suggested that their motivation might be, at least in part, altruistic.

Still, several alternative explanations existed for the behavior of the later-borns. Perhaps the escape manipulation did not affect the behavior of later-borns because they were less attentive to or less able to understand the implications of the manipulation. (First-borns tend to score higher than later-borns on measures of intelligence.) Or perhaps because the person in need was similar to them, later-borns found escape relatively difficult even in the easy-escape condition. This second possibility is consistent with Stotland's (1969) suggestion that later-borns are particularly sensitive to the needs of similar others.

Conclusion

Results of this study provided no evidence that any of the four "altruistic" personality variables examined was actually associated with altruistic moti-

vation. The scales used to measure three of the personality variables—
self-esteem, ascription of responsibility, and empathic concern—did seem to
be associated with increased motivation to help. The pattern of correlations
with helping across the escape manipulation, however, suggested that, for
each of these three, the prosocial motivation was directed toward increasing
the helper's own welfare rather than the welfare of the person in need. When
it was relatively difficult to escape self-censure if one did not help, scores on
these scales were positively correlated with helping. When escape was
relatively easy, the positive correlations vanished.

This pattern of helping suggested underlying motivation reminiscent of
Lincoln's self-analysis after helping the pigs: "I did it to get peace of mind,
don't you see?" And, as Lincoln said of his own motivation, such motivation
seems to be "the very essence of selfishness." Only later-borns showed a
pattern of helping that suggested possible altruistic motivation.

Another Look for Altruism in the Altruistic Personality: Conflicting Claims (Eisenberg et al., 1989)

Eisenberg, Miller, Schaller, Fabes, Fultz, Shell, and Shea (1989) conducted a
study exploring the nature of the motivation to help associated with "altruistic" personality variables, and they claimed to find evidence contrary to that
obtained by Batson et al. (1986): "Our findings support the view that there is
indeed an altruistic personality" (p. 65). Specifically, they claimed evidence
that measures of three "altruistic" personality variables identified by Staub
(1974) or Rushton (1980) were associated with altruistic motivation to help:
social responsibility, ascription of responsibility, and dispositional empathy,
including the tendency to take another person's perspective.

Procedure

As in the previous study, each participant in the Eisenberg et al. study took
part in both a group questionnaire session and an individual laboratory
session. In the questionnaire session, participants completed a battery of
scales, including Berkowitz and Lutterman's (1968) Social Responsibility
scale, Schwartz's (1968) Ascription of Responsibility scale, and Mehrabian and
Epstein's (1972) Empathy scale (sample item: "It makes me sad to see a lonely
stranger in a group."). Birth order was also assessed.

One to two weeks later, participants returned individually for the laboratory session. Early in this second session, each participant completed Davis's
(1983) Interpersonal Reactivity Index, the same multidimensional scale measuring dispositional empathy used by Batson et al. (1986).

In the laboratory session, participants were told that they would be seeing
two actual, but unaired, TV newscasts. Each was told that he or she would be

the only participant to see these particular newscasts, and for each, their emotional and physiological reactions would be assessed. Once instructions were clear and the Interpersonal Reactivity Index was completed, participants watched and rated two videotapes. The first was a rather bland and boring newscast on local events; the second showed an interview (actually fictitious) with a local woman, Mrs. Fulton, who was seated in a hospital room with her injured children. Mrs. Fulton described a serious car accident, the injuries it caused her two children, and the adjustment problems they were having as a result. She emphasized her children's fears of getting behind in school and failing, and her problem as a single parent finding enough time to be with them in the hospital. After viewing this videotape, participants were given an opportunity to help Mrs. Fulton by assisting with household tasks (e.g., shopping, yard work) so that she could spend more time tutoring and supporting her children in the hospital.

Results

Relation of Personality Measures to Helping. Only 45% of the participants in this study volunteered to help Mrs. Fulton, rendering parametric statistical analysis of a scaled measure of amount of helping suspect. Therefore, even though Eisenberg et al. (1989) focused their attention on analyses of transformed scores of amount of helping, it seems more appropriate to limit consideration to association of the "altruistic" personality measures to a dichotomous measure of helping (0 = no help; 1 = help).

Table 11.4 presents point-biserial correlations between the seven "altruistic" personality measures taken in this study and helping, first for all participants and then separately for women and men. Recall that in the Batson et al.

TABLE 11.4
Point-Biserial Correlations Between Personality Measures and Helping
(Eisenberg et al., 1989)

Personality Measure	Both Sexes ($N = 78$)	Women ($n = 37$)	Men ($n = 41$)
Social responsibility	.24*	.02	.35*
Ascription of responsibility	.28*	.40*	.09
Mehrabian & Epstein Empathy Scale	.31**	.38*	.23
Interpersonal reactivity (Davis)			
Perspective taking	.21	.09	.28
Empathy fantasy	.17	.16	.13
Personal distress	.02	−.20	.15
Empathic concern	.31**	.20	.37*

*$p < .05$; **$p < .01$, two-tailed.

Note: Copyright 1989, *Journal of Personality.* Reprinted by permission of Duke University Press, Durham, NC.

(1986) study all participants were women. By including both women and men, Eisenberg et al. were able to compare correlations for the two sexes.

As can be seen from Table 11.4, all of the "altruistic" personality variables correlated positively with helping, although there was some evidence of variability across sex. Most notably, scores on the Social Responsibility scale correlated significantly positively with helping for men ($r_{pb} = .35, p < .05$), but near zero for women ($r_{pb} = .02$); there was a similar but weaker pattern for the Perspective Taking scale. This pattern was reversed for the Ascription of Responsibility scale; it correlated significantly positively with helping for women ($r_{pb} = .40, p < .05$), and near zero for men ($r_{pb} = .09$). Finally, Eisenberg et al. reported finding no relation between birth order and helping.

Eisenberg et al. concluded that the positive correlations they found between their personality measures and helping provided evidence that there is indeed an altruistic personality. You may wonder what led them to this conclusion. After all, the positive correlations with helping simply indicate evidence of increased motivation to help; they say nothing about the nature of that motivation.

Eisenberg et al. justified their conclusion by asserting that participants in their study were all placed in a situation comparable to the easy-escape condition used by Toi and Batson (1982), described in chapter 8; their participants had no reason to expect future exposure to the Fultons' suffering if they chose not to help. In the Toi and Batson study, a positive relation between empathy and helping under easy escape was used to infer that empathy evoked altruistic motivation. So, reasoned Eisenberg et al., would not a positive correlation in their study also be evidence of altruistic motivation?

Was Escape Easy?   Unfortunately, there are three problems with the assumption of Eisenberg et al. (1989) that escape was easy in their study. First, recall that the type of escape at issue in the Toi and Batson study, which was designed to test the aversive-arousal reduction alternative to the empathy-altruism hypothesis, was escape from continued exposure to the stimulus causing empathic arousal. The type of escape at issue in testing for an altruistic personality is escape from anticipated shame and guilt. In some helping situations, especially ones like the shock situation used by Batson et al. (1986), in which the need is not stereotypic and helping is sufficiently costly that a failure to help can be easily justified, physical escape may be sufficient to permit escape from shame and guilt. In other helping situations, escape from exposure to the suffering victim may be easy, whereas escape from anticipated shame and guilt remains difficult, at least for some participants. This possibility seems especially likely in helping situations, such as the one used by Eisenberg et al., in which potential helpers are presented with a direct request and helping is relatively low cost. Concern about just such a possibility led to the introduction of justification for not helping manipulations in the research described in chapter 9, which tested for motivation to escape anticipated shame and guilt using relatively low-cost, direct-request helping.

Second, Eisenberg et al. found that three of their "altruistic" personality scales—Ascription of Responsibility, Perspective Taking, and Empathic Concern—were associated with social desirability (measured by the Marlowe–Crowne scale, Crowne & Marlowe, 1964; sample item: "Before voting, I thoroughly investigate the qualifications of all the candidates."); the correlations ranged from +.39 to +.50. Although partial correlation analyses provided no clear evidence that Social Desirability scores mediated the association between these personality scales and helping, the correlations with Social Desirability further highlight the possibility that individuals scoring high on these "altruistic" personality measures may be especially concerned with their positive social and self-image. This could make them more sensitive to any threat of anticipated shame and guilt, making escape for them more difficult.

Finally, recall that Eisenberg et al. had their participants complete the Davis Interpersonal Reactivity Index just before exposure to the need situation and opportunity to help. This procedure could easily have made salient to high scorers on the Empathic Concern scale their self-image as caring, sensitive individuals, making escape from shame and guilt even more difficult.

If high scorers on the "altruistic" personality measures in the Eisenberg et al. study actually found escape from shame and guilt relatively difficult, then the apparent contradiction between the results of their study and the results of the Batson et al. (1986) study disappears. Recall that under difficult escape Batson et al. found positive correlations with helping for self-esteem, ascription of responsibility, and dispositional empathy, and they found no association between helping and birth order. Eisenberg et al. did not measure self-esteem, but they too found positive correlations with helping for ascription of responsibility and dispositional empathy, and they reported no association between helping and birth order. For social responsibility, Batson et al. found a nonsignificant positive correlation when escape was difficult ($r = .18$); Eisenberg et al. found a very similar correlation ($r = .24$), but because their sample was larger, this correlation was reliably different from zero.

Conclusion

If escape from shame and guilt was actually difficult for at least some participants in the Eisenberg et al. study, then far from contradicting the Batson et al. results, their results provide a replication, adding further evidence that the motivation to help associated with these "altruistic" personality variables is actually egoistic. Unfortunately, because Eisenberg et al. did not manipulate ease of escape, we do not know with any confidence how difficult their participants perceived escape from shame and guilt to be.

Without a manipulation of ease of escape from anticipated shame and guilt, the Eisenberg et al. (1989) results can only tell us, once again, that various "altruistic" personality variables are associated with motivation to help. They do not reveal the nature of the underlying motivation; it might be altruistic, or it might be egoistic. More constructively, by including men as well as women in their sample, Eisenberg et al. found that sex differences may exist in the relation between "altruistic" personality variables and the motivation to help. Dyck, Batson, Oden, and Weeks (1989) pursued these sex differences in a study designed as a follow-up to the study by Batson et al. (1986).

A Third Look for Altruism in the Altruistic Personality: Hers and His (Dyck et al., 1989)

Dyck et al. (1989) continued the search for evidence that "altruistic" personality variables are associated not simply with increased helping but with altruistic motivation to help. Batson et al. (1986) had noted two limitations of their study: (a) they had not measured all of the personality variables claimed by various researchers to contribute to the altruistic personality, and (b) their sample included only women. Dyck et al. sought to address these limitations by examining the nature of the motivation to help associated with several additional "altruistic" personality measures, and to do so for both women and men.

New Measures of "Altruistic" Personality Dimensions

Self-Report Altruism Scale. In 1981, Rushton, Chrisjohn, and Fekken introduced a new measure of the "altruistic" personality, the Self-Report Altruism Scale (SRAS). This scale lists 20 everyday helping behaviors (e.g., "I have given money to a charity." "I have given directions to a stranger.") and asks respondents to indicate the frequency with which they have performed these behaviors (from "never" to "very often"). Rushton et al. claimed that the SRAS provides a more valid measure of an altruistic disposition than did earlier, more subjective questionnaires.

Kohlberg's Principled Morality. Both Staub (1974) and Rushton (1980) claimed that Kohlberg's principled morality (Kohlberg & Kramer, 1969) is an important component of the altruistic personality. Rest (1979, 1983) has developed a pencil and paper measure of Kohlberg's stage model of moral development, the Defining Issues Test (DIT). The DIT presents six moral dilemmas, each followed by 12 statements expressing considerations reflecting different levels of moral reasoning. For example, one dilemma on the DIT is Kohlberg's classic, "Heinz and the Drug":

> In Europe, a woman was near death from a special kind of cancer. There was one drug that the doctors thought might save her. It was a form of radium that a druggist in the same town had recently discovered. The drug was expensive to make, but the druggist was charging ten times what the drug cost him to make. He paid $200 for the radium and charged $2,000 for a small dose of the drug. The sick woman's husband, Heinz, went to everyone he knew to borrow the money, but he could only get together about $1,000, which is half of what it cost. He told the druggist that his wife was dying, and asked him to sell it cheaper or let him pay later. But the druggist said, "No, I discovered the drug and I'm going to make money from it." So Heinz got desperate and began to think about breaking into the man's store to steal the drug for his wife. (Rest, 1979, p. 8)

On the DIT, respondents are first asked to decide whether Heinz should steal the drug. Next, they read the 12 statements expressing possible considerations, such as: "Whether or not the community's laws are going to be upheld." "Would stealing in such a case bring about more total good for the whole society or not." Respondents rate how important each of the 12 considerations was in making their decision about the dilemma, then they rank order the four considerations that were most important. To score the DIT, these rankings are summed for each stage across dilemmas. Rest (1983) recommends using the DIT principled score (score for Stages 5, 5A, and 6 combined) to measure principled morality. Of the two illustrative considerations quoted above, the first is not principled; it is Stage 4 (Law and Duty to the Social Order). The second is principled; it is Stage 5A (Adherence to Societally Agreed Upon Principles for Social Order).

Gilligan's Caring Morality.   Carol Gilligan (1982) has criticized Kohlberg's model of moral development for being based exclusively on an ethic of justice in which individual rights and fairness are stressed. She argues that Kohlberg's model fails adequately to reflect women's moral development, which is more often based on an ethic of care and interdependence. Dyck et al. (1989) wished to include measures of Gilligan's caring morality in their study but could find no established measure, so they created several.

Gilligan (1982, pp. 73–74) had identified three different caring perspectives that she claimed form a developmental sequence:

1. *Self-Concern.* Development of caring morality begins with an exclusive focus on caring for oneself. Operating with this first perspective, moral decisions are based solely on what is good for the decider. Gilligan saw this perspective as selfish.

2. *Other-Concern.* A second perspective focuses on caring for others, to the exclusion of self. Moral decisions are based on what is best for the other. Gilligan saw this as the stereotypic feminine or maternal moral perspective.

3. *Mutuality.* A third perspective focuses on the mutual interdependence of people and caring for both self and others. Moral decisions are based on what is best for everyone involved. Gilligan saw this as a more mature perspective than exclusive other-concern; it involves a reconciliation of femininity and adulthood so that the criterion for judgment shifts from goodness to truth and honesty. "Care becomes the self-chosen principle of a judgment that remains psychological in its concern with relationships and response but becomes universal in its condemnation of exploitation and hurt" (p. 74).

To create a measure of Gilligan's caring morality, Dyck et al. added a page after each of the six moral dilemmas and 12 considerations on the DIT. The page contained six more considerations, two reflecting each of Gilligan's three perspectives. For example, considerations for the Heinz dilemma included: "Whether he will feel lonely when his wife dies" (Self-Concern). "Whether Heinz would be hurting the druggist if he stole the drug" (Other-Concern). "Whether Heinz has tried to work out a compromise with the druggist" (Mutuality). Respondents rated the importance of each consideration for their decision about the dilemma; they then ranked the two considerations that were most important. As with the DIT, these rankings were summed, producing a score for each of the three perspectives.

Justice Versus Caring Perspectives. To provide another measure of Kohlberg's justice and Gilligan's caring morality, a two-item rating form was created by adapting one developed by Ford and Lowery (1986). On this form, which was attached at the end of the DIT, respondents rated on seven-point scales how much they used a Justice and a Caring perspective when making their decisions regarding the dilemmas on the DIT. Description of the *Justice perspective* read: "One way to approach thinking about a social problem is to see yourself in a *process of judging.* This includes *standing back* from the problem at hand to consider the most *fair* way to resolve the dilemma. . . . You seek what is *most just* by considering the *rights of all involved*" (Dyck et al., 1989, p. 9). Description of the *Caring perspective* read: "One way to approach thinking about a social problem is to see yourself involved *in relationship* with others. This means you have certain *responsibilities* to be *concerned for others* and to consider how what you do will *help or hurt* those involved . . . You seek a way to *respond* that will minimize the hurt to all involved" (Dyck et al., 1989, pp. 9–10). As had been true for Ford and Lowery's description of the Caring perspective, this description seemed to have more the flavor of Gilligan's other-concern perspective than of her mutuality perspective.

Procedure

To assess the correlations of these new "altruistic" personality measures with helping under easy and difficult escape, Dyck et al. (1989) employed the same need situation, helping response, and escape manipulation used by Batson et al. (1986), except that they used the male victim (Charlie) for male participants. As before, several weeks prior to the experimental session, participants took part in a questionnaire session in which they completed the personality measures and provided birth order information. In the experimental session, they were given a chance to help by taking the other participant's place, receiving the shocks in his or her stead. In the difficult-escape condition, participants expected that if they decided not to help, they would continue watching the other participant receive shocks. In the easy-escape condition, they did not expect to continue watching. The help opportunity was again presented over an audio intercom.

Results

Relation of Personality Measures to Helping. As before, to determine the nature of the prosocial motivation associated with the personality measures, it was necessary to look at the correlations between each measure and helping under easy and difficult escape separately. If a personality measure was associated with egoistic motivation, then it should correlate positively with helping in the difficult-escape condition, but not in the easy. If a personality measure was associated with altruistic motivation, then it should correlate at least as positively with helping in the easy-escape condition.

These correlations appear in Table 11.5. Overall, there were no significant correlations for any of the moral judgment measures. There was a weak positive correlation between the SRAS and helping in the easy-escape condition; this correlation was significant under difficult escape, suggesting that participants who reported being more "altruistic" on the SRAS helped out of an egoistic desire to maintain their helpful self-image. Birth order was significantly positively correlated with helping in both escape conditions. This finding only partially replicated the Batson et al. (1986) results for birth order; they had found a positive correlation under easy escape and no reliable association under difficult escape. The major difference between the two studies was that all participants in the earlier study were women.

A Closer Look at Gender Differences. Because Dyck et al. included men as well as women in their study, it is possible to take a closer look at the

TABLE 11.5

Point-Biseral Correlations Between Personality Measures and Helping
When Escape Is Easy or Difficult (Dyck et al., 1989)

Personality Measure	Ease of Escape Without Helping			
	Easy		Difficult	
Self-Report Altruism Scale	.20	(46)[a]	.33*	(47)
DIT principled score	.14	(37)	.10	(39)
Gilligan perspectives				
Self-concern	−.21	(39)	−.21	(36)
Other-concern	.19	(39)	−.03	(36)
Mutuality	.01	(39)	.20	(36)
Justice perspective	.03	(39)	.05	(41)
Caring perspective	.14	(39)	.08	(41)
Birth order	.30*	(46)	.35*	(47)

[a]Number of participants on which each correlation is based is reported in parentheses.
*$p < .05$; **$p < .001$.

correlations, examining gender differences. Doing so reveals evidence that sex-role expectations may be important in understanding the nature of the motivation to help associated with "altruistic" personality measures, especially the moral judgment measures. Table 11.6 presents the correlations for women.

For women, the pattern of helping associated with the DIT, a measure of Kohlberg's principled morality criticized by Gilligan as being more sensitive to men's moral ideals than to women's, appeared potentially altruistic, whereas the pattern associated with a measure of Gilligan's caring perspective (Ford & Lowery-based measure), considered more stereotypic of the

TABLE 11.6

Point-Biseral Correlations Between Personality Measures and Helping
When Escape Is Easy or Difficult—Women Only (Dyck et al., 1989)

Personality Measure	Ease of Escape Without Helping			
	Easy		Difficult	
Self-Report Altruism Scale	.07	(30)[a]	.49**	(25)
DIT principled score	.27	(24)	−.13	(24)
Gilligan perspectives				
Self-concern	−.22	(25)	.08	(24)
Other-concern	.07	(25)	−.05	(24)
Mutuality	.15	(25)	−.03	(24)
Justice perspective	.11	(25)	−.02	(24)
Caring perspective	.11	(25)	.24	(24)
Birth order	.35*	(30)	.20	(25)

[a]Number of participants on which each correlation is based is reported in parentheses.
*$p < .05$; **$p < .001$.

feminine ideal, appeared, if anything, egoistic. The pattern of helping associated with the SRAS, a self-report measure of readiness to help by, for example, contributing to charity or aiding a friend—acts more consistent with the female sex-role (Eagly & Crowley, 1986)—also appeared egoistic. These results suggest that on female sex-role congruent measures, high scores by women may not be associated with altruistic motivation so much as with an egoistic desire to conform to the female sex-role ideal. High scores on Kohlberg's principled morality (measured by the DIT), a female sex-role incongruent measure, may be associated with altruistic motivation.

Table 11.7 presents the correlations for men. As can be seen, the pattern for men was quite different. There was evidence from both the DIT-based Other-Concern measure and the Ford & Lowery-based Caring measure that higher scores on Gilligan's caring perspective (stereotypically feminine) might be associated with altruistic motivation for men, whereas higher scores on Kohlberg's principled morality (stereotypically masculine) and the DIT-based Mutuality perspective (more androgynous?) appeared to be associated with egoistic motivation. The pattern of helping associated with scores on the more stereotypically feminine SRAS also appeared altruistic.

In general, then, measures of forms of morality considered to be the stereotypic ideal for one sex seemed, if anything, to be associated with *egoistic* motivation to help for that sex, but with potentially *altruistic* motivation for the other sex. Dyck et al. (1989) sought to explain this unexpected but intriguing pattern by suggesting that high scores on sex-role congruent measures of "altruism" might reflect an egoistic desire to present oneself as appropriately moral, as a good girl or good boy. On the other hand, high scores on the sex-role incongruent measures, less subject to contamination by

TABLE 11.7

Point-Biseral Correlations Between Personality Measures and Helping
When Escape Is Easy or Difficult—Men Only (Dyck et al., 1989)

	Ease of Escape Without Helping			
Personality Measure	Easy		Difficult	
Self-Report Altruism Scale	.46*	(16)[a]	.11	(22)
DIT principled score	.05	(13)	.41	(15)
Gilligan perspectives				
Self-concern	−.24	(14)	−.85***	(12)
Other-concern	.39	(14)	−.02	(12)
Mutuality	−.23	(14)	.53*	(12)
Justice perspective	.00	(14)	.15	(17)
Caring perspective	.35	(14)	−.05	(17)
Birth order	.26	(16)	.52**	(22)

[a]Number of participants on which each correlation is based is reported in parentheses.
*$p < .05$; **$p < .01$; ***$p < .001$.

self-presentation concerns (Jones & Pittman, 1982), might tap a truly altruistic personality.

Dyck et al. cautioned against considering this post hoc interpretation conclusive, however, for three reasons. First, the observed in-role versus out-of-role gender differences were not predicted. Second, several of the measures they used—especially the ones used to measure Gilligan's moral perspectives—were of uncertain reliability and validity. Third, their samples were small, and in some cases the correlations on which the post hoc interpretation was based only approached statistical significance.

Conclusion

Even with these cautions in mind, the consistency of the pattern of correlations remains impressive. It raises a hypothesis that seems worth pursuing in future research: Personality assessment instruments designed to measure altruistic motives stereotypic for one gender may actually measure egoistic motives for that gender but altruistic motives for the other gender. "Her" altruistic personality may be more clearly revealed by what shows through on measures of "his" morality, and vice versa.

An Alternative Interpretation: Upholding Moral Principles

The results of the Dyck et al. study are also consistent with a quite different interpretation. Rather than the pattern of correlations for sex-role incongruent measures reflecting altruistic motivation with the ultimate goal of benefiting the person in need, this pattern may reflect motivation with the nonpersonal ultimate goal of upholding one's moral principles. Although one might uphold moral principles as an instrumental goal on the way to the egoistic ultimate goal of avoiding guilt, one also might uphold them as an end in themselves. If one comes to value a moral principle like justice or caring in its own right, then one may be motivated to rectify any situation that violates this principle. Relieving a victim's suffering may be an instrumental goal on the way to this ultimate goal. If so, then, as suggested in chapter 1, the motivation is neither egoistic nor altruistic; it is of a third, impersonal type. Pursuit of the impersonal goal of upholding moral principles should produce the same pattern of correlations in easy- and difficult-escape conditions as the pattern predicted for altruistic motivation.

This alternative interpretation of the apparent evidence for altruism in the Dyck et al. study receives some anecdotal support from the reasons for helping Jews in Nazi Europe offered by Oliner and Oliner's rescuers. A rereading of the list of reasons presented at the beginning of this chapter reveals frequent reference to the desire to uphold moral principles.

Because of this possible alternative interpretation, it would be premature to conclude that the Dyck et al. (1989) results provide clear evidence, even on cross-sex measures, of altruism in the altruistic personality. Their results do suggest that the motivation to help associated with these cross-sex measures is not directed toward the egoistic goal of avoiding shame and guilt. Further research is needed to determine whether the underlying motivation is truly altruistic, or is instead directed toward the impersonal goal of upholding moral principles. At this point, it remains possible that those scoring high on cross-sex measures of the "altruistic" personality have taken to heart Kant's (1785/1889) admonition that we should love our neighbor as ourself "not from inclination, but from duty" (Section 1, paragraph 12).

GENERAL CONCLUSION

What conclusion should we draw concerning "altruistic" personality dimensions as a source of altruistic motivation? Probably the only conclusion to be drawn at this point is that no conclusion can be drawn.

In part, this is because very little research sheds any real light on the question. It is also because what research there is highlights two major measurement difficulties. First, measures of "altruistic" personality dimensions involve having individuals self-report the degree to which they possess highly desirable attributes—self-esteem, social and personal responsibility, sensitivity to the point of view of others, concern and compassion for people in need, helpfulness in a variety of settings, moral principles affirming justice or caring, and so on. It is possible, of course, that at least some of these self-reports are veridical. It is also possible—indeed it seems quite likely—that some of the self-reports say more about how different respondents see themselves or want to be seen by others than about how they actually are.

To have an "altruistic" self-image or public persona is dramatically different from actually possessing altruistic attributes. An "altruistic" image may be associated with increased helping that is directed toward the egoistic goal of avoiding shame and guilt for failing to live up to the "altruistic" standard, either in one's own eyes or the eyes of others.

Indeed, for women, we have seen a pattern of correlations across easy- and difficult-escape conditions that suggests this kind of egoistic motivation does underlie helping associated with scores on five different "altruistic" personality measures: self-esteem, ascription of responsibility, dispositional empathic concern, self-reported altruism, and endorsement of a caring perspective (Ford & Lowery-based measure). For women, the only variables that produced the pattern of correlations suggesting altruistic motivation were birth order (the motivation of first-borns seemed clearly egoistic; that of later-borns seemed potentially altruistic) and the DIT principled score, a measure of the degree to which the individual considers a universal principle of justice important in thinking about moral dilemmas.

The pattern of correlations looked very different for men. For them, the pattern suggested that the motivation associated with birth order (i.e., being later born) and the DIT principled score was egoistic. Three measures that had produced patterns suggesting egoistic motivation for women produced patterns suggesting possible altruistic motivation for men: self-reported altruism and both measures of Gilligan's other-oriented, caring perspective.

These sex differences highlight a second measurement problem that compounds the first. The desirability of different "altruistic" personality attributes may vary with self and social definition. Precisely those measures that are designed to tap what would seem to be the most important moral dimensions for a given individual or social group are the measures most likely to be contaminated with self-presentation for that individual or group. Self-report measures of value-laden "altruistic" attributes should not be taken at face value.

Unfortunately, taking such measures at face value is a wide-spread practice in the research claiming to provide evidence of an altruistic personality. How can we get beyond this practice? One possibility is suggested by the evidence that scores on some counter-normative measure of the "altruistic" personality—Kohlberg's justice principle for women, Gilligan's caring principle for men—may be more diagnostic of a genuine altruistic disposition. This is, however, not a very satisfactory solution. What is really needed are less contaminated measures of the "altruistic" attributes that are central for a given individual or social class. To the best of my knowledge, no such measures exist at this time.

In addition to these measurement problems, conceptual ambiguities remain. There is still considerable fuzziness in our thinking about various "altruistic" personality variables and how they relate to one another. There is also the major alternative explanation for the pattern of correlations across an ease-of-escape manipulation predicted if the underlying motivation is altruistic: The pattern could be due to an impersonal motive to uphold moral or ethical principles. To test this alternative explanation against the altruistic hypothesis will require different research designs from those used in the studies reviewed in this chapter. It will require designs that can disentangle acting to uphold the principle from acting to relieve the person's need. For a justice principle, this might be done by having a person justly in need; for a caring principle, disentanglement seems more difficult.

Clearly, more work is needed before we have a persuasive answer to the question of whether there is any real altruism in the altruistic personality. To date, we have evidence that several "altruistic" personality variables are associated with increased helping. We also have some evidence that the motivation behind the helping associated with most of these variables is egoistic rather than altruistic. We may, however, have found this evidence of egoism because our measures of these personality variables have not really tapped the altruistic dispositions as much as they have tapped the desire to project an "altruistic" social or self-image. If we can overcome our measurement problems, we may find that there is indeed some altruism in the altruistic personality.

It is clear that some people—the rescuers of Jews in Nazi Europe, Mother Teresa, Albert Schweitzer—are more helpful than others. As yet, we do not know whether the helpfulness is, in any degree, the result of personality attributes evoking altruistic motivation. This important and challenging research question awaits a clear answer. We know even less about the other possible sources of altruistic motivation mentioned at the beginning of the chapter. Clearly, far more research is needed before we know the scope of our altruistic potential.

CHAPTER 12

Implications and Limitations of the Empathy-Altruism Hypothesis

Returning to the most persuasively documented source of altruistic motivation—empathic feelings for a person in need—this final chapter begins to explore the implications if the empathy-altruism hypothesis is true. As noted at the end of chapter 10, we do not yet have sufficient evidence to be fully confident that empathy evokes altruistic motivation. Indeed, the empirical nature of the altruism question prevents ever claiming full confidence. The possibility always exists that there is some as yet unconsidered nonaltruistic explanation for all of the evidence supporting the empathy-altruism hypothesis reviewed in chapters 8–10. As the quantity and diversity of supporting evidence increases, and as more and more seemingly plausible egoistic explanations for the empathy–helping relationship prove inadequate, the likelihood of finding a satisfactory nonaltruistic explanation becomes smaller and smaller. Yet it can never be completely ruled out.

This caution notwithstanding, it seems only prudent to look up from the trail of empirical evidence, note where this trail seems to be leading, and consider what it means. What are the implications if we are capable of acting with an ultimate goal of increasing another person's welfare, if the potential to be altruistically motivated is part of human nature? Specifically, what are the implications if empathic feelings for a person in need evoke altruistic motivation to maintain or increase that person's welfare, as the empathy-altruism hypothesis claims?

There are both theoretical and practical implications if the empathy-altruism hypothesis is true, and both merit consideration. At the same time, there are also limitations, and these need to be considered as well. Rather than joyously proclaiming the dawning of yet another Age of Aquarius, with "harmony and understanding, sympathy and trust abounding," we need to take a hard look at the benefits that can and cannot be expected from tapping our apparent altruistic potential.

THEORETICAL IMPLICATIONS OF THE EMPATHY-ALTRUISM HYPOTHESIS

Looking Again at Our Theories of Personal Motivation and Social Interaction

No one doubts that humans are highly social creatures. Virtually all of our thoughts and actions are directed toward or are responses to other people. Moreover, our thoughts and actions are often directed toward helping one another. Yet to what end? The near unanimous consensus among psychologists has long been that in our interactions with others we do not really care about them; the real target of our concern is always, exclusively ourselves. We value others instrumentally, caring for their welfare only to the degree that it affects ours. Our behavior may be highly social; our thoughts may be highly social; but in our hearts, we live alone. We are highly social egoists.

Contemporary Views of Personal Motivation and Social Interaction

In contemporary personality and social psychology, egoism is the implicit if not explicit foundation for virtually every attempt to understand why we think and act as we do. It is implicit in the profusion of *self theories* that flowered during the "me generation" of the 1970s and 1980s. These self theories include self-awareness (Duval & Wicklund, 1972; Wicklund, 1975), self-monitoring (Snyder, 1979), self-presentation (Jones & Pittman, 1982; Schlenker, 1980), self-handicapping (Berglas & Jones, 1978), self-deception (Sackeim & Gur, 1985), self-evaluation maintenance (Tesser, 1988), symbolic self-completion (Wicklund & Gollwitzer, 1982), self-affirmation (Steele & Liu, 1983), self-discrepancy (Higgins, 1987), self-expansion (Aron & Aron, 1986), and various self-esteem theories (Bowerman, 1978; Snyder, Higgins, & Stuckey, 1983; Wills, 1981). Each of these theories assumes motivation with an ultimate goal of maintaining or enhancing one's self-image; social encounters are essential, but only as the instrumental means to reach this self-serving end.

Even our explicitly *social theories* of interpersonal relations—including long-term close relationships—seem invariably to be built on the assumption that we are, at heart, only out for ourselves. The driving force in social comparison theory (Festinger, 1954) is evaluation of our own opinions and abilities. The motivational premise of social exchange (Homans, 1961) and equity (Adams, 1965; Walster, Berscheid, & Walster, 1973) theories is, as Walster et al. pointed out, that "Man is selfish" (p. 151). Interdependence models (Berscheid, 1983; Kelley, 1979) focus on the way each partner in a relationship depends on the other in order to meet his or her own needs, or on situations in which Partner A benefits Partner B because having B's needs met is personally rewarding to A. Social dilemmas are typically posed as conflicts in which my immediate interests conflict with my long-range interests, or my opportunity to gain material rewards conflicts with my opportunity to gain social or self-rewards (Beggan, Messick, & Allison, 1988; Dawes, 1980; Hardin, 1968). Rarely is the possibility even entertained that the conflict is between wanting to meet my own needs and wanting to meet others' needs (but see Orbell, van de Kragt, & Dawes, 1988).

The concept of a communal as opposed to exchange relationship, a concept developed by Clark and Mills (1979) that at first glance seems to imply altruistic concern for the partner's welfare, on closer inspection appears to be yet another subtle expression of egoism. Clark and her colleagues have stated that in a communal relationship "members benefit one another in response to [the other's] needs" and that there is "a greater desire to meet the other's needs" (Williamson & Clark, 1989, p. 722). These statements certainly seem to suggest that in communal relationships we are concerned about not only our own but also our partner's welfare. Yet is the partner's welfare an ultimate or an instrumental goal? Clark and her colleagues have not been entirely clear on this point, but they imply that even in communal relationships concern for our partner's welfare is instrumental to enhancing our own welfare. The feature that distinguishes a communal from an exchange relationship is said to be a different set of rules: In communal relationships we are bound by a "norm of mutual responsiveness" (Clark & Mills, 1979, p. 13; also see Williamson & Clark, 1989). And why do we comply with rules or norms? Presumably, because we feel good when we do (Williamson & Clark, 1989) and fear external or internal sanctions when we do not (Schwartz & Howard, 1984). Even in the concept of a communal relationship, then, it all seems to come back to looking out for "Number One."

As a general statement, Donald Campbell's (1975) assessment seems as apt today as it was at the time of his 1975 Presidential Address to the American Psychological Association: "Psychology and psychiatry . . . not only describe man as selfishly motivated, but implicitly or explicitly teach that he ought to be so" (p. 1104). Contemporary personality and social psychology implicitly accepts the view of human nature inherited from its functionalist, psychoanalytic, and behaviorist ancestors. We may be social in thought and action, but in motivation we are capable of caring only for ourselves.

Need for a New Look

If the empathy-altruism hypothesis is true, then we need to take a new look at personal motivation and social interaction. For then, the egoist assumption that underlies all of these contemporary self and social theories is wrong. If we are capable of being altruistically motivated, then we can care about others' welfare as an ultimate not just an instrumental goal; we can seek their welfare for their sakes and not simply for our own. If this is true, then our range of personal motives is broader than we have thought. We are more social creatures than our psychological theories, including our most social social-psychological theories, would lead us to believe.

It is not that the existing theories are wrong in what they affirm; it is that they are seriously incomplete. There is part of our nature and potential that they ignore. We need a new, broader look at personal motivation and at social interaction, a look that takes account of our capacity to be altruistically as well as egoistically motivated.

Limits on the Theoretical Significance of Altruism

How General is the Empathy-Altruism Relationship?

Before we begin construction of elaborate new theories, however, it is only prudent to ask how serious the omission of altruistic motivation from our current theories really is. Looking back over the research conducted to test the empathy-altruism hypothesis, the omission may seem minor. Clear evidence for the existence of altruism has come to light only through a concerted search in a rather remote corner of human experience—elaborately contrived laboratory experiments in which college undergraduates are confronted with someone in apparent need under conditions systematically varied to permit inference about the ultimate goal of helping. If these are the only conditions under which empathy evokes altruistic motivation, then the failure of current psychological theory to take account of this motivation is of little import.

There is, however, no reason to think that just because evidence for altruism has been clearly observed only in the laboratory, altruism exists only there, any more than there is reason to believe that just because evidence for the swarm of subatomic particles has been clearly observed only under highly artificial laboratory conditions, these particles exist only there. Recall that the research designed to test the empathy-altruism hypothesis is cast in a Galilean not an Aristotelian mold (see chapter 5); it is designed to test a hypothesized relation between genotypic psychological constructs—empathic emotion and altruistic motivation—not to discover the prevalence of some phenotypic empirical phenomena, such as the amounts of empathy and helping evoked by seeing an undergraduate react badly to electric shocks.

As is characteristic of Galilean science, the hypothesized relation between empathic emotion and altruistic motivation is assumed universal. Whenever and to the extent that empathic emotion is felt, altruistic motivation is hypothesized to follow. This universality makes it appropriate to test the empathy-altruism hypothesis in contrived laboratory situations. The empathy-altruism relation should occur anywhere and everywhere, including the laboratory.

Our reason for retreating to the laboratory to look for the empathy-altruism relation was the same as Galileo's reason for retreating to the laboratory to study acceleration of falling bodies. The relation may not be detectable in less controlled situations, due to the presence of other factors and the absence of necessary comparison conditions. In the laboratory one can gain sufficient control over extraneous variables and make relevant comparisons so that underlying relations can be seen.

Only if there is some good reason to believe that the select sample of humans we have been studying is qualitatively different from the rest of humanity in their capacity to experience empathy or in the relationship of empathic emotion to altruistic motivation, which seems unlikely, need we worry. Generality is provided by the theory being tested, not by the samples or situations in which the testing takes place. How general is the empathy-altruism relationship? Until we have evidence to the contrary, it is appropriate to assume that it is universal.

Relative Importance of Egoistic and Altruistic Motives: Parsimony Lost

To persist, however, even if the empathy-altruism relation is accepted as universal, how important is it? As noted in chapter 6, conditions that evoke empathy and hence altruistic motivation are likely to evoke egoistic motives as well. Is not the force of the altruistic motivation likely to be trivial compared to the force of the egoistic motives, much as the gravitational force on a leaf is trivial as it is blown high into the sky on an autumn afternoon? This question has both theoretical and practical implications. We consider the latter in a moment; for now, let us focus on the former.

Just as for gravity, the most important point about altruistic motivation is its existence, regardless of whether we can detect its effect in a given situation. Although not apparent, the weak force of gravity is still acting on the high-flying leaf, just as this "weak" force keeps the earth in orbit. Knowing this, our understanding of the effect of one physical object on another is altered. Similarly, if altruistic motivation exists, then our understanding of human motivation and human nature is altered. If we are capable of adopting another person's welfare as an ultimate goal, then we are more social than we have imagined. This remains true even if in a given situation the force of altruistic motives is totally obscured by other, more powerful motives.

In addition, once we conclude that altruistic motivation exists, parsimony is no longer on the side of egoism. This has important theoretical consequences. As noted in chapter 1, when we help others it is typically not at all clear what our motives are. A mother rushes across the playground to comfort her child, who has fallen and skinned a knee. A middle-aged man tearfully decides to acquiesce to the quiet plea of his cancer-riddled mother and have the life-supports turned off. You sit up all night comforting a friend who has lost a job or a relationship. A friend contributes money to help famine victims in Africa, or to save whales. In each of these cases, and virtually any other case in which we help, we can think of possible egoistic motives to explain why we helped. The empirical evidence is equivocal.

As long as we lack clear evidence that altruistic motives exist, the logic of the problem is as depicted in the left-hand side of Fig. 12.1. There are some cases of helping where the motivation is clearly egoistic; there are a large number of cases where the motivation might be egoistic, altruistic, or both. All of the cases can be explained in terms of egoistic motives, and only some

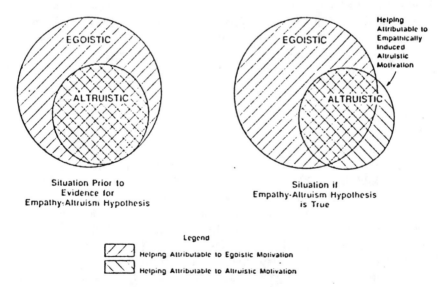

Situation Prior to
Evidence for
Empathy-Altruism Hypothesis

Situation if
Empathy-Altruism Hypothesis
is True

Legend

Helping Attributable to Egoistic Motivation

Helping Attributable to Altruistic Motivation

FIG. 12.1 Logical relation of egoistic and altruistic explanations of why we help others.

can be explained in terms of altruistic motives. Under these circumstances, parsimony clearly favors an exclusively egoistic explanation, and the prudent inference is to accept universal egoism.

If, however, the empirical tests of the empathy-altruism hypothesis lead us to conclude that empathic emotion evokes altruistic motivation—that there are some cases of helping in which the motivation is at least in part clearly altruistic and not egoistic—then the situation is changed. Then it is as depicted in the right-hand side of Fig. 12.1. To have only a small part of the altruistic circle lie outside the egoistic circle may seem like a minor change, but it has major implications. Now we must accept the existence of both egoistic and altruistic motives, and parsimony becomes irrelevant. There is no longer any logical reason to favor an egoistic interpretation of those cases in which the motivation might be egoistic, altruistic, or both. Prudence no longer gives egoism exclusive credit for the large area of overlap of the two explanations. Rather, this area becomes disputed territory, with both egoism and altruism having legitimate claims.

It is, of course, possible that in the research to date we have marched the entire width and breadth of the altruistic domain. Perhaps altruistic motivation is limited to situations in which one person feels empathy for another, and all of the overlapping area in the right-hand side of Fig. 12.1 is the exclusive province of egoism. Perhaps, but there is no a priori reason to assume this.

With parsimony lost, other possible sources of altruistic motivation need to be given careful consideration, just as we have done for empathy. Often, no doubt, it will be found that disputed territory belongs to the egoistic domain, as we found in the preceding chapter may be true for much of the helping associated with "altruistic" personality variables. Still, for each possible source of altruism, we need to look and see. As long as parsimony clearly favored universal egoism, there was no compelling reason to take claims of altruism seriously. Now there is.

The Domain of the Empathy-Altruism Hypothesis

In addition to considering other possible sources of altruism, we also need to explore more fully the uniquely altruistic territory that now exists. In the right-hand side of Fig. 12.1, the part of the altruistic circle that lies outside the egoistic circle is attributable to the empathy-altruism relationship. This is because the support for the empathy-altruism hypothesis is the only persuasive evidence we have at this time for the existence of altruistic motivation. Figure 12.1 depicts this part of the altruistic circle as relatively small; most of the altruistic circle still overlaps the egoistic one. At present, however, we really do not know the range and scope of empathic feelings, so we do not know how large the part of the altruistic circle that lies outside the egoistic circle is. We do not know how easy it is for us to become empathically aroused by another person's plight. Clearly, if empathy is a source—perhaps *the* source—of altruistic motivation, then we need careful and extensive investigation to find out.

Forces Limiting Empathy.   On reflection, there certainly seem to be strong forces working against the arousal of empathy. The three-path model in Fig. 6.1 identified perception of another person's need and adoption of that person's perspective as necessary conditions for the arousal of empathy. So, according to that model, the forces inhibiting arousal of empathy should include anything and everything that makes it difficult for us to attend to another person's need or adopt that person's perspective. These forces include (a) self-preoccupation or absorption in an ongoing task; (b) seeing the other as an object or "thing," as a statistic and not a person who cares about his or her own welfare; and (c) seeing the other as a person but as different from ourselves, as one of "them" not "us," as Black not White, male not female, Arab not Jew, Catholic not Protestant. Under the influence of such forces we may find ourselves, like Rousseau's (1782/1945) princess, responding to those who have no bread by coolly suggesting that they eat cake instead. As William James (1890) said, they "may be hanged for aught we care" (p. 318). The Holocaust reminds us how true these words can be.

Our Capacity for Empathy.   Yet, in spite of these pressures against empathy, we seem to have a remarkable capacity to respond empathically to the needs of others. In the experiments reviewed in chapters 8–10, simply exposing undergraduates facing no other pressing demands to a peer's suffering—a peer whom they had not seen before and need never see again—proved sufficient to evoke considerable empathy. And think about our capacity to feel for characters in novels, movies, and on TV. We may have known these characters only for minutes, and we know they are fictitious. Still, we find ourselves churning inside when they are in danger, yearning when they are in need, weeping over their losses and successes.

Some psychologists have suggested that our empathic emotions have a genetic base in the response of mammalian parents to their helpless offspring (e.g., Hoffman, 1981a; MacLean, 1973; McDougall, 1908). It may be true that we are especially likely to perceive the needs and adopt the perspective of offspring. If this is true, then it is apparently also true that we can cognitively "adopt" a wide range of non-kin, bringing them under our umbrella of empathic concern. Indeed, it seems that we often must take steps to avoid feeling empathy, whether for the homeless, those starving in Africa and Cambodia, or refugees from Central America. Lest we feel too much, we turn the corner, switch channels, flip the page, think of something else. This apparent necessity to defend ourselves against feeling empathy suggests the breadth of our susceptibility to empathic emotion and, as a result, to altruistic motivation.

Empathy in Other Mammalian Species: Compassionate Dogs?   The potential for empathy-induced altruism may even extend beyond the bounds of our species to at least some other mammals. We cannot at this point presume to know the nature of the underlying motivation, but the helpfulness of other species raises the altruism question, just as our own helpfulness does.

Elephants injured by a falling tree, weapon, or in a fight may be aided by other elephants, who cluster around and use their foreheads, trunks, and tusks to help it rise. Once on its feet, the injured elephant may be supported by others walking or running alongside. Why? Porpoises have been seen risking their lives to support a harpooned porpoise on the surface so that it can breathe. There are also reports of porpoises rescuing drowning humans in the same way. Why? Orphaned infant chimps have been adopted and reared by their adult brothers and sisters. Chimps in captivity have been observed pulling other chimps' hands back as they reach toward potential danger. Why? Such examples provide no answer, but they raise the question of whether members of some other species may be capable of empathic concern.

And why are dogs considered our best friends? Darwin (1872), himself a dog lover, was convinced that dogs are capable of a wide range of emotions, including pity and compassion (also see de Rivera, 1979). Certainly, examples of canine helpfulness are both numerous and dramatic. Betsy Weiderhold gave this account:

> One summer I lived alone with my dogs on a small island off the coast of Maine. I had made a trip to the mainland without them, and it was late at night; the fog and drizzle were thick as I motored out of the harbor. I tried following the lobster markers, but that became impossible as the sea swells grew larger. Finally, I could not see beyond the bow of the boat and I had to rely on my sense of direction, as there was no compass on the boat. Suddenly, I knew I had overshot the island. To collect my thoughts, I put the motor into neutral. By mistake, I hit the choke and the engine died! I tried to start the motor, but it would not cooperate. I tried again. I slumped down in my seat and dissolved into tears. My boat sloshed about, with water pouring over the sides. I then let out a frantic call for help.
>
> What makes animals sense danger or trouble long before human beings react? I am certain that by the time I cried out, Ursa was already in the water. From the rocks she plunged into that black, cold, angry water, with only her instincts to guide her. At first I heard her bark and thought she was on land, so I called her name over and over, trying to paddle the boat in her direction. Then my light caught her brown eyes riveted on me. As I reached over to help hold

her up to rest, she kept trying to grab my old canvas hat, which she always wanted to carry when I came back to the island from a jaunt. I frantically tied it to the painter, shoved it in her mouth, and yelled, "Let's go home, Ursa!" I gave the motor one more chance—and it caught!

Ursa swam ahead of my boat, just within the circle of my light, but the going was tedious. I became so discouraged when she finally refused to swim any further. Holding her tightly in my arms, crying into her wet, salty fur to tell her it was okay, I was struck on the side of the head by the big white mooring ball. No wonder she wouldn't swim anymore. Ursa had brought me home. (from Cohen & Taylor, 1989, p. 16)

It is possible, of course, that Ursa's behavior was driven by blind instinct, that it was not goal-directed at all. This is possible, but it seems unlikely. It is also possible that her behavior was motivated by a nascent egoistic concern that her major source of sustenance and affection was heading out to sea. This is possible, but a similar motive cannot easily account for the behavior of Red, described in the following newspaper story:

Mr. and Mrs. Bruce R. Morris of Harvester, Missouri, left their two-year-old daughter, Margaret, asleep in the car while they visited a dealer's showroom to look for a new car. Red, a stray Irish setter which the Morrises had adopted three weeks earlier, was also left in the car. The old car suddenly burst into flames, apparently as a result of faulty wiring. Red quickly jumped through the window to safety. Margaret, awakened by the smoke, stood up in the back seat, swinging her arms in fright. Mr. Morris, who witnessed the incident from the showroom reported, "As soon as Red hit the ground, he jumped up, put his paws on the side of the car and reached his head through the smoke coming out of the window." Red grabbed Margaret's coat collar with his teeth and dragged the little girl out of the window, then pushed her away from the car. Flames quickly engulfed the car. Margaret was taken to a hospital where she was treated for minor burns and released. Red suffered singed hair and a slight cut on his nose. (Batson, 1983, adapted from Associated Press story in Lawrence Journal-World, May 10, 1976)

Why did Red turn back to the car? It is possible, of course, that his behavior was just a fluke. This is possible. Yet is it too farfetched also to entertain the possibility that not only had the Morrises adopted Red into their family, but that Red had adopted them—that for him Margaret had cognitively become part of his family or pack and that as a result he felt empathic concern for her and was motivated to reduce her distress? If it is not too farfetched, then we need to extend the scope of our research on the empathy-altruism relation considerably. The domain of the empathy-altruism hypothesis may be much larger than we have imagined.

PRACTICAL IMPLICATIONS
OF THE EMPATHY-ALTRUISM HYPOTHESIS

Faced with empirical evidence for the existence of altruistic motivation evoked by empathy, and having some clues about the scope and power of our empathic feelings, and recognizing the possibility that even more of the motivation for helping that has been assumed to be egoistic might actually be altruistic, we are ready to turn to what Jean Piaget called, "the American question," the question of practical utility. If empathy-induced altruism exists, what is it good for? Before considering the practical promise of altruism, let us consider some practical problems.

Practical Problems with Empathy-Induced Altruism

It May Be Harmful to Your Health

Viewed from the perspective of personal survival and narrow self-interest, altruistic motivation is potentially dangerous. As the sociobiologists are fond of reminding us (e.g., Dawkins, 1976; Wilson, 1975), altruism may incline us to incur risks and costs in time and money that can be seriously damaging, even life threatening. When 28-year old Lenny Skutnik was asked why he dove into the ice-strewn Potomac River to rescue a drowning plane-crash victim, he said, "I just did what I had to do." We do not, of course, know the extent to which the motivation that impelled Skutnik's action was altruistic, but we do know that whatever motive made him have to leave the safety of his own car very nearly cost him his life.

Unfortunately, the outcome was worse for an elderly couple from Topeka, Kansas. As reported in my local newspaper the day after I wrote the preceding paragraph, the couple went to check on a neighbor's house because they had become concerned about her welfare. Inside, they found an armed burglar. He forced them into a car, drove them to a deserted area, and shot them dead.

Not only can altruism be dangerous for the person doing the helping, it can be harmful for the person receiving the help too. There is no reason to assume that altruistic motivation will always be accompanied by sensitivity and wisdom. Genuine concern for another's welfare may lead to provision of help that humiliates or suffocates the recipient. Balzac, one of our most astute observers of human nature, graphically portrayed this irony in his classic novel, *Pere Goriot* (1834/1962). Goriot's selfless love spoiled his daughters, drove them from him, and, ultimately, destroyed both them and him. Balzac's message: Altruism may be part of human nature, but it, like aggression, must be held carefully in check. It is potentially destructive.

Graham Hancock makes a similar point in his scathing indictment of international aid programs in *Lords of Poverty* (1989). He condemns the efforts of such esteemed agencies as the World Bank, UNICEF, UNESCO, the United Nations Development Organization, the United Nations Food and Agriculture Organization (F.A.O.), the European Development Fund, and A.I.D.

Many people would admit that the aid efforts of these organizations are less successful than one might wish. Hancock's attack is more fundamental; he claims that, even when motivated by genuine concern, international aid is nothing more than a transaction between bureaucrats and autocrats, in which corruption and self-defeating dependency are inevitable. To justify his attack, Hancock cites numerous examples, including the aid-financed dam in Guatemala that led to a 70% rise in residential electricity prices; the Sudanese sugar refinery turning out sugar sold in the Sudan at significantly higher prices than imported sugar; and the World Bank resettlement schemes in Brazil and Indonesia that have destroyed rain forests, contributed to the greenhouse effect, obliterated native cultures, and often left settlers poorer than before. Such examples are not the whole story about international aid, of course, but they are too numerous and too tragic not to sensitize us to inherent dangers in even the best-intentioned relief efforts.

Even when helping is clearly appropriate, empathy-induced altruism can at times make matters worse. This is especially true when the behavior needed to relieve a person's suffering requires a light and delicate touch. Think, for example, of the work of a surgeon. It is no accident, argues neurophysiologist Paul MacLean (1967), that surgeons are prohibited from operating on close kin or friends. The problem is not that they feel no empathic concern for these people; quite the opposite. They feel much empathy and presumably much altruistic motivation, too much. When operating on one's sister rather than "a patient," the high level of empathic concern and strong desire to benefit may cause a normally steady hand to shake. Empathy-induced altruistic motivation could cost the sister her life.

It May be Immoral

At a somewhat deeper level, how we answer the question of what altruism is good for depends in no small part on the moral status we accord to altruism. As pointed out several times in the preceding chapters, the existence of altruism is an empirical question, not a moral one. Still, how we feel about the existence of altruism is likely to be determined by our moral assumptions. There are a range of possibilities.

Some people may be delighted by the prospect that altruism exists; they may feel it offers hope for a more caring, humane society. For others, to learn that altruism is part of human nature may be a cause for concern rather than hope. Social commentators such as Freud (1930) and Konrad Lorenz (1966) consider the human potential for aggression to be a moral flaw in our nature;

other social commentators consider our potential for altruism to be a moral flaw as well.

Nietzsche and, more recently, Ayn Rand have stated the moral argument against altruism most forcefully. Their concern is not simply that unbridled altruism may backfire, doing more harm than good; they believe that altruism is a moral evil. Our altruistic impulses are the worst part of our natures; they erode our character and prevent us from realizing our true potential. Recall from chapter 2 that for Nietzsche (1888/1927) the "morality of unselfing" was a sign of weakness. Ayn Rand (1964) shared Nietzsche's belief in the degradation of the human spirit produced by altruism:

> Man must live for his own sake, neither sacrificing himself to others nor sacrificing others to himself. To live for his own sake means that *the achievement of his own happiness is man's highest moral purpose.* (p. 27)
>
> Altruism holds *death* as its ultimate goal and standard of value—and it is logical that renunciation, resignation, self-denial, and every other form of suffering, including self-destruction, are the virtues it advocates. And, logically, these are the only things that the practitioners of altruism have achieved and are achieving now. (p. 34)

Nietzsche's and Rand's critiques of altruism as immoral are, of course, based on their own beliefs about what are the highest human values: individual self-expression and power for Nietzsche; rationality, productivity, and self-esteem for Rand. To the extent that one accepts these values as the moral ideal, the assessment of altruism as immoral seems well founded.

Even if one adopts more egalitarian and collectivist values, believing that self-interest should be made subservient to the common good, there is reason to question the degree to which altruistic motivation evoked by empathic feelings is a force for good. To the extent that the common good is best served by the impartial allocation of resources such as is possible from John Rawls's (1971) "initial position of equality," empathy-induced altruism is a problem. Justice may be blind, but our empathic feelings clearly are not. We feel more sympathy and compassion for those close to us than for those who are more remote (Hume 1740/1896; Krebs, 1975). Hence, empathy-induced altruistic motivation is likely to promote favoritism and, thereby, injustice rather than justice. Think, for example, of the mother who, although she would advocate severe penalties for drug dealers, tearfully pleads with the judge to give her son, an admitted dealer, another chance. If justice is adopted as the highest moral principle, then this mother's act is immoral. Her plea is not for justice; it is for mercy.

Chilling testimony to the moral limits of empathy-induced altruism is offered by survivors of the death camps in Nazi Europe. In the camps, members of the underground could not save everyone. At times, they were faced with having to decide who would live and who would die. Survivors reported that empathic feelings interfered with making such decisions:

Compassion was seldom possible, self-pity never. Emotion not only blurred judgment and undermined decisiveness, it jeopardized the life of everyone in the underground. . . . Hard choices had to be made and not everyone was equal to the task, no one less than the kind of person whose goodness was most evident, most admired, but least available for action. . . . On no account could they be placed in situations where they had to take part in making decisions vital to the very existence of the camp. (Des Pres, 1976, pp. 153–154, quoting Kogon, 1953, p. 278)

Limits on the Needs Evoking Empathy

A third practical problem with empathy-induced altruism is that many of the pressing social problems we face today do not involve personal needs of the sort likely to evoke empathy. Our empathic feelings are usually felt for people, although we may also feel empathy for individualized members of other species, especially mammals. (Think of our feelings for our pets.) Yet many of today's needs, such as environmental protection, endangered species, energy conservation, nuclear disarmament, and population control, are global. They are not personalized needs of the sort that evoke empathy; they are broader and more abstract. It is hard to feel empathy for an abstract concept like the environment, world population, or the planet, although personalizing metaphors like "Mother Earth" may move us in that direction.

Not only is it hard to evoke empathy for these pressing global needs, many of these needs cannot be effectively addressed with a personal helping response. Issues like environmental protection, population control, and nuclear disarmament must be addressed, at least in part, in political arenas and through institutional and bureaucratic structures. The process is long and slow, not the sort for which emotion-based motivation, like empathy-induced altruism, is likely to be very effective.

The less personal, large-group nature of these global needs and of their possible remedies has led Garrett Hardin (1977) to question the usefulness of empathy-induced altruism as a potent force in addressing them:

Is pure altruism possible? Yes, of course it is—on a small scale, over the short term, in certain circumstances, and within small, intimate groups. In familylike groups one should be able to give with little thought "of nicely calculated less or more." But only the most naive hope to adhere to a noncalculating policy in a group that numbers in the thousands (or millions!), and in which many preexisting antagonisms are known and many more suspected. . . .

When those who have not appreciated the nature of large groups innocently call for "social policy institutions [to act] as agents of altruistic opportunities" they call for the impossible. In large groups social policy institutions necessarily must be guided by what I have called the Cardinal Rule of Policy: *Never ask a person to act against his own self-interest.* (pp. 26–27)

The only hope for dealing with issues like ecology, the greenhouse effect, and overpopulation is, Hardin concludes, a form of enlightened egoism based on heightened awareness of the long-term costs to self of actions that have short-term benefits.

A Fragile Flower, Easily Crushed

Not only do we have to worry about the preferential nature of empathic emotions and the limited scope of an empathy-induced altruism, but we must also question the stability of the altruistic motivation evoked by empathy. Recall that in the last study discussed in chapter 8 it was found that if the cost of helping was high (taking shocks that were "clearly painful but of course not harmful"), the motivation even of individuals who had previously reported high empathy for the person in need appeared to be egoistic. This finding led to the suggestion that concern for others is "a fragile flower, easily crushed by self-concern."

There seems little doubt that even if we have concern for others, we often do not act on it. It is overridden by other, more pressing concerns. Presumably, these self-concerns direct our attention away from a focus on the needs of the other person and toward our own needs, increasing feelings of personal distress relative to empathy and, hence, egoistic motivation relative to altruistic.

Of course, this is not all bad. Our lives would be decidedly awkward if we were only looking out for others' concerns and not our own. It would be, as one philosopher has suggested, like a community in which everyone tries to do each other's washing. No one's washing would get done.

The ease with which self-concerns can override altruistic concern for another is almost certainly a function of the strength of the altruistic motivation. In the study just mentioned, the potential helper and the person in need were undergraduate students who had never met; the empathic response was based on watching over closed-circuit TV as the person in need reacted with obvious discomfort to a series of electric shocks. With stronger emotional attachment between the helper and the person in need, the blossom of altruism may be less fragile. Think, for example, of a father's response at seeing his daughter toddling into the path of an oncoming car. Even though the situation involves considerable personal danger, the father's focus may well remain riveted on the child and her needs, with relatively little attention paid to the threat to his own life.

In summary, these four practical problems make it clear that altruistic motivation is not a panacea. Even if we consider selfless concern for the welfare of others to be morally good, which not everyone does, the range of people and problems that evoke empathy and, thereby, altruistic motivation is limited; altruistic motivation is not always adaptive; and altruistic concerns can be and often are overridden by self-concerns. These observations set bounds on what altruism is good for. Still, just as it would be wrong to try to bottle altruism as a patent medicine that is "good for whatever ails you," it would be wrong to conclude that it is good for nothing. Altruistic motivation is a potentially important psychological resource that, if harnessed and put to work, may yield important practical benefits.

The Promise of Empathy-Induced Altruism

More, and More Sensitive, Help

The most obvious practical benefit that empathy-induced altruistic motivation offers is increased help for individuals in need. The various egoistic motives for helping discussed in chapter 6 are certainly important in their own right, but often they are not enough. If we wish to build toward a more caring, humane society, one in which we are more responsive to one another's needs, then altruistic motivation is a key resource.

As already noted, altruistic motivation has no built-in failsafe; it can produce harm as well as benefit, and it is not likely to be useful in addressing all needs. Still, because it is directed toward the goal of enhancing the welfare of the person in need rather than one's own welfare, it is likely in many situations to motivate behavior that is more sensitive and responsive to the victim's need. The egoistic goals of gaining rewards and avoiding punishments can often be reached even if the help offered does not actually relieve that needy individual's suffering. "It's the thought that counts." But the altruistic goal is to have the needy individual's suffering relieved. For altruistic motivation, it's the result not the thought that counts.

In addition to producing more sensitive helping, altruistic motivation is also likely to be less fickle than egoistic motivation. Recall that in the experiments reviewed we found that individuals experiencing relatively low empathy and, hence, a relative predominance of egoistic over altruistic motives were far less likely to help when they could easily escape exposure to the victim's need without helping (chapter 8) or when they could easily justify to themselves and others a failure to help (chapter 9). The practical implications of these findings are more than a little troubling. Easy escape and high justification for not helping are common characteristics of many of the helping situations we face. In the booming, buzzing confusion of modern life, we can almost always find a way to direct our attention elsewhere or to convince ourselves that inaction is justified.

Given this, the practical potential of empathy-induced altruistic motivation looks promising indeed. In the experiments reviewed, individuals experiencing relatively high empathy showed no noticeable decrease in readiness to help even under conditions of easy escape and high justification.

Inhibition of Aggressive Behavior

A second promising practical implication of the empathy–altruism relation is the inhibition of aggression. To the degree that feeling empathy for someone evokes altruistic concern to maintain or increase that person's welfare, then feeling empathy should inhibit any inclination to aggress or harm that person. Empathic feelings should not, of course, be expected to inhibit all aggressive impulses, only those directed toward the target of empathy. Indeed, it is easy to imagine a situation in which empathy for Person A evokes increased aggression toward Person B, if B is perceived to be a threat to A's welfare.

Based on a meta-analysis, Miller and Eisenberg (1988) reported some support for the idea that empathy can inhibit aggression, although they admitted that the support is, as yet, rather limited and spotty. Assuming that future research will provide further support for this idea, some speculation about practical implications seems in order. How might we use the idea that empathy can inhibit aggression to address problems of intergroup conflict and hostility, such as conflicts among racial, ethnic, and religious groups, or conflicts among nations?

Using Personalizing Contact Via Superordinate Goals.   The empathy–altruism hypothesis suggests that a key strategy for counteracting intergroup tension and hostility may be to establish personalizing contact between members of the conflicting groups. *Personalizing contact* refers to interaction in which members of one group are led to deal with members of the other group on a personal, individual basis, not simply as one of "them." Such contact should encourage empathy for members of the outgroup in two ways. First, it should increase the likelihood of accurately perceiving the other's needs—his or her hopes and fears. Second, it should increase the likelihood of taking the other's perspective. As Fig. 6.1 indicates, these two conditions are assumed necessary and sufficient for the experience of empathy.

How can we create personalizing contact among individuals on opposite sides of a conflict? Obviously, it is not easy. More is required than simply bringing antagonists together; mere contact is likely to invite further hostility and aggression. The technique that has proved most effective in creating personalizing contact and thereby reducing intergroup conflict and hostility has been to introduce superordinate goals (Sherif, Harvey, White, Hood, & Sherif, 1961). *Superordinate goals* are ones that both parties in conflict want to reach but can reach only if they join forces and work together. Under these circumstances, potential antagonists find themselves in the same group, united in the effort to reach the common goal. Strange bedfellows, perhaps, but bedfellows nonetheless.

Think of the psychological consequences. To work together toward a common goal, members of one group must attend to and understand what members of the other group value, what the others want and need. Moreover, to coordinate efforts in pursuit of the goal, members of each group must attend to the perspective of members of the other group. The combined effect of these two consequences should be an increased likelihood of feeling empathy for members of the outgroup.

A classic demonstration of the effectiveness of superordinate goals in reducing intergroup conflict was provided by Sherif et al. (1961). In their Robber's Cave experiment, superordinate goals were used to eliminate the open hostility that had erupted between competing groups of 12- to 14-year-old boys at a summer camp. This experiment dramatically demonstrated the effectiveness of superordinate goals, but revealed little about why they work.

Racial Tension and Conflict in Educational Settings.   More relevant for our present concern, and more revealing of the underlying psychological process, is the use of superordinate goals in the Jigsaw Classroom. The Jigsaw Classroom is a learning technique developed by Elliot Aronson and his colleagues to try to overcome racial tension and animosity in desegregated schools (Aronson, Blaney, Stephan, Sikes, & Snapp, 1978). In such a classroom, students are placed in racially mixed groups (ideally, five to six students per group), and each group is given a learning task. Within a group, each member is given one, but only one, part of the information the group needs to complete the task. As a result, the group must rely on the contribution of each member to succeed.

Aronson et al. reported that liking for groupmates increased as a result of the jigsaw experience. Unfortunately, Aronson et al. did not report the effect specifically on interracial liking. In an earlier award-winning study, however, Weigel, Wiser, and Cook (1975) did report the effects of interdependent, ethnically mixed (White, Black, Mexican-American) student work groups on cross-ethnic liking, conflict, and helping. Results of that study indicated that working together in interdependent groups significantly increased both cross-ethnic liking and helping behavior, and it reduced cross-ethnic conflict (see also Johnson & Johnson, 1987).

Why does cooperative interaction in jigsaw groups increase liking and prosocial behavior? Aronson et al. (1978) believed that empathy is "one of the crucial mechanisms underlying the effects" (p. 118). Supporting this belief, Diane Bridgeman (1981), in a dissertation study under Aronson's direction, found that students from a jigsaw classroom were better at a perspective-taking task than were students from a traditional classroom. The task tested students' ability to adopt the perspective of characters in brief stories, seeing the story situation from the character's rather than their own point of view.

Importantly, results of this study indicated that the perspective-taking abilities learned in the jigsaw groups generalized to use in other situations as well.

International Tension and Conflict.   In international conflicts, the threat of mutual destruction, especially nuclear annihilation, introduces the fundamental superordinate goal of survival. Pursuit of this goal has led to a number of opportunities for personalizing contact between political leaders, at times with dramatic results—as in the agreement between Anwar Sadat and Manachem Begin forged at Camp David in September, 1978. Pursuit of the superordinate goal of economic success can also lead to personalizing contact, as in the formation of the European Economic Community.

Less dramatic examples of the use of personalizing contact to reduce international conflict include international exchange programs and international sporting events, such as the Olympics. These programs may help members of one group see members of the outgroup as persons like themselves, increasing the potential for empathic feeling.

Unfortunately, the superordinate goal in these international encounters is often too remote to have any effect; competition is more salient than cooperation. The empathy-altruism hypothesis suggests that these encounters would be more effective in reducing the potential for aggression if more immediate superordinate goals were introduced and the contact was designed to induce both awareness of the needs and adoption of the perspective of the other. For example, rather than national teams facing one another in international competition, as in the Olympics, it would be more effective to have competition between international teams, each composed of members from different nations. To share with a potential target of aggression "the thrill of victory and the agony of defeat" is likely to be more conducive to building a base for aggression-inhibiting empathy than is watching them rejoice at our defeat, or us rejoicing at theirs.

The aggression-inhibiting potential of personalized contact seems promising indeed. Still, there are limits. In some conflict situations the barriers of hostility are too high to make available superordinate goals effective. What common goals can we introduce between Arabs and Israelis, between Blacks and Afrikaans in South Africa, or between Protestants and Catholics in Northern Ireland? Doubtless, personalizing contacts do occur even in these situations. The shared tragedy of conflict can even become the occasion for mutual understanding and care between antagonists, as is said to have occurred between British and German soldiers who celebrated together in the trenches in France on Christmas Day, 1914. Without some common goal, however, these occasions are apt to be rare.

Abuse.   One form of aggression that empathy-induced altruism may be especially likely to inhibit is abuse, especially child and spouse abuse. It is a common observation made by those who study abusing parents that these parents seem to lack attachment and empathy (Egeland & Sroufe, 1981; Steele, 1980). Norma Feshbach (1987) summarized results of three studies that provide some empirical support for this observation. To cite but one, Frodi and Lamb (1980) found that, relative to nonabusers, abusive mothers displayed more physiological distress to a videotape of a crying infant and, unlike nonabusers, also displayed distress to a videotape of a smiling infant. Consistent with these physiological reactions, abusive mothers reported more annoyance and less sympathy than nonabusive mothers when observing the videotape of the crying infant.

It is also known that abused children are more likely to become abusing parents. Providing a possible clue to this perpetuation of child abuse across generations, Miller and Eisenberg (1988) found a relatively strong negative relation ($-.46, p < .001$) between *receipt* of abuse and children's expression of empathy for a suffering peer. In addition, Howes and Eldredge (1985) found that abused children were more likely than nonabused to respond to peers' distress with aggression. These findings suggest that training in perspective taking and recognition and acceptance of empathic feelings may be useful in combating abuse.

Derogation of Victims of Injustice.   Finally, in his classic work on the just-world hypothesis, Melvin Lerner found that research participants were likely to derogate a person whom they perceived to be an innocent victim of suffering (Lerner & Simmons, 1966). This derogation presumably served to maintain participants' belief that people get what they deserve and deserve what they get. Protecting our belief in a just world in this way can lead to what William Ryan (1971) has called *blaming the victim*. Ryan argues that we are likely to react to the victims of unjust discrimination and oppression in our society by unconsciously blaming them: If they have less, they must deserve less; that is, they must be less deserving. Ryan suggests that the prototypical victim blamer is the middle-class person who is fairly well off financially. By blaming the victims of poverty and social injustice, middle-class persons can reconcile their own relative advantage with their belief that the world is just.

Derogation and victim-blaming are all too well-known and chilling alternatives to caring about the suffering of others; these alternatives can lead to smug acceptance of the pain of others as just and right. Empathy-induced altruism may counteract this tendency. In an important follow-up to the study by Lerner and Simmons (1966), Aderman, Brehm, and Katz (1974) instructed some persons watching an innocent victim suffer to imagine how the victim was feeling. Aderman et al. found that these perspective-taking instructions, which we have seen used so often to evoke empathy, eliminated derogation of the innocent victim.

Improved Psychological and Physical Health

In the endless search in Western society for "The Good Life," attention has shifted in the past few decades from acquisition of possessions to gaining and maintaining psychological and physical health. Anything that makes me happier and more satisfied, that makes me feel better about myself, is good; anything that does not is bad. Anything that makes my body last longer and look better is good; anything that does not is bad. Many of us find ourselves engaged in a holy quest for what has variously been called self-acceptance, self-realization, self-determination, self-actualization, self-fulfillment, or simply, meaning in life. Our eating, drinking, smoking, and exercise habits have become highly sensitive to the latest word from the Office of the Surgeon General or the F.D.A.

Given this concern for personal health, it is not surprising that the potential benefits of empathy-induced altruism that are most likely to arouse interest are not the benefits for others—more, and more sensitive, help; less harm. The potential benefits most likely to arouse interest are the health benefits that accrue to the practitioner of altruism. There is growing evidence, rather uneven in quality, that empathy-induced altruism can indeed contribute to the altruist's psychological and even physical health.

For example, Allan Luks (1988), Executive Director of the Institute for the Advancement of Health in New York City, reported results of a survey of over 1,700 women involved regularly in helping others. Analogous to feelings experienced during and after vigorous exercise, many of these women reported feeling a "high" while helping—a sense of stimulation, warmth, and increased energy—and a "calm" afterward—a sense of relaxation, freedom from stress, and enhanced self-worth. Interestingly, these reports came only from those situations in which helping involved close personal contact with the person in need, not from anonymous donations of time and money, suggesting that empathy may be involved.

To explain these reports of the psychological and physical effects of helping, Luks quoted Harvard cardiologist Herbert Benson: "For millennia, people have been describing techniques on how to forget oneself, to experience decreased metabolic rates and blood pressure, heart rate, and other health benefits. Altruism works this way, just as do yoga, spirituality, and meditation" (p. 42). Reflecting on the results of this survey and other research, a group of biological and behavioral scientists headed by psychologist Neal Miller concluded that, "There is considerable evidence of various kinds to suggest that doing good may indeed be good for you. The probability that this is true is great enough . . . to justify research specifically aimed at determining the conditions that will maximize such an effect" (Luks, 1988, p. 42).

Anecdotal and self-report testimony to the meaning-providing elixir of altruism run the range from Dickens's classic fictional depiction of the happiness and self-fulfillment experienced by Ebenezer Scrooge after his transformation from stinginess to concern for others in "A Christmas Carol" (1843/1913), to the following words of an elderly widow who adopted a dog from her local Humane Society: "Six months a widow, I had found my empty home unbearable. Adopting Mandy was my answer, and I became her savior as well. . . . She was malnourished and dehydrated. The steadfast love and loyalty we have given each other has been a quiet joy unlike any other!" (Cohen & Taylor, 1989, p. 2).

There is even testimony that empathy-induced altruism may reduce the risk of heart disease. Dean Ornish (1989) reported that most heart patients he studied experienced emotional isolation, feeling apart from the world rather than a part of it. One of the strategies that Ornish found effective in alleviating this loneliness was to increase patients' interest in the welfare of others and in doing things for them. Ornish reported that such strategies not only led patients to report feeling better; they actually led to reduced coronary artery blockage.

In a similar vein, Redford Williams (1989) reviewed extensive evidence suggesting a link between heart disease and the hostile and cynical elements of Type A (coronary prone) behavior. The antidote to these life-threatening elements, claimed Williams, is the development of a "trusting heart." In addition to reduced cynical mistrust of the motives of others and reduced frequency and intensity of feelings of anger, irritation, and frustration, this trusting heart involves thinking of others and treating them with kindness. Specifically, Williams advised practicing putting yourself in the other person's shoes, because this will lead to feeling empathy for rather than anger toward others when their difficulties inconvenience you.

Second Thoughts

But if empathy-induced altruism is an antidote for meaninglessness and tension, then this antidote comes with a warning label on the bottle. Just as too much of almost any medicine will do you harm, too much selfless concern for others may lead to what has recently been labeled "compassion fatigue." It appears that the most concerned doctors, social workers, hospice workers, and therapists, those who take on an especially heavy load of other people's burdens, are vulnerable to a form of burnout in which they feel they have run dry and have nothing more to give. One cause of this syndrome may be that there is a limit to the number of times in a given period that we can take another person's perspective and become empathically aroused. Our emotional capacity is not a bottomless well. Just as we can feel only so much fear or pain, we may be able to feel only so much compassion and concern. There may be biological and psychological limits to the health-giving properties of empathy-induced altruism.

Even more disturbing, there is good reason to believe that those who turn to altruism as an antidote for meaninglessness and tension, will find the medicine bottle empty. As pointed out by Wallach and Wallach (1983) among others, to use altruism as yet another self-help cure, providing a means to the ultimately self-serving ends of self-actualization, self-fulfillment, more meaning in life, or better health, involves a logical and psychological contradiction. As soon as benefit to the other becomes an instrumental rather than an ultimate goal, the altruistic motivation evaporates. Only egoistic motivation remains. If it is empathy-induced altruism—rather than simply doing something nice for someone—that produces the health benefits, then intentional pursuit of these benefits will almost certainly fail. Altruism may enhance health as serendipitous consequence, but it cannot be used as a means to this end.

So, if we are to advocate increased attention to altruism on the pragmatic basis of what it is good for, then we shall have to restrict our attention to the benefits for others. Pursuit of these benefits—more, and more sensitive response to those in need; less aggression and hostility—may well bring important self-benefits, including improved psychological and physical health. Yet these self-benefits cannot be actively pursued. If we are to decide that altruistic impulses are worth developing, then our decision must be based on a desire to benefit others, not ourselves. But is this not as it should be? After all, a desire to benefit others is what altruism is all about.

Increasing Empathy-Induced Altruism

If we believe the potential benefits to others are sufficient to justify attempting to increase altruism in the society, then how might this be done? Two avenues seem worth exploring: (a) socializing for empathy and altruism and (b) stopping the undermining of altruistic impulses.

Socializing for Empathy and Altruism

Promise them tempting treats, and toddlers will share their toys. A few years later, your praise when these children are thoughtful and your displeasure when they are not are sufficient to make them more thoughtful. Even later, you need offer nothing; the intrinsic self-reward of seeing themselves as helpful, caring people and the anticipated self-punishment of shame and guilt are enough to lead the now-socialized adolescents to help at least some others.

As long as we assume that prosocial motivation is limited to reward seeking, punishment avoiding, and aversive-arousal reduction, as depicted on Paths 1 and 2 of Fig. 6.1, then standard socialization practices based on social-learning theory, like the ones just described, seem entirely appropriate. These socialization practices, which rely exclusively on the development of egoistic prosocial motives, are widely recommended by psychologists today (see, for example, Bandura, 1977; Bar-Tal, 1976; Bar-Tal, Sharabany, & Raviv, 1982; Rushton, 1980).

If, however, empathy-induced altruistic motivation is within the human repertoire, then the possibility arises for quite different socialization practices as well, ones designed to tap and amplify altruistic motives. Perhaps the easiest way to think about socialization strategies that might increase empathy-induced altruism is to link them to four key steps on Path 3 of Fig. 6.1:

1. perception of the other's need,
2. adoption of the other's perspective,
3. experiencing empathic emotion, and
4. enacting behaviors to reach altruistic goals.

Perception of the Other's Need. If children are to learn to react empathically to the suffering of others, then they must first learn to perceive the suffering of others. Parents' inclination may be to shield their children from unpleasant and potentially upsetting situations, hiding others' needs. But if children are to learn to perceive others' needs, a more appropriate response may be to point out need situations and help children understand how the people in need feel. This requires exposure to, not insulation from, the suffering of others.

Obviously, such exposure should be handled with care and sensitivity, being tuned to a child's age and ability to handle stress. Some needs, such as the needs of seriously injured accident victims or starving refugees, may evoke so much fear and aversion that nothing beneficial can be learned. Most children are, however, able to deal with a fairly wide range of needs, so long as they feel secure, are in the presence of a trusted adult, and the adult does not appear frightened or upset.

Examples of needs to which children might be exposed include sick or injured siblings or friends, homeless people on the street, and lonely elderly people in nursing homes. In addition to these real needs, fiction provides a ready vehicle for exposing children to others in need in an easily controlled, relatively secure context. The enduring interest in fairy tales depicting need—"Hansel and Gretel," "Little Red Riding Hood," "Cinderella"—and movies and TV programs with similar themes—*Bambi, The Wizard of Oz, Peter Pan,* "Lassie"—testifies to the strength of children's desire to play through issues of need and response to need.

Having and helping care for pets can also be an excellent way for children to gain exposure to and develop a sensitivity to others' needs, especially to needs that are different from their own. Because relationships with pets usually extend beyond single, brief encounters, they provide an opportunity for children to see needs grow, as well as to see what happens when needs are and are not met.

Adoption of the Other's Perspective.   As outlined on Path 3 of Fig. 6.1, perception of the other as in need is a necessary but not sufficient condition for the experience of empathy. Also necessary is adoption of the other's perspective, perceiving the situation from the point of view of the other's wants and desires and imagining how the other feels about the situation.

Adoption of the other's perspective requires considerable cognitive sophistication. It requires the ability to view the need situation from a point of view other than one's own and the ability to imagine how someone else is feeling or will feel. These inferences must often be made using limited information about the situation and limited verbal and nonverbal cues. The complex cognitive skills required involve what Jean Piaget (1953) called *formal operations.* Piaget originally estimated that the capacity for formal operations did not develop before about 10 years of age. Subsequent research has led to this estimate being revised downward, but it seems clear that before age 3 or 4, these skills are largely absent.

It also seems clear that among those capable of formal operations, development of these skills can be facilitated. Probably the best articulated and documented proposal for facilitating perspective taking in social development is Martin Hoffman's (1977) induction technique. This technique goes beyond simply reinforcing prosocial and punishing antisocial behavior. In situations in which a child's behavior has hurt or helped someone else, induction involves having the socializing agent explain to the child, or ask the child to explain, how the behavior has made the affected person(s) feel. Central to this induction technique is giving the child practice at, and reinforcing the child for, adopting the other's perspective.

Labeling Empathic Emotions.   If Path 3 in Fig. 6.1 is correct as drawn, then perception of the other's need and adoption of the other's perspective are sufficient conditions for children to experience empathic emotion. Initially, this emotional experience is likely to be vague and diffuse—a general sense of uneasiness, yearning, and sadness. Children need concepts and language in order to think about and differentiate among this and other vicarious emotional states such as distress, irritation, fear, and sorrow.

Socializing agents can facilitate this process both by describing their own feelings when confronted with someone in need and by asking children to describe their feelings. With a little attention to children's descriptions of different subjective states—e.g., "feeling tight in my tummy," "heavy and tired," "all warm inside"—and with the introduction of appropriate labels and distinctions, children can learn to recognize different vicarious emotions and to develop a vocabulary to think and talk about them.

Learning Viable Behavioral Means for Reaching Altruistic Goals.   Children also need to learn what behavioral means are and are not effective in reaching the goals of empathy-induced altruistic motives. To some degree, this learning proceeds on a trial and error basis, but socializing agents can also structure specific experiences for children in which various behavioral strategies are tried. Strategies might include (a) ignoring others' needs, (b) escaping from the situation, and (c) helping in more or less effective ways.

Naturally, one would want to allow children to try these different strategies only in situations in which, although the consequences of nonhelpful responses would be apparent, the consequences would not be irrevocable. Appropriate situations might include (a) response to the need of convalescing siblings or friends for visits and entertainment, (b) response to the need of a pet for feeding and exercise, or (c) response to the need for charitable contributions of refugee children in foreign lands. To facilitate exploration of various behavioral options, the socializing agent might suggest or even model different possibilities. By trying and then talking about the effects of different behavioral responses to those for whom one feels empathy, children can gain a clearer understanding of the nature of altruistic motivation. They can learn that the goal of this motivation is to increase the other's welfare rather than their own, and can learn effective behavioral means for achieving this goal.

Stopping the Undermining of Altruistic Impulses

When we consider factors that lead to underutilization of our altruistic potential, failure to socialize for altruism is only one side of the coin. On the other side are psychological forces that erode or undermine the altruistic impulses that do develop.

A powerful force undermining altruism is fueled by two cultural beliefs that psychology has strongly promoted. One is the belief, already discussed in detail, that all human motivation is ultimately egoistic. The second is the belief that it is important to have an honest, accurate, critical self-assessment—to know thyself, warts and all. Honest self-knowledge, even if this knowledge is painful, is a hallmark of most modern psychotherapies and self-help schemes. We are called to recognize and accept that we have self-serving desires and impulses, perhaps including a self-serving desire to transcend self-serving desires and to be, or at least to see ourselves as being, altruistic. Those of us who answer the call to honest self-knowledge become critically self-reflective; we seek to ferret out the real reasons for our actions and to avoid any self-deceptions or self-serving biases.

Perhaps the easiest way to understand how these two beliefs can work together to undermine altruistic motivation is to consider a hypothetical example. Imagine that you are at least in part altruistically motivated to provide the lonely elderly people who live in the nursing home down the street with some social contact on Saturday afternoons. It is often hard to make yourself go, but you feel it is important, and you feel considerable satisfaction when you do; the pats on the back you give yourself are well deserved. Material and social rewards for your visits are, by comparison, trivial; an occasional smile, a sparkle in the eye, a word of thanks. More often, you are greeted by hollow glassy stares, complaints, and even accusations. Still, you are not making these visits to get rewards. You care; your goal is to provide these elderly people with some light in the growing darkness of their lives, and you feel good about it.

Now imagine that you also want to be honest with yourself. You begin critically to self-reflect on the reason for your Saturday visits to the nursing home. Is it *really* because you care for the residents, or is it because of the self-benefits you receive? Is your motivation altruistic or egoistic? As we have seen, it is very difficult to ascertain whether another person's motivation is in any degree altruistic, but it is at least as difficult to make this determination about your own motivation. When trying to decide whether your motivation is altruistic, you will almost certainly be faced with ambiguous data. And if you are trying to be self-critical—trying to be careful not to see your motives as better than they are—an attributional bias may result. In an attempt to avoid a self-serving bias, you may replace it with a *self-deprecating* bias. This self-deprecating bias may lead you to make a selfish attribution for your helping, even if this attribution is wrong.

Asking yourself why you are really making the visits, you remind yourself that you were not born caring; you were socialized into it. Is it not true that your concern for the elderly is simply a product of your internalized values? And is it not true that you feel good when you make the visits and would feel guilty if you did not? Is this not the real reason you go? It all begins to appear little more than a self-serving charade in which "all is vanity and striving after wind."

If you pursue this logic, much of the satisfaction from your visits will disappear. Your concern for the elderly may become something that, although a part of you, is perceived to be outside you, controlling your behavior. You no longer see your visits as evidence of your altruistic concern for others, but of your need to see yourself as altruistic. The satisfaction from the visits, if not entirely gone, is certainly diminished. Quite likely, so are the visits. Not only is there now the cost associated with the behavior—time, effort, discomfort, and so on—but also the cost of seeing yourself as the kind of person whose goodness is for sale.

The combined effect of beliefs in universal egoism and in the importance of critical self-reflection is, then, that perceptions of ourselves as kind and altruistic, even when true, are likely to be replaced by the perception that our concern for others is guided by a self-serving ulterior motive, the motive to see ourselves as altruistic. We are likely to apply to ourselves Gheslin's (1974) acid observation: "Scratch an 'altruist' and watch a 'hypocrite' bleed" (p. 247). No longer can we take pleasure in caring for others; instead, we wince at our hypocrisy and vow: Never again. Critical self-reflection may turn the belief that all human motivation is egoistic into a self-fulfilling prophecy.

Consistent with this speculative analysis, two experiments have provided evidence that simply asking people to reflect on reasons why they helped someone in need was enough to lead them to perceive their helping to be less altruistically motivated. Moreover, as expected, this undermining of self-perceived altruism was most apparent among individuals who placed a high value on honest self-knowledge (see Batson, Fultz, Schoenrade, & Paduano, 1987).

How are we to combat these forces that threaten to undermine altruistic motivation? If the empathy-altruism hypothesis is correct, then we have a ready and powerful weapon: knowledge that the cultural belief in universal egoism is false. If you must accept that your motivation for helping others may be egoistic, altruistic, or both, then ambiguous data concerning your true motives and the desire for honest self-knowledge need not combine to produce a self-deprecatory bias. If you must honestly admit that your reason for visiting the nursing home may be, at least in part, because you care about the patients' welfare, then your altruistic motivation should not be undermined.

LOOKING TOWARD THE MORAL HORIZON

To surrender the belief in universal egoism is, however, not without cost. This belief, especially when combined with critical self-reflection, carries with it an important freedom. It permits us unashamedly to just say no when given the opportunity to help someone in the absence of clear self-benefits. There need be no remorse or guilt for failing to care for others if we know that our caring is not really sincere, if it is only an attempt on our part to feel good about ourselves or to avoid feeling bad. Indeed, there is a sense of relief in knowing ourselves, selfish desires and all, and in not being suckered into trying to act good. This knowledge considerably narrows our moral scope. If we cannot really care for others, then surely there is no reason to try.

But if altruistic motivation exists, then our moral horizon is not nearly so narrow. We can no longer excuse our callousness and insensitivity to the needs of others by explaining that it is unrealistic to expect more. If we have the capacity to care for others for their sakes and not simply for our own, then we can expect more.

This broadening of our moral horizon need not, however, be experienced as a burden. Altruism is not a moral prescription for what we should do; it is a motivation, a desire. As such, it does not demand that we care for others; it leads us to want to do so. To the degree that we are altruistically motivated, we cannot help caring. Quite the opposite of Kant's moral principles, altruistic motivation prompts us to care for one another not from duty but from inclination. Rather than a source of obligation, it seems a cause for—admittedly guarded—hope and celebration.

The ticket to this celebration, and to all the theoretical and practical implications outlined, is an affirmative answer to the altruism question. Audacious as it may sound, I believe that we now have an affirmative answer, based on the evidence for the empathy-altruism hypothesis. Admittedly, this answer is still tentative, but the evidence does seem strong enough that we should start looking for the party hats.

References

Adams, J. S. (1965). Inequity in social exchange. In L. Berkowitz (Ed.), *Advances in experimental social psychology* (pp. 267–299). New York: Academic Press.

Aderman, D., & Berkowitz, L. (1970). Observational set, empathy, and helping. *Journal of Personality and Social Psychology, 14,* 141–148.

Aderman, D., Brehm, S. S., & Katz, L. B. (1974). Empathic observation of an innocent victim: The just world revisited. *Journal of Personality and Social Psychology, 29,* 342–347.

Ainsworth, M. D. S., Blehar, M. C., Waters, E., & Wall, S. (1978). *Patterns of attachment: A psychological study of the strange situation.* Hillsdale, NJ: Lawrence Erlbaum Associates.

Allport, G. W. (1968). The historical background of social psychology. In G. Lindzey & E. Aronson (Eds.), *The handbook of social psychology* (Vol. 1, pp. 1–80). Reading, MA: Addison-Wesley.

Aquinas, T. (1917). *The summa theologica* (Vol. 2, Part II). (Fathers of the English Dominican Province, Trans.). New York: Benziger Bros. (Original work produced 1270)

Archer, R. L. (1984). The farmer and the cowman should be friends: An attempt at reconciliation with Batson, Coke, and Pych. *Journal of Personality and Social Psychology, 46,* 709–711.

Archer, R. L., Diaz-Loving, R., Gollwitzer, P. M., Davis, M. H., & Foushee, H. C. (1981). The role of dispositional empathy and social evaluation in the empathic mediation of helping. *Journal of Personality and Social Psychology, 40,* 786–796.

Aristotle. (1911). *The Nicomachean ethics* (D. P. Chase, Trans.). New York: E. P. Dutton.

Aristotle. (1932). *The rhetoric of Aristotle* (L. Cooper, Trans.). New York: Appleton-Century-Crofts.

Aron, A., & Aron, E. N. (1986). *Love and the expansion of self.* New York: Hemisphere.

Aronfreed, J. (1968). *Conduct and conscience: The socialization of internalized control over behavior.* New York: Academic Press.

Aronson, E., Blaney, N., Stephan, C., Sikes, J., & Snapp, M. (1978). *The jigsaw classroom.* Beverly Hills, CA: Sage.

Balzac, H. de (1962). *Pere Goriot* (H. Reed, Trans.). New York: New American Library. (Original work published 1834)

Bandura, A. (1977). *Social learning theory.* Engelwood Cliffs, NJ: Prentice-Hall.

Bandura, A., & Rosenthal, L. (1966). Vicarious classical conditioning as a function of arousal level. *Journal of Personality and Social Psychology, 3,* 54–62.

Bar-Tal, D. (1976). *Prosocial behavior: Theory and research.* Washington, DC: Hemisphere.

Bar-Tal, D., Sharabany, R., & Raviv, A. (1982). Cognitive basis for the development of altruistic behavior. In V. J. Derlega & J. Grzelak (Eds.), *Cooperation and helping behavior: Theories and research* (pp. 377–396). New York: Academic Press.

Batson, C. D. (1983). Sociobiology and the role of religion in promoting prosocial behavior: An alternative view. *Journal of Personality and Social Psychology, 45,* 1380–1385.

Batson, C. D. (1987). Prosocial motivation: Is it ever truly altruistic? In L. Berkowitz (Ed.), *Advances in experimental social psychology* (Vol. 20, pp. 65–122). New York: Academic Press.

Batson, C. D. (1990). How social an animal?: The human capacity for caring. *American Psychologist, 45,* 336–346.

Batson, C. D., Batson, J. G., Griffitt, C. A., Barrientos, S., Brandt, J. R., Sprengelmeyer, P., & Bayly, M. J. (1989). Negative-state relief and the empathy-altruism hypothesis. *Journal of Personality and Social Psychology, 56,* 922–933.

Batson, C. D., Batson, J. G., Slingsby, J. K., Harrell, K. L., Peekna, H. M., & Todd, R. M. (in press). Empathic joy and the empathy-altruism hypothesis. *Journal of Personality and Social Psychology.*

Batson, C. D., Bolen, M. H., Cross, J. A., & Neuringer-Benefiel, H. (1986). Where is the altruism in the altruistic personality? *Journal of Personality and Social Psychology, 50,* 212–220.

Batson, C. D., & Coke, J. S. (1981). Empathy: A source of altruistic motivation for helping? In J. P. Rushton & R. M. Sorrentino (Eds.), *Altruism and helping behavior: Social, personality, and developmental perspectives* (pp. 167–187). Hillsdale, NJ: Lawrence Erlbaum Associates.

Batson, C. D., & Coke, J. S. (1983). Empathic motivation of helping behavior. In J. T. Caccioppo & R. E. Petty (Eds.), *Social psychophysiology: A sourcebook* (pp. 417–433). New York: Guilford Press.

Batson, C. D., Darley, J. M., & Coke, J. S. (1978). Altruism and human kindness: Internal and external determinants of helping behavior. In L. Pervin & M. Lewis (Eds.), *Perspectives in interactional psychology* (pp. 111–140). New York: Plenum Press.

Batson, C. D., Duncan, B., Ackerman, P., Buckley, T., & Birch, K. (1981). Is empathic emotion a source of altruistic motivation? *Journal of Personality and Social Psychology, 40,* 290–302.

Batson, C. D., Dyck, J. L., Brandt, J. R., Batson, J. G., Powell, A. L., McMaster, M. R., & Griffitt, C. (1988). Five studies testing two new egoistic alternatives to the empathy-altruism hypothesis. *Journal of Personality and Social Psychology, 55,* 52–77.

Batson, C. D., Fultz, J., & Schoenrade, P. A. (1987). Distress and empathy: Two qualitatively distinct vicarious emotions with different motivational consequences. *Journal of Personality, 55,* 19–39.

Batson, C. D., Fultz, J., Schoenrade, P. A., & Paduano, A. (1987). Critical self-reflection and self-perceived altruism: When self-reward fails. *Journal of Personality and Social Psychology, 53,* 594–602.

Batson, C. D., O'Quin, K., Fultz, J., Vanderplas, M., & Isen, A. (1983). Self-reported distress and empathy and egoistic versus altruistic motivation for helping. *Journal of Personality and Social Psychology, 45,* 706–718.

Baumann, D. J., Cialdini, R. B., & Kenrick, D. T. (1981). Altruism as hedonism: Helping and self-gratification as equivalent responses. *Journal of Personality and Social Psychology, 40,* 1039–1046.

Beggan, J. K., Messick, D. M., & Allison, S. T. (1988). Social values and egocentric bias: Two tests of the might over morality hypothesis. *Journal of Personality and Social Psychology, 55,* 606–611.

Bentham, J. (1876). *An introduction to the principles of morals and legislation.* Oxford: The Clarendon Press. (Original work published 1789)

Berger, S. M. (1962). Conditioning through vicarious instigation. *Psychological Review, 69,* 450–466.

Berglas, S., & Jones, E. E. (1978). Drug choice as a self-handicapping strategy in response to non-contingent success. *Journal of Personality and Social Psychology, 36,* 405–417.

Berkowitz, L. (1972). Social punishments, feelings, and other factors affecting helping and altruism. In L. Berkowitz (Ed.), *Advances in experimental social psychology* (Vol. 6, pp. 63–108). New York: Academic Press.

Berkowitz, L., & Lutterman, K. (1968). The traditionally socially responsible personality. *Public Opinion Quarterly, 32,* 169–185.

Berscheid, E. (1983). Emotion. In H. H. Kelley, E. Berscheid, A. Christensen, J. H. Harvey, T. L. Houston, G. Levinger, E. McClintock, L. A. Peplau, & D. R. Peterson, *Close relationships* (pp. 110–168). San Francisco: W. H. Freeman.

Borke, H. (1971). Interpersonal perception of young children: Egocentrism or empathy? *Developmental Psychology, 5,* 263–269.

Bowerman, W. R. (1978). Subjective competence: The structure, process, and function of self-referent causal attributions. *Journal for the Theory of Social Behavior, 8,* 45–75.

Bowlby, J. (1969). *Attachment and loss: Vol. 1. Attachment.* New York: Basic Books.

Brehm, J. W. (1966). *A theory of psychological reactance.* New York: Academic Press.

Brehm, J. W., & Cole, A. H. (1966). Effect of a favor which reduces freedom. *Journal of Personality and Social Psychology, 3,* 420–426.

Bridgeman, D. L. (1981). Enhanced role-taking through cooperative interdependence: A field study. *Child Development, 52,* 1231–1238.

Brown, J. S. (1953). Problems presented by the concept of acquired drives. In M. R. Jones (Ed.), *Current theory and research in motivation: Nebraska symposium on Motivation* (Vol. 1, pp. 1–21). Lincoln, NE: University of Nebraska Press.

Butler, J. (1896). Upon the love of our neighbor. Sermon 11 in *The works of Joseph Butler, D. C. L.* (Vol. 2). Oxford: Clarendon Press. (Original work published 1729)

Campbell, D. T. (1975). On the conflicts between biological and social evolution and between psychology and moral tradition. *American Psychologist, 30,* 1103–1126.

Campbell, D. T. (1978). On the genetics of altruism and the counterhedonic components in human culture. In L. Wispé (Ed.), *Altruism, sympathy, and helping: Psychological and sociological principles* (pp. 39–57). New York: Academic Press.

Cassirer, E. (1921). *Substance and function* (W. C. Swabey, Trans.). Chicago: Open Court. (Original work published 1910)

Christie, R., & Geis, F. (Eds.). (1968). *Studies in Machiavellianism.* New York: Academic Press.

Cialdini, R. B., Baumann, D. J., & Kenrick, D. T. (1981). Insights from sadness: A three-step model of the development of altruism as hedonism. *Developmental Review, 1,* 207–223.

Cialdini, R. B., Darby, B. L., & Vincent, J. E. (1973). Transgression and altruism: A case for hedonism. *Journal of Experimental Social Psychology, 9,* 502–516.

Cialdini, R. B., & Kenrick, D. T. (1976). Altruism as hedonism: A social development perspective on the relationship of negative mood state and helping. *Journal of Personality and Social Psychology, 34,* 907–914.

Cialdini, R. B., Schaller, M., Houlihan, D., Arps, K., Fultz, J., & Beaman, A. L. (1987). Empathy-based helping: Is it selflessly or selfishly motivated? *Journal of Personality and Social Psychology, 52,* 749–758.

Clark, M. S., & Mills, J. (1979). Interpersonal attraction in exchange and communal relationships. *Journal of Personality and Social Psychology, 37,* 12–24.

Clark, R. D., & Word, L. E. (1972). Why don't bystanders help? Because of ambiguity? *Journal of Personality and Social Psychology, 24,* 392–401.

Clark, R. D., & Word, L. E. (1974). Where is the apathetic bystander? Situational characteristics of the emergency. *Journal of Personality and Social Psychology, 29,* 279–288.

Cohen, D., & Taylor, L. (1989). *Dogs and their women.* Boston: Little, Brown.

Coke, J. S., Batson, C. D., & McDavis, K. (1978). Empathic mediation of helping: A two-stage model. *Journal of Personality and Social Psychology, 36,* 752–766.

Comte, I. A. (1875). *System of positive polity* (Vol. 1). London: Longmans, Green & Co. (Original work published 1851)

Craig, K. D., & Lowery, J. H. (1969). Heart-rate components of conditioned vicarious autonomic responses. *Journal of Personality and Social Psychology, 11,* 381–387.

Craig, K. D., & Wood, K. (1969). Psychophysiological differentiation of direct and vicarious affective arousal. *Canadian Journal of Behavioral Science, 1,* 98–105.

Crowne, D. P., & Marlowe, D. (1964). *The approval motive.* New York: Wiley.

Darwin, C. (1859). *On the origin of species.* London: J. Murray.

Darwin, C. (1952). *The descent of man.* Reprinted in R. M. Hutchins (Ed.), *Great books of the Western World* (Vol. 49, pp. 253–600). Chicago: Encyclopaedia Britannica, Inc. (Original work published 1871)

Darwin, C. (1872). *The expression of the emotions in man and animals.* London: J. Murray.

Davis, M. H. (1983). Mesuring individual differences in empathy: Evidence for a multidimensional approach. *Journal of Personality and Social Psychology, 44,* 113–126.

Dawes, R. M. (1980). Social dilemmas. *Annual Review of Psychology, 31,* 169–193.

Dawkins, R. (1976). *The selfish gene.* New York: Oxford University Press.

de Rivera, J. (1979, August). *Biological necessity, emotional transformation, and personal value.* Paper presented at the meeting of the American Psychological Association, New York.

Des Pres, T. (1976). *The survivor: An anatomy of life in the death camps.* New York: Washington Square Press.

Dickens, C. (1913). *A Christmas carol in prose, being a ghost story of Christmas.* Boston: Houghton Mifflin. (Original work published 1843)

Dollard, J., & Miller, N. E. (1950). *Personality and psychotherapy.* New York: McGraw-Hill.

Dovidio, J. F. (1984). Helping behavior and altruism: An empirical and conceptual overview. In L. Berkowitz (Ed.), *Advances in experimental social psychology* (Vol. 17, pp. 361–427). New York: Academic Press.

Dovidio, J. F., Allen, J. L., & Schroeder, D. A. (1990). The specificity of empathy-induced helping: Evidence for altruistic motivation. *Journal of Personality and Social Psychology, 59,* 249–260.

Duval, S., & Wicklund, R. A. (1972). *A theory of objective self awareness.* New York: Academic Press.

Dyck, J. L., Batson, C. D., Oden, A., & Weeks, J. L. (1989, April). *Another look at the altruism in the altruistic personality: Hers and his.* Paper presented at the meeting of the Midwestern Sociological Association, St. Louis, MO.

Dymond, R. (1949). A scale for measurement of empathic ability. *Journal of Consulting Psychology, 13,* 127–133.

Eagly, A. H., & Crowley, M. (1986). Gender and helping behavior: A meta-analytic review of the social-psychological literature. *Psychological Bulletin, 100,* 283–308.

Egeland, B., & Stroufe, L. A. (1981). Attachment and early maltreatment. *Child Development, 52,* 44–52.

Eisenberg, N. (Ed.). (1982). *The development of prosocial behavior.* New York: Academic Press.

Eisenberg, N., & Miller, P. (1987). Empathy and prosocial behavior. *Psychological Bulletin, 101,* 91–119.

Eisenberg, N., Miller, P. A., Schaller, M., Fabes, R. A., Fultz, J., Shell, R., & Shea, C. L. (1989). The role of sympathy and altruistic personality traits in helping: A re-examination. *Journal of Personality, 57,* 41–67.

Eisenberg, N., & Strayer, J. (1987). Critical issues in the study of empathy. In N. Eisenberg & J. Strayer (Eds.), *Empathy and its development* (pp. 3–13). New York: Cambridge University Press.

Epictetus. (1877). *The discourses of Epictetus: with the Encheiridion and fragments* (G. Long, Trans.). London: George Bell & Sons.

Feshbach, N. D. (1987). Parental empathy and child adjustment/maladjustment. In N.

Eisenberg & J. Strayer (Eds.), *Empathy and its development* (pp. 271–291). New York: Cambridge University Press.

Festinger, L. (1954). A theory of social comparison processes. *Human Relations, 7,* 117–140.

Festinger, L. (1957). *A theory of cognitive dissonance.* Stanford, CA: Stanford University Press.

Fischer, W. F. (1963). Sharing in preschool children as a function of amount and type of reinforcement. *Genetic Psychology Monographs, 68,* 215–245.

Ford, M. R., & Lowery, C. R. (1986). Gender differences in moral reasoning: A comparison of the use of justice and care orientations. *Journal of Personality and Social Psychology, 50,* 777–783.

Freud, S. (1920). *A general introduction to psychoanalysis* (G. S. Hall, Trans.). New York: Boni & Liveright. (Original work published 1917)

Freud, S. (1930). *Civilization and its discontents* (J. Riviere, Trans.). London: Hogarth.

Freud, S. (1959). Thoughts for the times on war and death. In *Sigmund Freud: Collected Papers* (Vol. 4) (E. C. Mayne, Trans.). New York: Basic Books. (Original work published 1915)

Frodi, A. M., & Lamb, M. D. (1980). Child abuser's responses to infant smiles and cries. *Child Development, 51,* 238–241.

Fromm, E. (1947). *Man for himself: An inquiry into the psychology of ethics.* New York: Fawcett.

Fultz, J., Batson, C. D., Fortenbach, V. A., McCarthy, P. M., & Varney, L. L. (1986). Social evaluation and the empathy–altruism hypothesis. *Journal of Personality and Social Psychology, 50,* 761–769.

Gaertner, S. L., & Dovidio, J. F. (1977). The subtlety of white racism, arousal, and helping behavior. *Journal of Personality and Social Psychology, 35,* 691–708.

Galileo. (1952). *Dialogues concerning the two new sciences* (H. Crew & A. de Salvio, Trans.). Chicago: Encyclopedia Britannica. (Original work published 1638)

Gelfand, D. M., Hartmann, D. P., Cromer, C. C., Smith, C. L., & Page, B. C. (1975). The effects of instructional prompts and praise on children's donation rates. *Child Development, 46,* 980–983.

Geller, V., & Shaver, P. (1976). Cognitive consequences of self-awareness. *Journal of Experimental Social Psychology, 12,* 99–108.

Gheslin, M. T. (1974). *The economy of nature and the evolution of sex.* Berkeley: University of California Press.

Gibbons, F. X., & Wicklund, R. A. (1982). Self-focused attention and helping behavior. *Journal of Personality and Social Psychology, 43,* 462–474.

Gilligan, C. (1982). *In a different voice: Psychological theory and women's development.* Cambridge, MA: Harvard University Press.

Gouldner, A. W. (1960). The norm of reciprocity: A preliminary statement. *American Sociological Review, 25,* 161–179.

Grusec, J. E. (1981). Socialization processes in the development of altruism. In J. P. Rushton & R. M. Sorrentino (Eds.), *Altruism and helping behavior* (pp. 65–90). Hillsdale, NJ: Lawrence Erlbaum Associates.

Hamilton, W. D. (1964). The genetic evolution of social behavior. *Journal of Theoretical Biology, 7,* 1–51.

Hamilton, W. D. (1971). Selection of selfish and altruistic behavior in some extreme models. In J. F. Eisenberg and W. S. Dillon (Eds.), *Man and beast: Comparative social behavior.* Washington, DC: Smithsonian Institution Press.

Hancock, G. (1989). *Lords of poverty: The power, prestige, and corruption of the international aid business.* New York: Atlantic Monthly Press.

Hardin, G. (1968). The tragedy of the commons. *Science, 162,* 1243–1248.

Hardin, G. (1977). *The limits of altruism: An ecologist's view of survival.* Bloomington: Indiana University Press.

Harris, M. B., & Huang, L. C. (1973). Helping and the attribution process. *Journal of Social Psychology, 90,* 291–297.

Hartshorne, H., & May, M. A. (1928). *Studies in the nature of character: Studies in deceit* (Vol. 1). New York: Macmillan.

Hartshorne, H., May, M. A., & Maller, J. B. (1929). *Studies in the nature of character: Studies in self-control* (Vol. 2). New York: Macmillan.

Hartshorne, H., May, M. A., & Shuttleworth, F. K. (1930). *Studies in the nature of character: Studies in the organization of character* (Vol. 3). New York: Macmillan.

Hatfield, E., Walster, G. W., & Piliavin, J. A. (1978). Equity theory and helping relationships. In L. Wispé (Ed.), *Altruism, sympathy, and helping: Psychological and sociological principles* (pp. 115–139). New York: Academic Press.

Heider, F. (1958). *The psychology of interpersonal relations.* New York: Wiley.

Higgins, E. T. (1987). Self-discrepancy: A theory relating self and affect. *Psychological Review, 94,* 319–340.

Hobbes, T. (1973). *Philosophical rudiments concerning government and society (De Cive),* Chapter 1. Reprinted in R. D. Milo (Ed.), *Egoism and altruism* (pp. 18–25). Belmont, Calif.: Wadsworth. (Original work published 1642)

Hobbes, T. (1651). *Leviathan: or the matter, form, and power of a commonwealth, ecclesiastical and civil.* London: A. Crooke.

Hoffman, M. L. (1975). Developmental synthesis of affect and cognition and its implications for altruistic motivation. *Developmental Psychology, 11,* 607–622.

Hoffman, M. L. (1976). Empathy, role-taking, guilt, and development of altruistic motives. In T. Lickona (Ed.), *Moral development and behavior: Theory, research, and social issues* (pp. 124–143). New York: Holt, Rinehart, & Winston.

Hoffman, M. L. (1977). Moral internalization: Current theory and research. In L. Berkowitz (Ed.), *Advances in experimental social psychology* (Vol. 10, pp. 86–135). New York: Academic Press.

Hoffman, M. L. (1981a). Is altruism part of human nature? *Journal of Personality and Social Psychology, 40,* 121–137.

Hoffman, M. L. (1981b). The development of empathy. In J. P. Rushton & R. M. Sorrentino (Eds.), *Altruism and helping behavior: Social, personality, and developmental perspectives* (pp. 41–63). Hillsdale, NJ: Lawrence Erlbaum Associates.

Hoffman, M. L. (1982). Development of prosocial motivation: Empathy and guilt. In N. Eisenberg (Ed.), *The development of prosocial behavior* (pp. 281–313). New York: Academic Press.

Hogan, R. (1969). Development of an empathy scale. *Journal of Consulting and Clinical Psychology, 33,* 307–316.

Homans, G. C. (1961). *Social behavior: Its elementary forms.* New York: Harcourt, Brace, & World.

Horney, K. (1950). *Neurosis and human growth: The struggle toward self-realization.* New York: Norton.

Hornstein, H. A. (1976). *Cruelty and kindness: A new look at aggression and altruism.* Engelwood Cliffs, NJ: Prentice-Hall.

Hornstein, H. A. (1978). Promotive tension and prosocial behavior: A Lewinian analysis. In L. Wispé (Ed.), *Altruism, sympathy, and helping: Psychological and sociological principles* (pp. 177–207). New York: Academic Press.

Hornstein, H. A. (1982). Promotive tension: Theory and research. In V. J. Derlega & J. Grzelak (Eds.), *Cooperation and helping behavior: Theories and research* (pp. 229–248). New York: Academic Press.

Howes, C., & Eldredge, R. (1985). Responses of abused, neglected, and maltreated children to the behaviors of their peers. *Journal of Applied Developmental Psychology, 6,* 261–270.

Hull, C. L. (1943). *Principles of behavior.* New York: Appleton-Century.

Hull, J. G., & Levy, A. S. (1979). The organizational functions of the self: An alternative to the Duval and Wicklund model of self-awareness. *Journal of Personality and Social Psychology, 37,* 756–768.

Hume, D. (1896). *A treatise of human nature.* (L. A. Selby-Bigge, Ed.). Oxford: Oxford University Press. (Original work published 1740)

Hume, D. (1902). *An enquiry concerning the principles of morals.* (L. A. Selby-Bigge, Ed.). Oxford: Oxford University Press. (Original work published 1751)

Hygge, S. (1976). Information about the model's unconditioned stimulus and response in vicarious classical conditioning. *Journal of Personality and Social Psychology, 33,* 764–771.

Isen, A. M., & Levin, P. F. (1972). Effect of feeling good on helping: Cookies and kindness. *Journal of Personality and Social Psychology, 21,* 344–348.

James, W. (1890). *Principles of psychology* (Vol. 1). New York: Henry Holt.

Johnson, D. W., & Johnson, R. T. (1987). *Learning together and alone: Cooperative, competitive, and individualistic learning.* Englewood Cliffs, NJ: Prentice-Hall.

Jones, E. E., & Davis, K. E. (1965). From acts to dispositions: The attribution process in person perception. In L. Berkowitz (Ed.), *Advances in experimental social psychology* (Vol. 2, pp. 219–266). New York: Academic Press.

Jones, E. E., & Pittman, T. S. (1982). Toward a general theory of strategic self-presentation. In J. Suls (Ed.), *Psychological perspectives on the self* (pp. 231–262). Hillsdale, NJ: Lawrence Erlbaum Associates.

Kahn, C. H. (1981). Aristotle and altruism. *Mind, 90,* 20–40.

Kant, I. (1889). Fundamental principles of the metaphysic of morals. In *Kant's Critique of Practical Reason and other works on the theory of ethics* (4th ed.) (T. K. Abbott, Trans.). New York: Longmans, Green & Co. (Original work published 1785)

Karniol, R. (1982). Settings, scripts, and self-schemata: A cognitive analysis of the development of prosocial behavior. In N. Eisenberg (Ed.), *The development of prosocial behavior* (pp. 251–278). New York: Academic Press.

Karylowski, J. (1982). Two types of altruistic behavior: Doing good to feel good or to make the other feel good. In V. J. Derlega & J. Grzelak (Eds.), *Cooperation and helping behavior: Theories and research* (pp. 397–413). New York: Academic Press.

Karylowski, J. (1984). Focus of attention and altruism: Endocentric and exocentric sources of altruistic behavior. In E. Staub, D. Bar-Tal, J. Karylowski, & J. Reykowski

(Eds.), *Development and maintenance of prosocial behavior* (pp. 139–154). New York: Plenum.

Kelley, H. H. (1979). *Personal relationships: Their structures and processes.* Hillsdale, NJ: Lawrence Erlbaum Associates.

Kenrick, D. T., Baumann, D. J., & Cialdini, R. B. (1979). A step in the socialization of altruism as hedonism: Effects of negative mood on children's generosity under public and private conditions. *Journal of Personality and Social Psychology, 37,* 747–755.

Kogon, E. (1953). *The theory and practice of hell* (H. Norden, Trans.). New York: Farrar, Straus.

Kohlberg, L. (1969). Stage and sequence: The cognitive-developmental approach to socialization. In D. Goslin (Ed.), *Handbook of socialization theory and research* (pp. 347–480). Chicago: Rand McNally.

Kohlberg, L. (1976). Moral stages and moralization: The cognitive-developmental approach. In T. Lickona (Ed.), *Moral development and behavior: Theory, research, and social issues* (pp. 31–53). New York: Holt, Rinehart, & Winston.

Kohlberg, L., & Kramer, R. (1969). Continuities and discontinuities in childhood and adult moral development. *Developmental Review, 12,* 93–120.

Krebs, D. L. (1970). Altruism—an examination of the concept and a review of the literature. *Psychological Bulletin, 73,* 258–302.

Krebs, D. L. (1975). Empathy and altruism. *Journal of Personality and Social Psychology, 32,* 1134–1146.

Krebs, D. L. (1982). Altruism—a rational approach. In N. Eisenberg (Ed.), *The development of prosocial behavior* (pp. 53–76). New York: Academic Press.

Krebs, D. L., & Miller, D. T. (1985). Altruism and aggression. In G. Lindzey & E. Aronson (Eds.), *Handbook of social psychology: Vol. 2. Special fields and applications* (3rd ed., pp. 1–71). New York: Random House.

Krebs, D. L., & Russell, C. (1981). Role-taking and altruism: When you put yourself in the shoes of another, will they take you to their owner's aid? In J. P. Rushton & R. M. Sorrentino (Eds.), *Altruism and helping behavior: Social, personality, and developmental perspectives* (pp. 137–165). Hillsdale, NJ: Lawrence Erlbaum Associates.

Kropotkin, P. (1902). *Mutual aid, a factor of evolution.* New York: McClure, Phillips.

Langer, E. J., & Abelson, R. P. (1972). The semantics of asking a favor: How to succeed in getting help without really dying. *Journal of Personality and Social Psychology, 24,* 26–32.

La Rochefoucauld, F., Duke de (1691). *Moral maxims and reflections, in four parts.* London: Gillyflower, Sare, & Everingham.

Latané, B., & Darley, J. M. (1970). *The unresponsive bystander: Why doesn't he help?* New York: Appleton-Century-Crofts.

Leeds, R. (1963). Altruism and the norm of giving. *Merrill-Palmer Quarterly, 9,* 229–240.

Lenrow, P. (1965). Studies of sympathy. In S. Tomkins & C. Izard (Eds.), *Affect, cognition, and personality* (pp. 264–293). New York: Springer.

Lerner, M. J. (1970). The desire for justice and reactions to victims. In J. Macaulay & L. Berkowitz (Eds.), *Altruism and helping behavior* (pp. 205–229). New York: Academic Press.

Lerner, M. J. (1982). The justice motive in human relations and the economic model of man: A radical analysis of facts and fictions. In V. J. Derlega & J. Grzelak (Eds.), *Cooperation and helping behavior: Theories and research* (pp. 249–278). New York: Academic Press.

Lerner, M. J., & Simmons, C. H. (1966). Observer's reaction to the "innocent victim": Compassion or rejection? *Journal of Personality and Social Psychology, 4,* 203–210.

Lerner, M. J., & Meindl, J. R. (1981). Justice and altruism. In J. P. Rushton & R. M. Sorrentino (Eds.), *Altruism and helping behavior: Social, personality, and developmental perspectives* (pp. 213–232). Hillsdale, NJ: Lawrence Erlbaum Associates.

Lewin, K. (1935). *Dynamic theory of personality.* New York: McGraw-Hill.

Lewin, K. (1951). *Field theory in social science: Selected theoretical papers.* New York: Harper.

Lewin, M. A. (1977). Kurt Lewin's view of social psychology: The crisis of 1977 and the crisis of 1927. *Personality and Social Psychology Bulletin, 3,* 159–172.

Lorenz, K. Z. (1966). *On aggression.* New York: Harcourt, Brace, & World.

Luks, A. (1988). Helper's high. *Psychology Today, 22*(10), 39–42.

Macaulay, J., & Berkowitz, L. (Eds.). (1970). *Altruism and helping behavior: Social psychological studies of some antecedents and consequences.* New York: Academic Press.

MacDonald, A. P. (1969). Manifestations of differential levels of socialization by birth order. *Developmental Psychology, 1,* 485–492.

MacDonald, A. P. (1971). Birth order and personality. *Journal of Consulting and Clinical Psychology, 36,* 171–176.

McDougall, W. (1908). *An introduction to social psychology.* London: Methuen.

McGuire, W. J. (1973). The yin and yang of progress in social psychology: Seven koan. *Journal of Personality and Social Psychology, 26,* 446–456.

Machiavelli, N. (1908). *The prince* (W. K. Marriott, Trans.). New York: E. P. Dutton. (Original work published 1513)

MacIntyre, A. (1967). Egoism and altruism. In P. Edwards (Ed.), *The encyclopedia of philosophy* (Vol. 2, pp. 462–466). New York: Macmillan.

MacLean, P. D. (1967). The brain in relation to empathy and medical education. *Journal of Nervous and Mental Disease, 144,* 374–382.

MacLean, P. D. (1973). *A triune concept of the brain and behavior.* Toronto: University of Toronto Press.

Mandeville, B. (1732). *The fable of the bees: Or, private vices, public benefits.* London: J. Tonson. (Original work published 1714)

Manucia, G. K., Baumann, D. J., & Cialdini, R. B. (1984). Mood influences on helping: Direct effects or side effects? *Journal of Personality and Social Psychology, 46,* 357–364.

Maslow, A. H. (1954). *Motivation and personality.* New York: Harper & Row.

Maslow, A. H. (1968). *Toward a psychology of being* (2nd ed.). New York: Van Nostrand.

Mathews, K. E., & Canon, L. K. (1975). Environmental noise level as a determinant of helping behavior. *Journal of Personality and Social Psychology, 32,* 571–577.

Mehrabian, A., & Epstein, N. (1972). A measure of emotional empathy. *Journal of Personality, 40,* 525–543.

Meindl, J. R., & Lerner, M. J. (1983). The heroic motive: Some experimental demonstrations. *Journal of Experimental Social Psychology, 19*, 1–20.

Midlarsky, E. (1968). Aiding responses: An analysis and review. *Merrill-Palmer Quarterly, 14*, 229–260.

Milgram, S. (1963). Behavioral study of obedience. *Journal of Abnormal and Social Psychology, 67*, 371–378.

Milgram, S. (1974). *Obedience to authority: An experimental view.* New York: Harper & Row.

Mill, J. S. (1861). *Utilitarianism.* London: Parker, Son, & Bourn.

Miller, P. A., & Eisenberg, N. (1988). The relation of empathy to aggressive and externalizing/antisocial behavior. *Psychological Bulletin, 103*, 324–344.

Milo, R. D. (Ed.). (1973). *Egoism and altruism.* Belmont, CA: Wadsworth.

Mischel, W. (1973). Toward a cognitive social learning reconceptualization of personality. *Psychological Review, 80*, 252–283.

Moran, G. (1967). Ordinal position and approval motivation. *Journal of Consulting Psychology, 31*, 319–320.

Moscovici, S. (1985). Social influence and conformity. In G. Lindzey & E. Aronson (Eds.), *Handbook of social psychology: Vol. 2: Special fields and applications* (3rd ed., pp. 347–412). New York: Random House.

Moss, M. K., & Page, R. A. (1972). Reinforcement and helping behavior. *Journal of Applied Psychology, 2*, 360–371.

Nagel, T. (1970). *The possibility of altruism.* Princeton, NJ: Princeton University Press.

Nietzsche, F. (1927). *Ecce Homo.* In *The philosophy of Nietzsche.* (C. P. Fadiman, Trans.). New York: Random House. (Original work published 1888)

Oliner, S. P., & Oliner, P. M. (1988). *The altruistic personality: Rescuers of Jews in Nazi Europe.* New York: The Free Press.

Orbell, J. M., van de Kragt, A. J., & Dawes, R. M. (1988). Explaining discussion-induced cooperation. *Journal of Personality and Social Psychology, 54*, 811–819.

Orne, M. (1962). On the social psychology of the psychological experiment: With particular reference to demand characteristics and their implications. *American Psychologist, 17*, 776–783.

Ornish, D. (1989). *The effects of lifestyle changes on coronary heart disease.* Unpublished manuscript.

Pascal, B. (1952). *Pensees.* (W. F. Trotter, Trans.). Chicago: Encyclopedia Britannica. (Original work published 1670)

Piaget, J. (1953). *The origins of intelligence in the child.* New York: International Universities Press.

Piliavin, I. M., Piliavin, J. A., & Rodin, J. (1975). Costs, diffusion and the stigmatized victim. *Journal of Personality and Social Psychology, 32*, 429–438.

Piliavin, J. A., Dovidio, J. F., Gaertner, S. L., & Clark, R. D., III (1981). *Emergency intervention.* New York: Academic Press.

Piliavin, J. A., Dovidio, J. F., Gaertner, S. L., & Clark, R. D., III (1982). Responsive bystanders: The process of intervention. In V. J. Derlega and J. Grzelak (Eds.), *Cooperation and helping behavior: Theories and research* (pp. 279–304). New York: Academic Press.

Piliavin, J. A., & Piliavin, I. M. (1973). *The Good Samaritan: Why does he help?* Unpublished manuscript, University of Wisconsin, Madison, WI.

Plamenatz, J. (1949). *The English utilitarians.* Oxford: Basil Blackwell.

Plato. (1893). *The Phaedrus, Lysis, and Protagoras* (J. Wright, Trans.). London: Macmillan.

Poplawski, W. T. (1985). On the origin of altruism and charitable behavior conceptions: Chosen ancient sources as a contribution to prosocial behavior theory. *Psychologia, 28,* 1–10.

Popper, K. R. (1959). *The logic of scientific discovery.* New York: Basic Books.

Powell, G. H. (1924). Introduction. In *The moral maxims and reflections of the Duke de la Rochefoucauld.* New York: Frederick A. Stokes.

Rand, A. (1964). *The virtue of selfishness: A new concept of egoism.* New York: New American Library.

Rawls, J. (1971). *A theory of justice.* Cambridge, MA: Harvard University Press.

Reis, H. T., & Gruzen, J. (1976). On mediating equity, equality, and self-interest: The role of self-presentation in social exchange. *Journal of Experimental Social Psychology, 12,* 487–503.

Rest, J. R. (1979). *Development in judging moral issues.* Minneapolis, MN: University of Minnesota Press.

Rest, J. R. (1983). Morality. In J. Flavell & E. Markham (Eds.), *Manual of child psychology: Vol. 3. Cognitive development* (P. Mussen, General Ed.) (pp. 556–629). New York: Wiley.

Reykowski, J. (1982). Motivation of prosocial behavior. In V. J. Derlega & J. Grzelak (Eds.), *Cooperation and helping behavior: Theories and research* (pp. 352–375). New York: Academic Press.

Ridley, M., & Dawkins, R. (1981). The natural selection of altruism. In J. P. Rushton & R. M. Sorrentino (Eds.), *Altruism and helping behavior: Social, personality, and developmental perspectives* (pp. 19–39). Hillsdale, NJ: Lawrence Erlbaum Associates.

Rogers, C. R. (1951). *Client-centered therapy: Its current practice, implications, and theory.* Boston: Houghton Mifflin.

Rogers, C. R. (1961). *On becoming a person.* Boston: Houghton Mifflin.

Rokeach, M. (1969). *Beliefs, attitudes, and values.* San Francisco: Jossey-Bass.

Rosenberg, M. (1965). *Society and the adolescent self-image.* Princeton, NJ: Princeton University Press.

Rosenhan, D. L. (1970). The natural socialization of altruistic autonomy. In J. Macaulay & L. Berkowitz (Eds.), *Altruism and helping behavior* (pp. 251–268). New York: Academic Press.

Rosenhan, D. L. (1978). Toward resolving the altruism paradox: Affect, self-reinforcement, and cognition. In L. Wispé (Ed.), *Altruism, sympathy, and helping: Psychological and sociological principles* (pp. 101–113). New York: Academic Press.

Rosenhan, D. L., Salovey, P., Karylowski, J., & Hargis, K. (1981). Emotion and altruism. In J. P. Rushton & R. M. Sorrentino (Eds.), *Altruism and helping behavior: Social, personality, and developmental perspectives* (pp. 233–248). Hillsdale, NJ: Lawrence Erlbaum Associates.

Rosenhan, D. L., Salovey, P., & Hargis, K. (1981). The joys of helping: Focus of attention mediates the impact of positive affect on altruism. *Journal of Personality and Social Psychology, 40,* 899–905.

Rousseau, J. J. (1945). *The confessions of Jean-Jacques Rousseau* (Book VI). New York: Modern Library. (Original work published 1782)

Rousseau, J. J. (1950). *A discourse on the origin of inequality.* In *The social contract and discourses.* (G. D. H. Cole, Trans.). New York: E. P. Dutton. (Original work published 1755)

Rushton, J. P. (1980). *Altruism, socialization, and society.* Engelwood Cliffs, NJ: Prentice-Hall.

Rushton, J. P. (1981). The altruistic personality. In J. P. Rushton & R. M. Sorrentino (Eds.), *Altruism and helping behavior: Social, personality, and developmental perspectives.* Hillsdale, NJ: Lawrence Erlbaum Associates.

Rushton, J. P., Brainerd, C. J., & Pressley, M. (1983). Behavioral development and construct validity: The principle of aggregation. *Psychological Bulletin, 94,* 18–38.

Rushton, J. P., Chrisjohn, R. D., & Fekken, G. C. (1981). The altruistic personality and the self-report altruism scale. *Personality and Individual Differences, 2,* 293–302.

Rushton, J. P., & Sorrentino, R. M. (Eds.). (1981). *Altruism and helping behavior: Social, personality, and developmental perspectives.* Hillsdale, NJ: Lawrence Erlbaum Associates.

Ryan, W. (1971). *Blaming the victim.* New York: Random House.

Sackeim, H. A., & Gur, R. C. (1985). Voice recognition and the ontological status of self-deception. *Journal of Personality and Social Psychology, 48,* 1365–1368.

Sagi, A., & Hoffman, M. L. (1976). Empathic distress in newborns. *Developmental Psychology, 12,* 175–176.

Schachter, S. (1964). The interaction of cognitive and physiological determinants of emotional state. In L. Berkowitz (Ed.), *Advances in experimental social psychology,* Vol. 1 (pp. 49–80). New York: Academic Press.

Schaller, M., & Cialdini, R. B. (1988). The economics of empathic helping: Support for a mood management motive. *Journal of Experimental Social Psychology, 24,* 163–181.

Schaps, E. (1972). Cost, dependency, and helping. *Journal of Personality and Social Psychology, 21,* 74–78.

Schlenker, B. R. (1980). *Impression Management.* Monterey, CA: Brooks/Cole.

Schroeder, D. A., Dovidio, J. F., Sibicky, M. E., Matthews, L. L., & Allen, J. L. (1988). Empathy and helping behavior: Egoism or altruism? *Journal of Experimental Social Psychology, 24,* 333–353.

Schwartz, S. H. (1968). Words, deeds, and the perception of consequences and responsibility in action situations. *Journal of Personality and Social Psychology, 10,* 232–242.

Schwartz, S. H. (1975). The justice of need and the activation of humanitarian punishments. *Journal of Social Issues, 31* (3), 111–136.

Schwartz, S. H. (1977). Normative influences on altruism. In L. Berkowitz (Ed.), *Advances in experimental social psychology* (Vol. 10, pp. 221–279). New York: Academic Press.

Schwartz, S. H., & Howard, J. (1982). Helping and cooperation: A self-based motivational model. In V. J. Derlega & J. Grzelak (Eds.), *Cooperation and helping behavior: Theories and research* (pp. 327–353). New York: Academic Press.

Schwartz, S. H., & Howard, J. (1984). Internalized values as motivators of altruism. In

E. Staub, D. Bar-Tal, J. Karylowski, & J. Reykowski (Eds.), *Development and maintenance of prosocial behavior* (pp. 229–255). New York: Plenum.

Sharp, F. C. (1928). *Ethics.* New York: Century Company.

Sherif, M. (1936). *The psychology of norms.* New York: Harper.

Sherif, M., Harvey, O. J., White, B. J., Hood, W. E., & Sherif, C. W. (1961). *Intergroup conflict and cooperation: The Robber's Cave Experiment.* Norman: University of Oklahoma Book Exchange.

Simner, M. L. (1971). Newborn's response to the cry of another infant. *Developmental Psychology, 5,* 136–150.

Simpson, G. G. (1966). The biological nature of man. *Science, 152,* 472–478.

Skinner, B. F. (1953). *Science and human behavior.* New York: Macmillan.

Smith, A. (1853). *The theory of moral sentiments.* London: Henry G. Bohn. (Original work published 1759)

Smith, A. (1872). *On the wealth of nations.* London: Alex Murray. (Original work published 1771)

Smith, K. D., Keating, J. P., & Stotland, E. (1989). Altruism revisited: The effect of denying feedback on a victim's status to empathic witnesses. *Journal of Personality and Social Psychology, 57,* 641–650.

Smith, T. W., Ingram, R. E., & Brehm, S. S. (1983). Social anxiety, anxious self-preoccupation, and recall of self-relevant information. *Journal of Personality and Social Psychology, 44,* 1276–1283.

Snyder, C. R., Higgins, R. L., & Stuckey, R. J. (1983). *Excuses: Masquerades in search of grace.* New York: Wiley.

Snyder, M. (1979). Self-monitoring processes. In L. Berkowitz (Ed.), *Advances in experimental social psychology* (Vol. 12, pp. 85–128). New York: Academic Press.

Snyder, M. L., Kleck, R. E., Strenta, A., & Mentzer, S. J. (1979). Avoidance of the handicapped: An attributional ambiguity analysis. *Journal of Personality and Social Psychology, 37,* 2297–2306.

Spencer, H. (1870). *The principles of psychology* (Vol. 1, 2nd ed.). London: Williams and Norgate.

Spencer, H. (1872). *The principles of psychology* (Vol. 2, 2nd ed.). London: Williams & Norgate.

Spinoza, B. de. (1910). *Spinoza's ethics and "de Intellectus Emendatione."* (A. Boyle, Trans.). New York: E. P. Dutton. (Original work published 1677)

Staub, E. (1971). Helping a person in distress: The influence of implicit and explicit "rules" of conduct on children and adults. *Journal of Personality and Social Psychology, 17,* 137–145.

Staub, E. (1974). Helping a distressed person: Social, personality, and stimulus determinants. In L. Berkowitz (Ed.), *Advances in experimental social psychology* (Vol. 7, pp. 293–341). New York: Academic Press.

Staub, E. (1978). *Positive social behavior and morality: Social and personal influences* (Vol. 1). New York: Academic Press.

Staub, E. (1979). *Positive social behavior and morality: Socialization and development* (Vol. 2). New York: Academic Press.

Staub, E., & Baer, R. S., Jr. (1974). Stimulus characteristics of a sufferer and difficulty of escape as determinants of helping. *Journal of Personality and Social Psychology, 30,* 279–285.

Steele, B. (1980). Psychodynamic factors in child abuse. In C. H. Kempe & R. E. Helfer (Eds.), *The battered child* (3rd ed., pp. 49–85). Chicago: University of Chicago Press.

Steele, C. M. (1975). Name-calling and compliance. *Journal of Personality and Social Psychology, 31,* 361–369.

Steele, C. M., & Liu, T. J. (1983). Dissonance processes as self-affirmation. *Journal of Personality and Social Psychology, 45,* 5–19.

Stotland, E. (1969). Exploratory studies of empathy. In L. Berkowitz (Ed.), *Advances in experimental social psychology* (Vol. 4, pp. 271–313). New York: Academic Press.

Stotland, E., Sherman, S. E., & Shaver, K. G. (1971). *Empathy and birth order: Some experimental explorations.* Lincoln: University of Nebraska Press.

Stroop, J. R. (1938). Factors affecting speed in serial verbal reactions. *Psychological Monographs, 50,* 38–48.

Tesser, A. (1988). Toward a self-evaluation maintenance model of social behavior. In L. Berkowitz (Ed.), *Advances in experimental social psychology* (Vol. 21, pp. 181–227). New York: Academic Press.

Thomas, G. C., & Batson, C. D. (1981). Effect of helping under normative pressure on self-perceived altruism. *Social Psychology Quarterly, 44,* 127–131.

Thomas, G. C., Batson, C. D., & Coke, J. S. (1981). Do Good Samaritans discourage helpfulness?: Self-perceived altruism after exposure to highly helpful others. *Journal of Personality and Social Psychology, 40,* 194–200.

Thompson, W. C., Cowan, C. L., & Rosenhan, D. L. (1980). Focus of attention mediates the impact of negative affect on altruism. *Journal of Personality and Social Psychology, 38,* 291–300.

Toi, M., & Batson, C. D. (1982). More evidence that empathy is a source of altruistic motivation. *Journal of Personality and Social Psychology, 43,* 281–292.

Tolman, E. C. (1932). *Purposive behavior in animals and men.* New York: Century.

Trivers, R. L. (1971). The evolution of reciprocal altruism. *The Quarterly Review of Biology, 46,* 35–57.

Underwood, B., & Moore, B. (1982). Perspective-taking and altruism. *Psychological Bulletin, 91,* 143–173.

Wallach, M. A., & Wallach, L. (1983). *Psychology's sanction for selfishness: The error of egoism in theory and therapy.* San Francisco, CA: W. H. Freeman.

Walster, E., Berscheid, E., & Walster, G. W. (1973). New directions in equity research. *Journal of Personality and Social Psychology, 25,* 151–176.

Weigel, R. H., Wiser, P. L., & Cook, S. W. (1975). The impact of cooperative learning experiences on cross-ethnic relations and attitudes. *Journal of Social Issues, 31*(1), 219–244.

Weiner, F. H. (1976). Altruism, ambiance, and action: The effect of rural and urban rearing on helping behavior. *Journal of Personality and Social Psychology, 34,* 112–124.

Weyant, J. M. (1978). Effects of mood states, costs, and benefits on helping. *Journal of Personality and Social Psychology, 36,* 1169–1176.

Wicklund, R. A. (1975). Objective self-awareness. In L. Berkowitz (Ed.), *Advances in experimental social psychology* (Vol. 8, pp. 233–275). New York: Academic Press.

Wicklund, R. A., & Gollwitzer, P. M. (1982). *Symbolic self-completion.* Hillsdale, NJ: Lawrence Erlbaum Associates.

Williams, R. (1989). *The trusting heart: Great news about Type A behavior.* New York: Random House.

Williamson, G. M., & Clark, M. S. (1989). Providing help and desired relationship type as determinants of changes in moods and self-evaluations. *Journal of Personality and Social Psychology, 56,* 722–734.

Wills, T. A. (1981). Downward comparison principles in social psychology. *Psychological Bulletin, 90,* 245–271.

Wilson, E. O. (1975). *Sociobiology: The new synthesis.* Cambridge, MA: Harvard University Press.

Wilson, E. O. (1978). *On human nature.* Cambridge, MA: Harvard University Press.

Wilson, J. P. (1976). Motivation, modeling and altruism: A Person X Situation analysis. *Journal of Personality and Social Psychology, 34,* 1078–1086.

Winer, B. J. (1971). *Statistical principles in experimental design* (2nd ed.). New York: McGraw-Hill.

Wispé, L. G. (1968). Sympathy and empathy. In D. L. Sills (Ed.), *International encyclopedia of the social sciences* (Vol. 15, pp. 441–447). New York: Free Press.

Wispé, L. G. (Ed.). (1978). *Altruism, sympathy, and helping: Psychological and sociological principles.* New York: Academic Press.

Wispé, L. G. (1986). The distinction between sympathy and empathy: To call forth a concept a word is needed. *Journal of Personality and Social Psychology, 50,* 314–321.

Wispé, L. G. (1987). History of the concept of empathy. In N. Eisenberg & J. Strayer (Eds.), *Empathy and its development* (pp. 17–37). New York: Cambridge University Press.

Woodworth, R. S. (1918). *Dynamic psychology.* New York: Columbia University Press.

Zuckerman, M. (1975). Belief in a just world and altruistic behavior. *Journal of Personality and Social Psychology, 31,* 972–976.

Author Index

247

Subject Index